Between the Fences

Between the Fences

Before Guantánamo, there was the Port Isabel
Service Processing Center

TONY HEFNER

Seven Stories Press
New York

A Seven Stories Press First Edition

Seven Stories Press
140 Watts Street
New York, NY 10013
www.sevenstories.com

In Canada: Publishers Group Canada, 559 College Street, Suite 402, Toronto, ON M6G 1A9

In the UK: Turnaround Publisher Services Ltd., Unit 3, Olympia Trading Estate, Coburg Road, Wood Green, London N22 6TZ

In Australia: Palgrave Macmillan, 15–19 Claremont Street, South Yarra, VIC 3141

College professors may order examination copies of Seven Stories Press titles for a free six-month trial period. To order, visit http://www.sevenstories.com/textbook or send a fax on school letterhead to (212) 226-1411.

Book design by Jon Gilbert

Library of Congress Cataloging-in-Publication Data

Hefner, Tony.
 Between the fences : before Guantánamo, there was the Port Isabel Service Processing Center / Tony Hefner.
    p. cm.
 ISBN 978-1-58322-912-5 (pbk.)
 1. Aliens--Government policy--United States. 2. Alien detention centers--Texas.
 3. Hispanic Americans--Texas. I. Title.
 JV6483.H396 2010
 325.73--dc22
                                              2010018469
Printed in the United States

9 8 7 6 5 4 3 2 1

■   ■   ■

Note: Last names and alpha numbers of detainees have been removed from this book to protect individual privacy. However, documents including all of this information are available from the author should there be an investigation into these incidents at the Port Isabel Detention Center.

This book is dedicated to Larry Conrady Jr.
January 15, 1982–March 2, 2008

For God shall bring every work into judgment, with every secret thing, whether it be good, or whether it be evil.

ECCLESIASTES 12:14

Contents

Preface

The United States of America represents a land of opportunity for many throughout the world, especially for the Hispanic people to our south. Reaching our borders is the dream of millions searching for a better life. This means more to me than most citizens of our great nation, as my father was an undocumented immigrant from Mexico.

I have had the same opportunity here in the United States as my father had in Mexico. His parents moved from Spain to Mexico when he was just a baby, and they became successful cattle ranchers there. Many years later, just a few months before my birth, my father was shot and killed crossing the Rio Grande a few miles from the city of Laredo, Texas, where I was born.

I have often asked myself what Mexico would be like today if its people had not crossed our borders. I have had a lot of time to consider this question, and I still don't have a satisfactory answer. For one thing, my father might still be alive. Many young Hispanic men have lost their lives crossing the Rio Grande. Some, like my father, were shot and killed by men on this side of the border who had no regard for human life and looked upon killing as a sport. On several occasions I have visited Mexico and seen the poverty there, and have met some of its hardworking people. During my five years—from 1983 to 1986 and then from 1988 to 1990—working inside the detention facility, I heard about the many reasons people risk their lives to cross our borders. They are the same reasons Americans have fought so hard to make our own country great: to create a better life for themselves and for their children.

Immigration detention is not a new phenomenon. Neither is abuse within those facilities. However, unlike the events at the Iraqi prison Abu Ghraib, the documented abuse that I have repeatedly presented to the Immigration and Naturalization Service (INS), to numerous US senators, and to Karl Rove under George W. Bush has passed from one official to another without an adequate response. Accounts of the abuse, torture, and homicide of prisoners held in Abu Ghraib were brought to the attention of an outraged public, but that same public remains oblivious to identical abuses occurring in our own detention centers here. I am sure government officials reading my reports must have seen the similarities between the abuses in Texas and those uncovered at Abu Ghraib and, later, Guantánamo Bay. We cannot leave the fate of the four hundred thousand immigrant detainees currently being held in the US to these politicians. We must make these abuses public on our own and put pressure on the INS to address these problems.

This is my own story as I saw it and recorded it in a series of notebooks during my employment inside the Port Isabel Service Processing Center, and an account of my many attempts to stop some of the inhumane abuses that went on within its walls. How can the American people be appalled at abuse committed during wartime across the ocean and yet not lift their skirts high enough to see the abuse going on beneath their own feet? How can we send armed servicemen and women to prison for abuse abroad and yet not hold federal officials accountable for the same crimes within our own borders? Immigrant detainees represent one of the fastest growing segments of the incarcerated population, yet there are no federal regulations governing the conditions of their detention. I hope this book will help bring public attention to the Port Isabel Service Processing Center and other detention centers around the country in which similar abuses are committed.

The stories I write about in this book may appall and shock you. Still, I firmly believe that border security is essential to our national security, and full border funding should be granted. In a post-9/11 world, I worry very much for our safety. Border security, however, does not require routine abuse and ill treatment of people who are only trying to better themselves and provide for their families. Americans will never be able to stand up against the abuse of human rights in other countries until we can account for our own actions here on our own soil.

Reach out and feel the victim's pain . . .
Let it touch your heart.
Wipe a tear or two away and you will learn,
as I have seen.
Beyond those soft and dark brown eyes. . . . belief in
justice, and a will to survive.

Tony Hefner
April 2010

Introduction

It is 1983, and war in Central America has forced hundreds of thousands to flee north to the United States to seek asylum. Many wind up here at Bayview, just outside of Los Fresnos, Texas, a detention facility for immigrants entering the country illegally.

I am in charge. I look up from my desk as two male Salvadoran detainees walk into the Four-Alpha dormitory in Building 4. The guard at Gate 3 radios to tell me that these men are returning from a meeting with their lawyer.

The guard asks, "You copy, Four-Alpha?"

"Ten-four," I confirm.

The two men give me their names to write into the daily logbook. Their foreheads are creased and their mouths turned down as they talk quietly to each other in Spanish. Carlos, a young detainee in the room, and I look at each other. When they leave, he interprets what they were saying for me. They gave all their money to the lawyer. They're afraid to be deported, afraid of what awaits them in El Salvador.

The detainees come from all over—China, Germany, Mexico, Africa, India, Libya—but most are from Spanish-speaking countries, some from as far south as Chile. I don't have much conflict with them. I don't speak their languages, but it doesn't matter. I treat them with respect, and they give me no trouble. In fact, most of the time, it's better than that.

"Jack Rabbit! Jack Rabbit!" radios the Gate 3 guard. "Jack Rabbit" is code for a detainee trying to escape.

A group of detainees rush to the nearest open window. They can see the escapee running. I order them back, lock the windows, and hurry to secure the rest of my post. Guards carry no guns or weapons inside the facility. Our only defense is a radio to call for help.

The men cheer on the Jack Rabbit. I push my way through the crowd and command them back to their beds. The INS requires me to conduct a roll call and head count when everything is under control again.

I look through the window. The detainee is young, around twenty-two. He is trying to scale the first fourteen-foot chain-link fence, about forty feet from where I stand. His orange uniform is distinct against the light blue sky. Not far behind him run several guards who work for Burns International Security, the contract company that also employees me. The man reaches the top of the fence. He is frantic. He must cross the V-shaped barbed wire on top. After this fence, another one looms ten feet away with the same barbed wire. He straddles the wire. His arms begin to bleed.

He jumps to the ground, and his knees buckle beneath him. His head darts back and forth as he crouches like a scared animal.

Men yell at him from both sides. Immigration officers in green race along the outside perimeter in the foot patrol area. Beyond them is the wildlife refuge. If the escapee can get there, the brush will hide him.

For a moment, he doesn't move. He seems to know that he is not going to make it. But in his panic, he tries anyway. He starts to run between the two fences. Roars from the dorm excite him. Then two officers rush through the gate. The men in green grab him and throw him into the dust.

The officers hold him down. Within seconds guards arrive. He lies motionless. One officer pulls the detainee's hands behind him while another thrusts his foot on his neck. They tie his hands. Another one kicks him repeatedly.

They pull him up from behind by his arms. The officers guide him from between the fences toward Processing in Building 9. As they walk past my dorm they jerk him from side to side. This behavior sends a message to other detainees: don't be our next example.

Two floors above, in Four-Bravo and Four-Charlie, other detainees call the officers names, "¡Asesinos perros, asesinos perros!" "Killer dogs, killer dogs!" Other voices echo through the dorm. I hear crying. Is any place worse than this?

I can't help but think about all the detained men and women I have talked with over the years. So many come to the Unites States because of poor conditions or fighting in their homeland. Some have seen parents and family members killed by their nation's armies. Others come looking for a better life.

I wonder about this young man. Why does he want to escape? Maybe he spent all his money just to get here and could not face being sent back penniless. Maybe the money he earned in America was necessary to his family back home. Maybe, if he were deported, soldiers would meet him at the airport, and he would join *los desaparecidos*, the disappeared ones. Or maybe it's the camp itself that he's trying to escape.

∎ ∎ ∎

This book is about the men, women, and children caught between the fences of US government policy and the degenerate power of its enforcers. It's about employees who worked for the government, the police force, and security companies and lost their jobs trying to stop the ongoing, widespread corruption. But mainly, this is the story about my battle to stop the evil that I saw destroying and maiming, as surely as any Salvadoran machete. It's about the conflict I faced in deciding to take a stand for my beliefs and for all those who still love the law and are frustrated when its spirit is broken in the courtrooms of America. It's a stand that I, my wife, and a handful of others took at the risk of our lives. In the aftermath, I found answers to the puzzle of my own mixed heritage.

I have been telling my story now for almost twenty years. The faces inside Port Isabel today are different. But the abuse I witnessed inside those walls, I know, continues. I want to tell my story so that the faces inside the center can finally be seen.

My campaign reached many: Karl Rove, senior adviser to former president George W. Bush, who ordered the new Department of Homeland Security (DHS) to investigate my allegations; Judge Linda Reyna Yañez, who sits on the Texas 13th Circuit Court of Appeals and filed a $1 million lawsuit against three of the perpetrators; former US Attorney General Janet Reno; Congressman James Sensenbrenner, former chairperson of the Judiciary Committee; Senator Carl Levin, the chairman of the Permanent Subcommittee on Investigations; Congressmen Dave Camp and Bart Stupak of Michigan, both of whom wrote letters to the chairman of the Judiciary Committee; Doris Meissner, former commissioner of the INS; Ann Richards, former governor of Texas; former Senator Phil Gramm; the US Equal Employment Opportunity Commission (EEOC); the Federal Bureau of Investigations (FBI); the Office of the Inspector General (OIG); and the House Judiciary Subcommittee on International Law, Immigration, and Refugees.

My legal complaints were initially thrown out of court on summary judgment by former 197th District Court judge Darrell Hester (known locally as "hang 'em high Hester") in Brownsville, Texas. They were, however, broadcast to an outraged public in newspapers, magazines, local news shows, and internationally. The television programs *Inside Edition*, the *María Laria Show*, *Ocurrió Así*, *Primer Impacto*, and *Cristina* all made public appeals. My lawsuit won in appeal in 1994.

The Whistleblower Protection Act protects government

employees who report corruption from retaliation. However, no such act exists to protect security guards employed by contract companies who work alongside government employees. If guards witness or are victims of wrongdoing on government property, they can and do lose their livelihoods by reporting it.

The documents and records that exist are extensive, and it simply isn't possible to tell each story and describe the impact these events have had on the lives of all those involved. But this book will provide a complete picture of some of the events I either witnessed or was told about and later corroborated. I hope they will serve as examples of the countless untold stories that remain in the shadows.

■ ■ ■

On February 8, 1995, two immigration officers and several other men were arrested for transporting drugs. Juan García Abrego, head of Mexico's powerful Gulf Cartel at the time of the September 1996 trial, was paying the officers. United States government immigration buses were used to haul millions of dollars' worth of cocaine through border checkpoints to avoid detection. During the twelve-year battle to stop corruption inside this facility, drugs were being smuggled into the country using our tax dollars. A police officer had informed a supervisor of deportation in October 1992 about the cocaine smuggling, but a high-ranking INS district official told him not to investigate. "Smuggling," the district official said, "is none of our business."

The abuse in this facility is horrifying. The only people who tried to do something about it lost their jobs. The others are still in charge.

1
The Reality of a Dream

Wetting a washcloth at the kitchen sink, I scrub the sweat and dirt off my face, trying to rub away the part of my heritage that makes me brown inside. My blood is half-Mexican but my skin is white, and deep down in my heart I don't know if I can ever make peace between the two after what has happened here.

I stare out the window at the mowed tufts of Bermuda grass where they meet the dirt of the paddock. Tan powdery dirt, the kind that clogs your pores in the humid heat of the south Texas summer and turns white skin brown, now infiltrates every crack and crevice of the mobile home my wife, Barbara, and I have shared for the past twelve years. A gritty film coats my boots, fills my pockets, and sticks to my neck like paint.

I walk back into the front room. I have no job, my marriage is struggling, my dream of a ranch ministry is like the crap I scrape off my boots coming out of the barn—all this to prove that my Mexican blood isn't tainted. Is that what I came down here to prove? I look at my arms where black hairs still dominate after forty-five years.

My arms are strong and dirty from digging. But all I see is the color, dark brown. I hate this feeling!

The phone rings. Maybe it's Barbara to say that she made it to work safely. Anxiety is making me paranoid.

A gruff voice answers, "Hefner?"

"Yeah?" My guts roll up in a knot.

"Doomsday is here."

"What?"

"You're a dead man." Click.

What I thought was a simple complaint reporting illegal activity within a detention center has now become life threatening. Do I take their daily death threats seriously? And are they going to follow through?

Cowards! Why don't they just come out here and get it over with? Show their faces like I show mine! But you can't mess with them because they're the government, boy! They can slander, intimidate, or frame you, or even blow you away, and nobody will ever know the truth. The government is made up of people like you and me, good and bad. They can tear up the paperwork, hang you in the barn, and walk away. I see it now. Up close and personal, upside down. Bad is good and good is bad, and the good guy is cracking up.

Fear gets me. I was raised on threats. I hate them, but I can manage. But how in God's name do I protect my wife?

I step back from the living room window into the shadows of the hallway, out of range, and slide down to the cool linoleum. Moist heat hangs like a blanket in the air. I hold my head in my hands, feeling my gold wedding ring against my forehead. I am small and ignorant and way, way out of my league. How did I ever think I could fight them? How did I wind up on the wrong side of everything?

The morning sunshine comes streaming in through the front window and breaks into tiny rainbows off the glass candy dish Barbara picked up at a yard sale back in Ohio. The Chachalaca birds repeat their call in the distance. Chachala, chachala, they sing, over and over, reciting the list of my failures. The big sign out front—Bearing Precious Seed Ranch—annoys me now. It stares at me with its childish letters, and the happy tune it once sang is now twisted and harsh. I was proud when we put it up. Now I'm going to chop it down.

The phone rings again. I crawl to it.

"Tony? I'm here," Barbara says in her soft voice. "There're three ledgers on my desk, so I can't really talk." Silence.

"Barbara?"

"Tony, don't talk to me about leaving Texas. Not on the phone."

"No, no. It's just . . . I'm sorry." Another long pause.

"Everything will turn out all right," she says.

Still an optimist. Every single investigation of the detention camp to date has been whitewashed. I look like an idiot.

"Good-bye, Barbara."

I know I'm a little guy, a nobody from nowhere. But I'm a citizen, aren't I, going way out of my way to do the right thing?

It comes down to this: Cynthia, Jovita, Beatriz, and the hundreds they represent along with me, a middle-aged half-Mexican who's passed as white since kindergarten, are too small for Texas-style justice. I didn't go to law school. I went to Bible school. Chachala.

God, how did this happen?

■ ■ ■

Summer 1981. The hot and humid air smelled of sharp pesticides from the crop duster a few miles away. Periodically, a breeze off the cattle ranch down the road gave me a lift, and I whistled as I left the barn and walked under a blazing blue sky toward our new mobile home. I liked it warm. I liked those cattle smells. Movement in the pasture caught my eye. Newborn foals were rearing up on spindly legs to paw the air like their fathers. The mares grazed under fifty-foot-tall rippling palm trees. Paradise.

Horses used to scare me. They were big and powerful, something I wasn't. I used to see them in the fields alongside the country road in Windham, Ohio, where I spent my younger days. They'd race our car when we drove beside the pasture, their manes flowing out and necks arched just so. I read about them and took a job in a stable during Bible school to cure myself of the phobia.

I had always wanted to be a cowboy and have a horse, but never in my craziest dreams was I on a ranch training and breeding horses. Appaloosas and Quarter Horses, masters of the sagebrush. I couldn't stop smiling.

Barbara and I came to the Rio Grande Valley of south Texas in the spring of 1981, a year after I graduated from the First Baptist Church's School of Scriptures in Milford, Ohio. I was thirty-three years old. I had planned to go into the mission field. A few short-term assignments to Mexico were very satisfying. My school was known for printing New Testament Bibles in many different languages. Other missionaries and I had taken them by horseback to remote Mexican villages in the mountains a hundred miles south of Monterey, reaching people that nobody else had.

I had had a born-again Christian experience at twenty-four, so telling people about God's love for them was a deep desire. I saw a need, and I wanted to help people like me who had no hope because of a brutal and unloved childhood.

My stepfather told me when I was six that because my real father was Mexican, I was worth less than the food and clothing it'd take to raise me. My mother was white. In his eyes I was a half-breed. I was taught to be embarrassed.

My mother, Betty Jean Pressdee, met my biological father, Antonio Robles, in Ohio where he worked illegally on the railroad. She said they got married and went to live in Texas, where she later found out that he already had a family in Mexico. I was christened Antonio Robles after him, because two months before I was born he was shot crossing the Rio Grande.

I was born in Laredo and lived in Texas for all of five days. As my mother told it, she got scared that Antonio's family would kidnap me and take me across the border, so she fled north on the only train out of town—a troop transport train full of Army Air Corps returning from World War II. A soldier gave up his seat so my mother could sit down with me. The soldier was Gene Autry, the singing cowboy movie star. When he held me he called me Pancho, a name and identity to which I would secretly cling.

In Ohio two years later, my mother married my stepfather, Jim, who adopted me and gave me his name, Hefner, but was ashamed of me. His mother and one of his sisters teased him, saying, "You had to go and marry someone who already had a kid not your own, and a half-breed at that." They thought Mexicans were the scum of the earth. How could a white woman have a child with one? Not all of Jim's sisters felt this way. One of them was more like a mother than an aunt to me. She, too, was a Christian and disapproved of my stepfather's abuse.

As a boy, Jim was nearly electrocuted by downed power lines during a storm in West Virginia. From that day on he suffered from depression and nervous breakdowns. During these episodes my mother usually took him to the hospital for shock treatments, but sometimes we were forced to keep him at home. I remember him pleading over and over again not to take him. Most of the time he couldn't work, so my mother held two jobs and got depressed a lot. Both of them drank and ran around and screamed at each other, sometimes about me. I became the whipping boy for everything Jim saw wrong with our lives. And it was my job to care for him. We received some welfare, lived in a housing project, and never had any money. Somehow that was my fault, too.

Childhood was put on hold. When I was old enough, I took care of my three half-siblings because I was the only one my mother trusted. The beatings and abuse would draw outside interest from child protective services. Our family could have been split up and put into foster care, so I took my responsibilities seriously. I was expected to have the chores done before my mother got home from work. Sometimes I told the school I was sick in order to go home early, wash the dishes, and make supper. That meal was usually bread and sugar with coffee poured over it or ketchup sandwiches, because Jim would hide the food from us.

One day, I was cleaning up in the kitchen when I felt someone watching me. Looking around, I saw Jim's eyes in the shadows of the pantry. He leaped out, fast and evil, with his black hair stringy around his eyes, his arms and legs grabbing, scaring me almost to death. Like a raging bull with wet stains under his armpits and the smell of cigarettes and liquor on his heavy breath, he said I was overfeeding the kids. He beat me with his fist around the head and neck and held me by the hair until I repeated that I was worthless and stupid. He said I was a nigger turned inside out, because that's what Mexicans were. Then he said he was going to beat the Mexican out of me.

When this type of thing happened, I would mentally separate myself from it, out of fear, knowing what he would do to me. I would put myself into a trance as a means of protection and bury the bad stuff away. Repression helped me manage the immediate pain, but throughout adulthood, I always wondered—was I normal?

To keep peace in the family, I learned early to do exactly what I was told, never look Jim in the eye, and keep the bruises covered and the family secrets secret. And every day he used to tell me that when I least expected it, he'd kill me.

Living in Ohio, I never saw Hispanic people. I only knew I was different from everyone else. My mother's brother, Uncle Louie, would call me "Pancho" on the sly because he knew I liked it. It was our secret. I wanted to be a cowboy like my heroes—justice-makers Gene Autry and Roy Rogers—and see Texas, where I imagined there'd be sagebrush and stagecoaches, but I kept this all to myself, wheedling bits of information out of my mother when we were alone.

When I started kindergarten and had just found out that I was adopted, I told my teacher that my father was a "wetback." I didn't even know what it meant. When she mentioned it to Jim, he screamed at my mother and threatened to get rid of me. My mother told me never to tell anyone who my real father was and not to bring any more humiliation to the family.

So, as an adult, after all the brainwashing and Latino-bashing, I wound up feeling compassion for Hispanics. They were my real father's people, and partly mine, though I felt no connection. It became important for me to prove that Hispanics weren't all those bad things I'd been told. I wanted to show poverty-stricken border Hispanics, who thought white-skinned people were better than them, that they were just as good, and that their children were worth more than gold to God. I wanted to show Jim and my siblings that Mexicans weren't dumb, the dirt of the earth, and unable to learn, as I had been told.

I gradually became more and more focused on the plight of children. As a young adult working with different churches and scouting organizations, I discovered that it was easier for me to communicate with children than with adults or authority figures. I grew up with a speech impediment because I was afraid that adults would hit me when I spoke to them. If they were nice to me, my emotions ran wild, wanting to be loved and accepted. To the children, I was a hero. They knew I cared.

One summer vacation, while driving busloads of boys and girls to the Bill Rice Ranch in Murfreesboro, Tennessee, for a week-long Christian retreat, I saw something that showed me the direction I wanted to go. This Christian ranch was a safe place, a perfect community that demonstrated adults could be loving and selfless toward children. In a place like that, kids could relax enough to think straight, enjoy the irresponsibility of childhood, and open up to allow themselves to be shaped. It showed the kids how life *could* be.

Once I put the ranch idea together with my compassion for Hispanic children, I knew what I wanted to do. The last thing on my mind was getting married. But then I met Barbara. I had dated lots of girls, and they seemed to like me. I was the kind of guy their fathers loved: home on time, no funny business, and mindful of the rules. Barbara was different, though. The petite and protected only child of an Irish deacon in the Baptist church, she was the first girl who didn't seem to chase after me. She attracted me with a whole new set of qualities. She was beautiful and honest, reserved and confident, and had a wholeness and innocence about her that I found fascinating and humbling. She was spiritual, ethical, and honest. I was so surprised to find out she liked me. The first time she saw me, I was in the First Baptist Church choir. She told me later, "I saw you up there in the tenor section, and I was wondering what your wife looked liked." I told her she should have looked in a mirror.

We married in May 1979. I was unsure about being a father, afraid I'd turn out like Jim. When I was eight I babysat a little guy, around two or three. When his father came home, the baby ran from his dad to me, and the dad told me to give him a smack and send him back to him. To me, a smack meant a hard and thorough beating. I hit the baby several times. The man became alarmed and said, "I only told you to give him a smack!" I didn't know any different. That's what scared me. But Barbara was selfless and understood the depth of my problem. Though she loved children, she agreed to wait.

When I asked her why she married me, Barbara said it was because I made her laugh and brought the unexpected into her life. But she was no pushover. Barbara felt that wherever we went, if it were God's will, she would be content no matter what the circumstances. When I told her I wanted to go to Texas and start a ranch ministry for Hispanic children and that it might be a hard life, she said, "I always wanted to live in Texas for some reason."

So in 1981, with faith and stars in our eyes, we opened the truck windows and drove to the flat bottomlands of the Rio Grande Valley. Several miles from the town of San Benito and about thirty from the Gulf coast, we leased an abandoned cattle ranch full of cactus and mesquite that was perfect for what we wanted to do.

■ ■ ■

The Bearing Precious Seed Ranch was established that fall with the help and labor of several local churches as a retreat for poor children. The last job on the ranch transformation was to pour cement into the holes that would hold the big sign welcoming the kids. Here they would ride horses, go on hayrides, learn the gospel, and experience kindness and caring first hand. When I looked at the sign I could almost hear circus music. It seemed so innocent and good.

The ranch was thirty acres of rolling, undeveloped land, surrounded by palm trees and pasture fences, with a gigantic aluminum pole barn and a small wooden house. We made a saddle room and office out of the house and bought a new mobile home to live in. Back in Ohio, we were given our first horse toward this ministry, a young Appaloosa stallion we named Faith. He grew to be enormous, but exceptionally gentle and intelligent. Soon after, others donated stallions and mares, both for riding and as a source of potential income from stud service. We had two top-notch horses with champion bloodlines. It was a great way to support the ministry. Barbara was never too keen on working with the horses (she was pretty much petrified of them), so she got a part-time job as a bookkeeper for a nice family business that owned Bicycle World, Just for Babies, and Terry's Que Pasta and left me to handle the horses. It seemed that all was falling into place perfectly, as though God had his hand on us.

We discovered that gaining the trust of the children's parents was not so easy. We worked through the young people's ministry at the local Baptist church but found that Hispanic families were suspicious of anyone wanting to treat their children in a special way. Especially white people. Some of the kids had even been taught to stay away from white children. Since I was officially pastor of the ranch ministry, had graduated from an established Bible school, and was backed by the Baptist church, my pastor gave me permission to introduce myself as a reverend to help ease their fears. As we went door to door in poor neighborhoods, we invited the parents and grandparents to come along to our ranch to watch their children. It was a good start.

For our first retreat, Barbara and other church ladies barbecued hot dogs while I took the children around the ranch on a hay wagon. I had to hitch the wagon to a tractor to get through the tangles of sagebrush and huisache. A lookout on Faith walked behind us to keep an eye on the children, and they would reach out for him over the yards between, as if trying to touch a dream. A reporter from the *San Benito News* wrote a story on the ministry, and a large picture of happy, waving children graced the front page of the Sunday morning edition.

We also took over the little Sunday school at the church, and through contacts with families and rides in the big yellow church bus on Sunday morning, the program grew from seven children to fifty. I didn't like to do anything halfway, so I worked to get as many kids as possible because I knew they needed the scriptures to teach them what was right, to help them stay off drugs, and to live productive lives. The kids responded by learning and paid us with big hugs and smiles.

Until this time, I had worked my whole life with Anglo children. I had no idea I would feel so different around Hispanics. I guess I expected the kids to be timid because they were brown or to behave as I had. But these Hispanic children laughed and ran and were themselves without shame. They did not even seem conscious of themselves. My own identity was stirred because of their freedom. I wanted to see myself in their eyes.

As our ministries grew, I advertised Hefner's Quarter Horses Stud Service in the *American Quarter Horse Journal* and in the local feed stores. On talking to Vicente Ramirez, a well-known trainer who lived not far from Los Fresnos, I discovered that we owned the two best stallions in the valley—Top Calibar and Three Auca

Spears—both descendants of Three Bars, a leading sire. Three Auca was also grandson of Go Man Go, a three-time world champion Quarter Horse, and Sugar Bars, a leading Quarter Horse sire.

Our horse population rose and fell as foals were born and sold into other states and Mexico. Toward the end of May 1982, after our first year, our best income ended with the breeding season. We had been expecting financial support from our church in Ohio and were troubled when they failed to respond. By August our funds had dropped below what we needed because we didn't want to give up the retreats and refused to charge money for them. We hoped other churches in the area would contribute because their children took part as well. We didn't ask for help, though, as they were poor churches and we were newcomers. We didn't want to start off with our hands out. So being a certified welder, I found a welding job in Port Brownsville that August. However, in three months' time the job was completed, and we were needy again.

I scouted for work throughout the county, but welding jobs were scarce. I found out that this four-county area—the Harlingen district of southeast Texas—was one of the poorest areas in the United States. The only job I could get was minimum wage.

Bob Anderson, a friend from church who worked as a detective for the sheriff's department in the McAllen area, found out that I was looking for work.

"Say Hefner, I've got some friends in security and heard they're doing some hiring at the detention center. Why don't you go out there?"

"What detention center?"

"The INS camp. I give courses. I'll give you one free, get you your security guard's certificate. You present that with my recommendation, and they'll hire you. Best job around."

"But I only know a little bit of Spanish."

"Doesn't matter. They have illegal immigrants there from all over the world."

I hadn't known such a place existed. I took his four-week class, and without knowing very much about the workings of the Immigration and Naturalization Service, I was hired by the private security company Burns International, which subcontracted additional security guards for duties with INS officers inside the detention facility at Bayview, also known as Los Fresnos Immigration Prison, Port Isabel Service Processing Center, and the *Corralón* ("the big corral") to inmates. It was the dusty, smelly, 347-acre former US naval base out on the edge of nowhere, at the end of a road on the Gulf of Mexico.

At that time, I hadn't thought much about immigration but believed that the United States should control immigrants coming into the country. I saw them come, whole families sleeping behind abandoned buildings in cardboard boxes, with bad food and no medicine for their children, whose eyes became infected because of the lack of sanitation. They didn't care about where they were going. They were scared of war and had heard that the streets of America were paved with gold and everybody worked. I believed that people coming here from other countries first needed to understand our laws and how to obey them, so I had no philosophical problem detaining those who wanted to bypass that. My job at the detention facility was to help them reorganize and keep the peace until their cases were decided. Barring fights between them, which were pretty common as some were enemies outside, too, I didn't see why the job couldn't flow in an orderly progression of justice, with US courts, officers, and government institutions ensuring that fair and impartial decisions were made for all.

Some very troubling things happened during my training at the camp. It was the first time I hadn't told Barbara everything, for fear of what she would say. Mr. Cecilio L. Ruiz Jr., the assistant district director for detention and deportation and the head of the whole thing, paid our classroom of twenty men and women trainees a visit. In his late forties, he was dressed impeccably in a light gray business suit, about five foot eight like me, of dark complexion, and built like a stone-carved Aztec. He swaggered to the front of the room and sat imposingly on the edge of a desk. He looked squarely at every woman there.

"Looking good. Looking very good. I have a very large appreciation for women. Understand? Very large."

Some of the women laughed and others shrank.

"Women are my passion. I am not homosexual. It is not allowed. No homosexuals will be running my camp. So if any of you are, you can forget it," Ruiz said. His leaden eyes glared at the men from under heavy brows, and then soon came to rest on a pretty girl.

"If you girls have any trouble at all, anything, anytime, you come to my office. Large number one on the side of the building." He pointed through the window at the offices on the hill beyond. "I will personally take care of you. Yes. Very good care." His face reddened. "But if one of you men darkens my doorstep asking for any help, I will fire you. Do you understand? I am not here to hold any man's hand. It is my camp, and those who are hired will soon learn how I want it run. That means no questions. That's all. Welcome to Bayview."

I was shocked. If this guy ever talked to my wife like that, I'd deck him. The inflections in his voice made every comment sexual. I didn't know what to expect. Maybe he was just trying to scare off the timid trainees. Maybe it was a test of some kind.

■ ■ ■

I started at Bayview in March 1983, after an unusually cold winter that froze the tops off our palm trees. The camp was about twenty miles from the ranch, and it took about a half hour to drive there. Barbara dropped me off in the parking lot before she went to work.

"That place gives me the creeps," she said, looking at the high fences and forbidding solidity of the buildings. "Hope it goes all right."

"Nothing will happen, Barbara. See you tonight."

She told me how important I looked in my blue uniform, her eyes twinkling reassuringly, and drove away.

But I was concerned. Could I do this without communicating in Spanish? What if I couldn't understand what someone needed in an emergency? I'd heard things about the men held here, that they came from all different walks of life—soldiers, guerillas, felons, farmers—and that when they were caged up together they behaved like animals of prey, the strong victimizing the weak. It was a different culture within the high barbed-wire fences. Now I was the one in uniform. Others would watch me in order to learn.

∎ ∎ ∎

The INS facility was long from one end to the other, the buildings two to three stories high and stacked next to each other like dominoes on the sandy delta about three miles from the Gulf of Mexico. Few trees grew, with mostly low brush, mesquite, and varieties of palm. Between the Gulf and the compound was the Sabal Palm Audubon Center, a sanctuary protecting 557 acres of palm and alligator habitat. Two fourteen-foot chain-link fences surrounded the camp, running parallel with ten feet of Bermuda grass between them. Each fence was topped with ten strands of barbed wire. The sky was big and hazy blue and the air was cool. I looked from one end of the place to the other, and then joined the rest of the guards as we passed through the double gates.

Most of the new guards and those I saw inside were brown-skinned Hispanics. They all spoke Spanish, and they looked at me suspiciously. One detainee made me laugh when he asked me if I was the only American employed there. For the first time in my life, I felt isolated because of my fair skin. But I also sensed respect, and I liked it.

We were led on a tour of the camp and shown the layout of male and female dorms, the mess hall, processing area, attorney rooms, solitary rooms, recreation yard, lock-up pens, and assorted offices of the guards and directors. The facility was originally designed to house 450 inmates, but because of changes in government policy toward Central America, which resulted in thousands of new migrations, by 1983 the building's capacity had been expanded to 600. We actually held more than 700.

The camp reminded me of a slaughterhouse I'd seen as a boy. The rancid smell of urine and feces, stale tobacco, and sweaty bodies packed tightly together permeated the concrete rooms and hallways. The smell came to mean sickness and perversion as my years there dragged on. In my mind it would always be the smell of corruption.

Detainees urinated against the walls of the recreation yard, which contributed to the stench. I was told that toilet paper was not flushed down with waste in many countries. Instead, the soiled paper was put in waste cans or thrown on the ground, and that intensified the odor even more.

Groups of prisoners—Mexicans, Central Americans, Ethiopians, Haitians, and others—were herded like sheep from one yard to another. I saw the expressionless faces of the other guards, the cold treatment they gave their charges, and heard their curses and ridicule in private. It was not a happy place. The shoving and profanity caused childhood memories to surface in me.

Another new guard, Frank Valdez, and I were assigned to work inside the male dorms. I was given a desk in a small glass-enclosed office. From there I could oversee the sleeping area, the television room, and the ping-pong table. Guards were not allowed to carry weapons within the facility because, technically, it was not a prison, but a detainment camp, although in every other way it seemed like the former. I had a radiophone to communicate with the control center that monitored all activities. We'd been taught the rudiments of self-defense—the disarming of an attacker, methods of physically handling detainees—and about the rights of those held on United States soil. It all sounded decent and fair. Treatment was based on the Geneva Convention: respect for each person's honor, convictions, and religion, and humane treatment with no violence to threaten their life, health, physical, or mental well-being.

The routine went basically like this: undocumented immigrants who were caught crossing into our country without documentation were usually brought from Border Patrol or the county jail to Bayview in patrol vans. They entered through Gate 1, the main double gates, and into the parking area in the heart of the facility. They were divided into male and female groups and taken to be processed in Building 9. Along the way, they would be taunted by loud shouts from the Four-Alfa recreation area on the other side of the parking lot. Their fingers grasping the chain-link fence, detained men would yell to the new male arrivals, "¡Vaselina, vaselina¡" Once inside, they were locked up in wire-divided rooms, then individually photographed and fingerprinted. Each one would sit down with an INS officer, be asked his or her name and any aliases, their country of origin, and if they'd ever been in the United States. They were also asked if they brought children with them, and if they had any relatives living here in the US.

They'd fill out the Form to Show Cause, on which the detainee had to state why he or she shouldn't be deported. A bond was set, usually two to three thousand dollars. If paid, the person would be set free to move about as long as he or she didn't work. Though it was their right, if they wanted to apply for political asylum, the officers would discourage them.

Hardly anyone but Nicaraguans got asylum in those days. They received special treatment because our country recognized responsibility for their civil war due to our support of the rebel Contras. The Salvadorans and Guatemalans, who were also at war, would nearly always get deported. Sometimes they chose to fight it with a lawyer and remain at the camp, because they faced beatings or death as traitors back home. I spoke with INS officers who had confirmed with police officials in other countries that the detainees were considered traitors when they arrived.

If a detainee's request for asylum was rejected or he couldn't pay his bond within a certain time frame, he was deported. Some were petrified of going home. Others welcomed it after living in the fields behind Brownsville or being at the camp, especially if they got a plane ride home. It was much easier than walking through Mexico where both bandits and police raped, robbed, and kidnapped them.

While assisting the officers processing new inmates, I heard horror stories. One man, a young Brazilian with shiny black eyes, told me that when he was five his father was killed and his mother received some insurance money. Her brother, his uncle, wanted it, but she wouldn't give it to him. Right in front of the little boy, his uncle took a machete and butchered her. He spared the boy but took him along with the money, molesting him until he was old enough to escape. Eventually, the boy became religious and came to the US to work with some Catholic missionaries, but was picked up by Border Patrol. He didn't even know he was here illegally.

After filling out forms, the men were given a shower and sprayed for lice. They were given an orange jumpsuit to put on. Their personal belongings were checked into burlap bags. They were allowed to keep a watch and maybe twenty dollars. If they had more money than that, an officer would take it to the vault.

The officers made it clear that if the detainees did exactly as they were told, there wouldn't be any trouble. After a few days on the job, I was getting the hang of it. Some of the detainees lived so far from the modern world that running water was foreign to them. One man didn't know what a toilet was. Others had told him it was a drinking fountain. I tried to explain that he shouldn't drink from it. The detainees from Pakistan would wash their feet in the sinks before they prayed. It was a religious practice. The detainees from

Mexico always got into an uproar over it, complaining that they brushed their teeth in the messy sinks. Another guy had no knowledge of personal hygiene, so with Frank Valdez as witness to avoid any misunderstanding, I told the man how to clean himself with soap. Each time we sent him to the clinic, the man came back telling us the doctor wouldn't look at him. "The doctor said I was abusing myself."

After several weeks, I had gained the men's trust. When they asked for a clean towel or some deodorant, I gave it to them. If they asked a question I could understand, I answered them. It was my policy not to ask them to do anything I wouldn't do myself. I respected them as people, and in turn, they respected me. Do unto others, as you'd have them do unto you. A simple thing. Even so, I came to be known as the "Reverend."

I acted as any ethical man or woman would under the circumstances. But the more time I spent around the other guards, watching them shove and curse the detainees and listening to their lewd jokes about visiting the female dorms at night, the more I realized that Frank and I and a few others were outnumbered. My reputation for getting along with the detainees hadn't gone unnoticed by my superiors, and I was warned not to be so easy on them. They laughed at me and said I was too softhearted.

■　■　■

It didn't take long before I was awakened to the level of abuse at Ruiz's camp. One night, after I'd worked there a few months, I witnessed the late-night happenings there. I was working the midnight shift, eleven to seven. My post was on the second floor of the two male dorms in buildings 32 and 34. They were separated from the female dorm in Building 35 by a fourteen-foot chain-link fence. My assignment was to do hourly head counts, enforce lights out, and see that all men were alone in their bunks.

At 1:30 a.m. I took my walkie-talkie and called in the head count to Control in Building 9, far across the camp. Similar calls came in from all dorms and patrol areas over the radio at this time. Guards posted outside the facility checked in every thirty minutes. Procedure was to call in all movement and activities.

As I strolled away from the sleeping bodies to the television area, I yawned. I'd been pulling a lot of graveyard shifts lately. Guards on night duty were not allowed to read or watch television, so I had to keep myself awake. The only light in the room came from a soda machine and a small desk lamp back in the office. Outside the window, mercury-vapor lights clearly illuminated the area between the male and female dorms. I stood by the window and yawned again. The muffled purr of an engine drew my attention to a green INS van that had pulled up to the gate outside the women's recreation area. Its lights were off. Nothing came over my radio. Why didn't foot patrol call Control to advise them of activity?

A female guard walked out of Building 35. I saw her unlock the gates and open them wide as the van pulled in. After relocking them, she went to the van and stood talking to the officer. She laughed loudly, and then the van drove up to the entrance of the building. That laugh belonged to Juanita Flores, a guard I'd met recently. She'd worked there for two and half years—fairly long for a guard. We'd just started to nod hello in passing.

Juanita went back inside and returned with a young female detainee, dressed in her camp orange jumpsuit with a T-shirt underneath. The girl was a fair-complexioned Hispanic, slender and wearing makeup. She strode to the van with her head cocked alluringly to one side, opened the door, and got in. I recognized the man in the van as Salazar, a tall, slim INS officer who once told me about his habit of picking up immigrant women at night, having sex with them, and dropping them off in front of my ranch because he knew we would give them a drink of water and a phone call. Juanita reopened the gate and the INS van disappeared into the darkness.

What had just happened? Where was he taking her? I started to pace. I couldn't help but think the obvious, but perhaps another explanation existed. I hadn't seen a female security guard in the van. Female guards escorted female detainees, without exception. Better get back to business. I bet I wasn't supposed to see that.

An hour later I was at the window by chance when a different guard escorted the same girl back to Building 35 by way of the opposite gate and turned her over to Juanita Flores. Now I was really confused.

When I got home that morning, Barbara told me over breakfast about the scare she'd had that night. Alone in the house, she'd been awakened by noises. She got up and tiptoed to the living room where she heard male voices speaking in Spanish outside. She'd watched aghast as the front door knob shook and turned against its lock. She had run for the shotgun, even though she detested it and knew I hadn't bought any shells. The intruders left without breaking in, but she'd been scared out of her wits and wished to high heaven I'd been there. We knew that undocumented immigrants sometimes knocked on our door and ran through our yard at night, but it hadn't been a big deal. Now I just stared at her white face. Suddenly our lives had become complicated. Once again, as when I was abused, I had a nasty secret. I couldn't confide my fears in Barbara because she had enough of her own, and she was depending on me. I always thought that I could live by the rules I believed in and loved, and feel blameless and good about myself. But as I put my arms around her to quiet her fears, I knew I wouldn't tell her what had happened at the camp. Maybe she'd want me to quit. Maybe she'd want to leave.

Two weeks later, I was on the midnight shift again. This time I was alone on foot patrol outside the facility, walking the perimeter and watching for escapees. I'd just turned the corner from behind the women's dorm walking north on the road that ran the length of the camp when I saw the green van facing me with its lights out. Salazar was driving again. I came up to the driver's-side window.

"Hey, Hefner, I have to go over to Building 35. Control knows I'm out here, so don't call them on the radio."

My face flushed. I didn't like being pressured to break the rules. But I understood keeping secrets. Salazar sat there above me in his pressed green uniform. So confident. I replied in a small voice, "Ten-four."

Salazar drove the van and waited for Juanita to open the gate. I walked along and stood far enough away to see but avoid being seen. When the darkened van drove past me again, a different young Hispanic woman sat in the front seat. I caught Salazar's gaze following me as they went by. I knew he didn't trust me to keep his secret. Other guards already saw me as a preacher who been known to stand up for the rights of others. After all, that was my responsibility as a kid, caring for my siblings. The van traveled north on the road and turned off up the small hill where Building 1 stood. Ruiz's office was there; the INS's offices were also there. From a distance I watched the van sitting in the parking lot and tried to rationalize away my complicity. Half an hour later the van started up again and drove down the hill and around to the other side of the camp. My memories of that night are much like my memories of the day I saved my little two-year-old sister from drowning in the creek when another sibling pushed her in. I was five and didn't even know how to swim, but I was able to keep her head above water until my parents arrived. Now I am sick to my stomach and don't know what it's going to take for me to jump in *again*.

Remember that story of the little boy with his finger in the dike? My dike was developing cracks, and water was seeping through. Oh, they were small cracks, a lie of omission to Barbara here, looking the other way with Salazar's flings there. I was afraid that before long, I might allow a full-fledged flood.

Every day at muster, when our supervisors explained the day's activities to the guards, we were warned not to ask questions about what we saw going on. "Don't see anything, don't look twice, just accept what happens. Don't talk to the media about what you see because they would only misinterpret and blow it all out of proportion." We always wondered what they were talking about, but it was eerily like another family secret. My conscience hurt over deceiving Barbara.

One day, as I took my break in the snack room, Juanita Flores walked over to the vending machines. She asked me for a quarter. It was the first time she'd spoken to me. Male and female guards rarely saw each other enough to become acquainted.

I smiled and flipped the coin to her. She bought a fruit pie and a soda then came over to my table and sat down. Juanita was rough and worn looking, giving the impression that she'd lived a hard life. Her dark hair was pulled back and mostly hidden under her uniform cap.

"Man, I can't stand this place. It's startin' to get to me. INS men think they run the world."

"Yeah, things are pretty crazy right now," I responded, surprised by her confiding in me. I told a few jokes and made her laugh, which displayed gaps where her teeth were missing. She relaxed. Would she tell me what was going on?

"Say, Juanita, " I began hesitantly. "Where did Salazar take the female detainee you brought out to the van the other morning?"

Juanita frowned. I'd hit a nerve. She asked me how I knew about that so I told her. She looked hard at me. A wall had formed. "You should know better than to ask questions. Someday you'll ask the wrong person."

I could feel my face flush red. Juanita took a long drink of her soda, then set it down and stared at the ice. She took a breath as if to speak but exhaled uneasily. Her forehead furrowed. Then she looked at me and spoke in a whisper.

"We are told that the girl is being taken to Processing to clean the offices, but she comes back and tells us differently. She told us the officers promised to get her out of here earlier if she has sex with them."

My mouth fell open. Juanita glared at me. "All you guys think the same way."

I reassured her we weren't all the same, but she was skeptical. As I stood up to leave, she grabbed my arm and asked me not to say that she had told me anything, because her husband was out of work and they had kids to support.

From her reaction I guessed that lying to detainees for sex might be more widespread. I believed that those officials involved would be fired if their supervisors discovered it, but what could they do to Juanita?

"But how can this be going on? Do any supervisors know?"

"Hefner, just drop it. You'll get us both fired."

"Why would we be fired? We didn't do it."

I left the break room and returned to my post, getting more and more angry. Why were these men able to take advantage of desperate women without being reported? It was infuriating news. But the real question seemed to be, what was I going to do about it?

2

The Conspiracy

Windham, Ohio, where I grew up, was mostly rural. Forest, fields, and lakes dotted the area where my stepfather would go to hunt when he wanted to be alone. Watching him go off meant it was up to me to handle the kids and any trouble that came up, but seeing him come back would make me bite my fingernails and think of how to humor him. It must be true that those who have been beaten by their parents still love them in spite of it. Acceptance and understanding is the key to escape. You keep on forgiving and trying to forget. I can honestly say that I loved and needed him and desperately wanted his approval.

Still, I didn't understand him. He was a "children should be seen and not heard" man and would enforce that with a swift backhand to the mouth, but then he would take neighborhood children for wagon rides while I had to sit on the porch and watch. The adult neighbors would comment on how much I looked like him with my black shaggy hair. "You can't say this one's not yours." Jim would laugh a little, but there was bitterness in it. He taught his other children that I wasn't their brother, and they grew up feeling superior. The adults seemed to think he was a good-enough guy, but the neighborhood kids knew better and would tease me, never allowing me to forget he was crazy.

Proving myself to my stepfather became a real obsession. He was always yelling about how I wasn't good enough, so "being good" became my goal. My mother's love and approval of him erased any doubts about his state of mind. At fourteen, I witnessed some teenagers looting a railroad car. I called the police, who were able to reclaim the stolen items, and they congratulated me on my quick thinking. That made me feel better than I ever had. Jim had taught me respect for the uniform, especially the police, and he couldn't condemn what the police praised. It became my habit to indulge anyone who held authority over me.

After I had been a guard for three years, detention camp life with its horror stories and abuses had become pretty commonplace. My niche was joke teller and nice guy, and I tried not to think about the rest. I did what I was told. But I wasn't proud of myself for staying silent. Now and then I'd see a woman's haunted face and wonder if I were responsible for some of that anguish. But it was more important to stay submissive to my employers and be accepted than to point out abuse. It was a confusing time when I couldn't quite see the larger issue. Guilt was a familiar and accepted weight. I rationalized that there wasn't much I could do without the cooperation of the other guards who knew, and they were all afraid for their jobs. I tried to be kind and gentle with the detainees while on duty and not participate in any activity I found questionable. And my job was important, too, paying for so many good things. Our ministries were established, and Barbara and I, with no children of our own, felt as though each child we cared for was ours. Barbara opened like a rose in the company of the children. Surely God didn't want me to lose my job.

I went on this way for many years—feeling horrified by the abuse I witnessed but not knowing what I could do about it. But then, in July 1986, we experienced a series of events that would test our faith in God and our belief in the victory of truth. On July 3, the fuel pump in my truck broke, and I had to have it towed to a nearby garage. Because of the Fourth of July holiday, it couldn't be fixed until the fifth. It was all right, though, as I didn't have to be at work until 3:00 p.m. that day, and I'd just ask my neighbor for a ride.

The morning of the fifth, I was preoccupied as I worked Three Auca Spears, our prize stud, on a tether rein in the paddock next to the barn. It was already hot and flies were hatching all around. I was thinking about an incident at work and a warning I'd received from my Burns supervisor, Abel Zavala. Zavala was a fair man. He went to one of the local churches and loved his family. He told me that our superior, Captain Danny Santana, wanted to "get rid of me." Apparently, a meeting was held with all the Burns supervisors at which I had been discussed as a "threat" to the Hispanics. Zavala told me that the others felt that because I was Anglo I might be promoted faster and rise higher in the company than they would. The fact that I was well respected strengthened this argument. "Apparently," Zavala said, "you're leaning toward helping the detainees and caring too much."

Zavala had argued that nevertheless, I was a good worker with no performance complaints and others seemed to like having me around, so I was spared for the time being. But he warned me to be careful.

The warning rankled me. Nobody knew I was half-Mexican. Would this problem go away if they knew I was one of them? But I got automatic respect because of the white color of my skin. I'd been discriminated against for my Hispanic blood as a child. Did I want to trash what was my advantage now? Only it wasn't quite an advantage if they wanted to sack me. I just couldn't win.

After Zavala and I had spoken, he walked toward Gate 3 while I exited through the control room on my way outside to the parking lot. Three female guards came running out of a small room not scanned by security cameras. Two of the guards were laughing and giggling, but the other stomped out angry. It was Juanita Flores. She was bristling because "that bastard pulled out his privates and was chasing us. He wanted us to touch it." The other women demurred that "he was just joking with us."

The door opened and a male voice with a throaty laugh said, "Come back in. I promise I'll be good."

I was face to face with Salazar, who stood there in the doorway, rumpled and round eyed, trying to shut his zipper.

Salazar had exposed himself and yet had complete job security. Meanwhile, my friend Frank had just lost his job. Frank reported to the Wage and Hour Division at the Department of Labor that the guards were not getting paid for the extra fifteen minutes at muster. Wage and Hour conducted an investigation and forced Burns to pay us for those extra minutes or be fined by the government agency. Frank eventually resigned because of pressure from Captain Danny Santana. Santana had kept him posted outside during the daytime when it was really hot, so he would have to stand in the sun for hours. Frank couldn't take it anymore. Now I was on the line. What kind of man did they want working at the camp, anyway?

I used the tether rein to slow down Three Auca Spears to a walk. The horse kicked at a fly, and his leg struck the metal siding on the barn. It ripped his leg. A serious gash started to bleed on his left pastern just above his hoof. I quickly tied him and examined the cut. It was a deep slice with clean edges and was bleeding like an open tap. I yelled out to Barbara to call the veterinarian and hoped she could find one fast on the Fourth of July weekend. Barbara came out to look, saw the blood, and headed back to the house saying, "Oh my God." I found a towel and wrapped it tightly around the leg, knowing that it was difficult to stop bleeding from this type of cut without stitches.

When Barbara returned, I was in the stall on my knees. Blood was all over my pants and shirt, and I could see her gulp back her nausea. I told her to stay out of the stall. "The vet said to apply pressure. He'll be here as soon as he can," she said. "He's got another emergency." Poor Barbara hates needles and shots and gets faint at the sight of blood.

"Honey, you'll have to call the camp and tell them I'll probably be late today. Tell them what happened," I said.

A few minutes later Barbara was back, upset and teary eyed, but not from squeamishness. "Your supervisor wants to talk to you."

"But I can't right now."

"You don't understand. He wants you to come to the phone right now if you want your job. Hurry, Tony, he's waiting."

She had no idea why my supervisor was being unreasonable. I tried to reassure her. I retied the towel as tightly as I could and ran to the house to pick up the phone. It was Lieutenant Eloy Huerta, one of my Burns supervisors. He said that if I wasn't at work by 3:00 p.m., I wouldn't have a job. He said, "You have to make up your mind. It's either your horse or your job."

Great, this was the excuse they were looking for. I told him I'd call him back and ran to the stall again. I saw the horse in pain and could not abandon him.

By five o'clock the vet had come and gone, and the horse, though he'd lost a lot of blood, would recover. I was exhausted. Three Auca Spears was part of our livelihood. I leaned on Barbara as we walked back to the house. Her silence meant she wanted some kind of explanation about this job mess.

"Well, maybe you guessed things aren't all roses at the camp," I said.

"Kinda figured that out."

I told her they were looking to fire me and leveled with her about the camp situation. I wasn't surprised that she didn't believe me.

"You're probably making mountains out of molehills."

I called the camp and asked to speak to Lieutenant Huerta. He made me sweat for a while on hold, and when he finally picked up the phone, he said that I had made my choice and to call Captain Danny Santana in a few days.

And that was that. I was out. Barbara was aghast. I was worried she would blame me, but after she thought about it she said something wonderful: "Tony, if you say you're being treated unfairly, it must be so." I didn't ever wonder if she blamed me in the awful months that followed.

On the seventh, Santana said he wanted to see me on the tenth at 2:00 p.m. sharp. Okay. Surely he would understand the circumstances. It wasn't like I was neglecting my responsibilities.

At 2:00 p.m. on the dot I walked into Santana's office. The captain, sitting at his desk, seemed preoccupied and didn't get up to shake my hand.

"This does not look good, Hefner," he said as he rifled through some papers. He picked up a report. "We gave you an opportunity to come to work, and you refused a direct order. You give us no other choice but to fire you. You can go."

My first inclination was to get out because I was mad, but when I saw him avoiding eye contact, I stopped. For three years I worked the night shift at this place. I knew who should be fired, and it wasn't me.

"You're really gonna fire me for this?"

"We will not bend the rules for you or anyone else. You can pick up your last check when you return the uniforms."

I knew why I'd been fired. But I wasn't going to let them do it. I had more than just a job at Bayview. I was delivering Spanish New Testaments through the mailroom to the detainees. It was good to see them reading it instead of fighting or jumping into bed with each other. And they needed a guard who'd give them soap when they asked for it, not laugh in their faces or shove them with a billy club. I would fight for my job.

After starting to collect unemployment benefits, I contacted the Equal Employment Opportunity Commission, the EEOC, to see if they could help me get my job back. Their representative, Mrs. Carlo Byers, guided me in filling out the claim form as I explained to her why I was fired. She was very helpful and understanding and sent the form to San Antonio to be processed. She said Burns had two weeks to oppose the benefits I was receiving. I'd hoped at least to collect unemployment from them until I found a new job or got my job back, but they appealed and forced a hearing for September 23, 1986, about two months away.

At the hearing, Captain Santana and a Burns district manager argued against me for two hours, saying I had no transportation and no intention of even going to work that day. After the mediator, Mrs. Jody Gómez, decided in Burns's favor, she ruled that:

> The claimant acted willfully and deliberately against the interest of his employer when he elected to absent himself from work in order to care for his horse and in not taking responsible actions to make arrangements for his transportation in order to report to work.

Willfully and deliberately? Pretty strong words. I was denied unemployment and told to pay back the Texas Employment Commission the $2,184.00 I had already received. Where was I going to get that? Everywhere I applied for work, I had to list Burns as my last employer. Burns naturally gave me a poor recommendation.

On September 29, after I'd been off nearly three months, I was in the front pasture doing fence repairs when Abel Zavala drove up. It wasn't unusual to see him because he went to church in San Benito and dropped by our place now and them. But this time, after a little small talk, he handed me a sworn, notarized letter.

"Read it," Zavala said.

I wiped my hands on my jeans and held the letter at arm's length to get focused. In it, Zavala swore that Captain Santana fired me because of a racial conspiracy.

Another Burns supervisor had come forward to my aid. He wrote a letter stating that I was dependable and had a good attitude toward my fellow workers. The letter was ammunition. I then asked the mechanic who worked on my truck to write a letter explaining the breakdown and the veterinarian who worked on Three Auca Spears to write yet another letter.

Then I called the Humane Society of Hidalgo County. Their investigator, Cindy Milton, averred in her letter:

Mr. Hefner is not in violation of Penal Code 42:11 because on July 5th of this year he made sure that his seriously injured horse was taken care of. If Mr. Hefner had chosen to go to work and leave the injured horse unattended, he would have been in violation (of the law).

The penalty for leaving Three Auca Spears alone and untreated, had he died, was a fine of two thousand dollars and one year in jail. I sent copies of all the letters to the Equal Employment Opportunity Commission in San Antonio and felt sure I'd get my case reopened. The mediator's words at the hearing, that I'd acted willfully and deliberately against the interest of my employer, still hurt. It just hadn't been that way. Truth and the courts would vindicate me.

After my unemployment was stopped we relied on Barbara's part-time job to put food on the table. It was pretty meager. Both of us had been taught to live by hard work and faith, but when it comes down to a steady diet of refried beans and bananas at five pounds for a dollar, trusting God isn't easy. It seemed he always waited until you were past what you thought you could bear.

As time passed and bills went unpaid, I couldn't find any work anywhere. The collapse of the Mexican peso had affected all the businesses in the Valley so there were more boarded-up stores than open ones. You couldn't even get a bad job. Barbara was still carrying the financial load, and every day it felt worse. Our mobile home payments were months behind, and we were at the point where we thought we'd lose the ranch.

We were forced to sell some good riding horses. Two mares, Hope and Charity, had given us nice, healthy foals, and were as sweet as could be. It was hard to sell them.

Worst of all, we couldn't hold retreats anymore. One day we were at the grocery store and saw one of our favorite families, Mrs. De la Cruz, a single mom, and her eight children. Last Christmas we'd collected some money to buy presents for the kids and took the packages to their grandmother's house so they wouldn't know who bought them. They'd been so excited at Sunday school. "Somebody gave us presents," they said and talked to Barbara about the toys they got and how they never got toys at Christmas but always "new" coats from the Salvation Army. "I just hate the Salvation Army," said Miguel, who was now a chunky little boy of nine. He and his seven-year-old twin sisters, Anabel and Anita, ran to us and hugged us. "When do we get to come on another retreat and go hayriding with the horses?" they asked.

Looking down at those big, trusting brown eyes, I felt so bad I wanted to cry. "We'll have one again real soon," I lied. I felt so guilty but couldn't explain. I'd stand by the wooden paddock fence and just stare down the road into the nothingness where it all blurred together. I began asking myself, why? Some reason had to justify this hardship. I hated feeling like a helpless and silly child. As I stood there picking splinters out of the fence I resolved to fight Burns with every legal resource available.

In the midst of our troubles our kind neighbor, Alice Hopperstad, helped us. Alice went to the bank with me and paid off the mobile home. She arranged to charge us a little interest but was willing to accept payments when we could make them, and she was easy to please. Barbara made a lot of banana cream pies over the months to show her our gratitude. So at least we had a house, and we weren't starving. But it would take a lot more to lift our depression.

■   ■   ■

In July 1988, two years after I had been fired, Mrs. Byers from the EEOC called. She told me to report to work the next day, because I had my job back. After two years! I could hardly believe it and felt confused. They had humiliated and wronged me. I needed a job and needed to see whether fighting them had been worth it. Yet if I'd won my case, why did it take Burns two years to rehire me?

To my knowledge, no one who had gotten fired had ever won his job back through the legal system. Canned employees had either messed up and taken the consequences or accepted that they weren't wanted around. It seemed to be the south Texas mind-set to accept failure with a shrug and move on. I'd heard enough to know the kind of thinking that was typical. They all thought I was Anglo and had more education and resources than they did. I had a ranch and horses—considerable possessions. I'd gone beyond high school (which counted for brains), and I was white skinned, which meant I knew my rights and was able to use the law to protect them. That's the notion that got me fired in the first place. White people use the laws, and US laws are the enemy in this no-man's-land of southeast Texas. The Anglos and Hispanics living here make up the law themselves, doing things the way they've been done for a hundred years.

Now that I was back, I knew that the camp dictators would be gunning for me. Part of the deal was that I would get a lump sum of back pay as reparations, but that I would sign a secret agreement with Burns not to tell anyone about it. I guess they didn't want others suing for the same thing.

Reporting to work the next day, I was told I'd be working the day shift this time. I didn't like it because I couldn't see what was going on at night anymore, but they didn't offer me a choice. Many new Burns guards were there, and some experienced ones had been promoted to INS jobs, which were more prestigious. The supervisors that had fired me, Captain Danny Santana and Lieutenant Eloy Huerta, had both been promoted. Huerta went up to the INS and Santana to Border Patrol, which was considered a higher sector of the INS. I also found out that Cecilio Ruiz, the head of the camp, had pushed for their promotions when he found out I was coming back. Ruiz had it in for me. I think he was personally insulted that the EEOC was forcing his company to rehire someone he didn't want around. Instead of allowing his buddies at Burns, Santana and Huerta, to eat crow and work with me again, he had them promoted. I wasn't hired back until they were gone.

Ruiz didn't hide his disfavor. He called me "Swabbie" in front of the other guards during muster. He said I reminded him of someone in the Navy, and since he was an ex-marine and hated the Navy, it was supposed to be an insult. It was common knowledge that he despised white people, and he flaunted his power over them whenever he could. It seemed to me that he felt inferior because his skin was very dark. Even though he had white friends, as a group they signified privilege and oppression. He had suffered much discrimination growing up. Ruiz had originally been in Border Patrol, but during a skirmish with drug runners, he took six bullets. His position at the camp was a reward for spilling his blood and in no way reflected his experience or expertise in the administration of the camp. He was vindictive and macho, and had to sexually dominate every female around him—ugly, beautiful, fat, old, it didn't matter to him. We all had to "humor" him or risk our jobs.

Surprisingly, I saw and heard much more on the day shift than I ever did at night. Not only were detainees being abused, but so were female guards. I bumped into Vicente Ramirez, the horse trainer I knew outside the camp, that first day back. He was lying on a desk sleeping and looked irritated when I came in and woke him up. I had called him a friend in our dealings with horses, and I had recommended him as a trainer and relied on his advice. But he was arrogant, and when my stud fees seemed too high to him, he wasn't above slamming the quality of my horses to persuade me to lower my fees. He had been hired in my absence. This was no surprise because he was an old friend of the new captain at Burns, Ernesto Rubio, and lived down the road from Juanita Flores. Ramirez, a dark-haired bronco with Spanish good looks, had a body he was proud of.

"Well, well, look who's back," he said as if he'd worked there all along. He stood up, grimaced, and stretched, throwing his chest out and flexing his biceps for my inspection. He reached way down into his pants to retuck his uniform shirt, then left without another word. If he intended to make me feel small, he succeeded.

Eduardo Payan, the new INS supervisor of detention and deportation, who'd been transferred just before I came back, was a pleasant, tall, grandfatherly man with a full head of white hair. He sympathized with my plight at Bayview. I had met him when I applied for permission to give the dean of the School of Scriptures, Reverend Verlis Collins, a tour of the camp. Reverend Collins wanted to see the detainees who had received the Spanish New Testaments the church was sending me. Before we left Payan's office that day, Payan put his hand on my shoulder and complimented me on my ministry and on my fight to get my job back. I'm sure that pleased the dean. Payan also said he'd like to talk to me later.

Several months passed before Payan reminded a supervisor to have me contact him, and we finally got around to discussing the sordid atmosphere at Bayview and discovered that we were on the same side.

One day he told me about a scene he had witnessed in Ruiz's office. A female guard on duty had used Wite-Out on the daily logbook to cover up a small mistake she'd made. The INS manual gives the following as cause for the termination of an employee:

> Falsification or unlawful concealment, removal, mutilation, or destruction of any official documents or records, concealment of material facts by willful omission from official documents or records . . .

Captain Rubio used this as an excuse to fire her. The woman happened to be beautiful, outspoken, and flamboyant. Two days later, Ruiz invited her to his office to discuss the possibility of rehiring her. Another female INS officer named Norma Rangel accompanied her there.

Payan and two other INS employees were standing at Ruiz's door when he opened it for the woman to leave. They noticed that her eyes were puffy and red from crying. Ruiz then said in their presence that he was putting her back on Burns's payroll because "the bitch gave the best head I ever had."

This wasn't the first I'd hear of the affair. Before Payan told me about the incident, I had innocently asked the girl about her rehiring. "Only a few days off, and you're back to work . . ." She was not pleased to recount the story but couldn't believe I hadn't heard it. Maybe it was the unexpected look on my face that made her go on. "Ruiz, without any clothes on, looks like a big fat bullfrog." She complained that Captain Rubio was also pressuring her for sexual favors because he claimed that he had a lot to do with helping her get her job back.

Her Wite-Out mistake was an excuse to blackmail her for sex. I was dumbfounded. Rubio used to be a Burns guard like myself, a pretty good guy with whom I'd become friends. I'd had his children and wife out to my ranch for a barbecue during a retreat. He had a drinking problem, but he'd been able to control it for years until he was promoted and started working under Ruiz. Now he sometimes came to work drunk.

Barbara wondered how in the world these women could take this kind of treatment. Was a mere job worth it? Two years after the Wite-Out incident, the other female INS officer, Norma Rangel, who'd escorted the women into Ruiz's office, quit her job because of Ruiz's sexual demands. After working to be promoted from a Burns guard to an INS officer, Norma was giving up a high-paying job.

Ruiz made sure he had control over every female guard, whether they worked for him or for the contract company. He actually had no direct influence on hiring or firing other than recommendations, but because he controlled who could come into the camp under a "clearance" exemption (guards and other staff members were not required to answer questions about their criminal record if they received this exemption), Ruiz would threaten female guards with having their clearances lifted if they refused to "date" him. Payan confirmed this: "I was ordered by Ruiz to terminate clearance for guards and one in particular for not meeting him for lunch . . . He told me, 'Fire the bitch, nobody stands me up.'" Payan did not terminate her clearance, but the demands for sexual favors continued and the reputation of Ruiz, Rubio, and Ramirez—known as the three "R's"—grew.

Other grounds for dismissal included disorderly conduct, use of abusive or offensive language, intimidation by word or action, engaging in disruptive activities that interfered with the moral and efficient operation of the government, theft, vandalism, immoral conduct, or any criminal actions. All were disregarded in Ruiz's camp. His rules were simpler: play along, don't interfere with our "privileges," or you're out.

I'd gained a reputation for standing up for myself when I fought Burns for my job. Some guards were glad I was back. They'd become discouraged because nothing had changed; in fact, things had gotten worse. Guards and detainees now came to me with their problems and confided what they'd seen or asked me for help. They seemed to be looking to me for moral strength, as if I were some kind of crusader. But all I did was write down what they told me. So far, it was a notebook crusade.

The next couple of years revealed what a battleground the camp had become. The fight for justice intensified as wave upon wave of undocumented immigrants crossed the border fleeing the violence in Nicaragua, El Salvador, and Guatemala. By 1989, the camp had swollen from seven hundred to ten thousand refugees.

3

Death of a Detainee

> The mishandling of detainees' property can create
> resentment and distrust. Therefore, the INS offi-
> cers conducting inspections and/or shakedowns
> should take care not to damage or destroy the
> property of detainees. Every effort should be made
> to return articles to their original place, leaving the
> area as it was found prior to the search, except
> items determined to be contraband, which are
> then removed.
>
> —INS RULES AND REGULATIONS

I would often be in the dorm with detainees who were assigned
cleaning duties. Their daily chores were to sweep floors, mop, wash
windows, and scrub bathrooms, for which they were paid one
dollar a day. I often had to encourage the men not to quit. The foul-
ness of the waste sometimes made the job unbearable.

Periodically, INS officers carrying black batons and wearing
camouflage uniforms and visored helmets would enter the dorm
to search for drugs and weapons. Usually four or five officers would
start in different sections of the room and strip the beds, tossing
the bedding and mattresses onto the floor. When they searched the
small metal cabinets holding the men's possessions, valuable
papers needed for court were often crumpled and scattered.

The INS officers performing the shakedowns were friends of
mine, and sometimes ones with whom I had just shared lunch or

discussed a family problem. So it grieved me deeply when on one occasion these officers, in my presence, ordered the workers assigned to cleaning duties to sweep up all the papers they had just strewn about, put them into large black plastic bags, and take them out to the dumpsters. Then they ordered the men to clean up the dorm again. I watched the INS officers pocket money from the beds they had torn apart.

The detainees who were in the recreation yard outside pressed up against the gate watching bags of their belongings being taken to the dumpster. The INS posted security guards around the dumpster area to prevent anyone from going through the trash.

The officers left me with the detainees frantically returning to the dorm to hunt for their valuables. Many cried over lost pictures, missing legal papers, and phone numbers of family back home. Their belongings were lost. The looks on their faces haunted me for years.

■ ■ ■

Eduardo Payan, with whom I was becoming close, was the new supervisor of detention and deportation. He received formal complaints from detainees with grievances and was responsible for entering them into the system. After we had been friends for a while and had often shared our disapproval of what we saw occurring at the camp, he began to tell me about these official complaints—to relieve his sense of impotence and disgust, I think. Their content floored me, but I was encouraged to see that some detainees were brave enough to come forward. Some knew they were being exploited and realized they had no control over their destiny. Though Payan forwarded the complaints diligently, they were rarely taken seriously and little came of them. He felt it was wrong to victimize the immigrants at the camp, yet his efforts were being stopped on all sides because of Ruiz. Payan had to walk a fine line to maintain a good relationship with Ruiz.

. . .

In July 1988, five women—Ana and Miwa of El Salvador, Concepción and Santa of Honduras, and Beatriz of Nicaragua—filed a joint complaint. It stated that the women were upset about being required to go to Building 1 after 9:30 p.m. to "clean offices." Once inside, they were expected to provide sexual favors to INS officers and security supervisors.

Another detainee, Berta from Honduras, was escorted many times to the parking lot outside Building 1 by security guard Lydia Dillard. Once in the parking lot the female guards left the women there with no one in sight. Later the guards were informed that they were to pick up the detainees. Again, the women were left standing unattended in the parking lot, where the guards would find them and transport them back to the dorm. The same orders were delivered on weekends. Berta told Lydia she was having sex with the recently promoted Burns supervisor Vicente Ramirez. In fact, she'd written a letter to camp head Cecilio Ruiz on July 7, 1988, asking to speak with him as soon as possible because she was pregnant. Shortly before she was to deliver, Berta was deported. She contacted Lydia once more to report that she had given birth to a baby girl. Payan told me she had confessed the story to him as well.

Another detainee, Barbara, wrote to an INS official on July 26, 1988, to complain about detainees forced to have sex with INS officers. Payan gave me a copy of her letter.

On July 25, 1988, Payan received another complaint from a detainee named Ana. She stated, "The females are taken out nightly at 9:30 to Building 1 and returned at 10:30." She said that the center is not a detention center but a jail for prostitution.

Payan himself filed a complaint about these various violations with the district office but was thwarted by the INS, his employer. On July 28, 1988, the acting district director, George T. Summerville

Jr., wrote a memorandum to all Harlingen district sections. In it he states, "In the future, any report made to OPR (Office of Professional Responsibility) will be documented in writing. You will continue to report any allegations to OPR as in the past, but will forward a report to this office. Please ensure that the report contains the following subject matters: 'Time and date of alleged incident, office and agent reported to.'"

As Payan said, in a memorandum he wrote that day and passed along to me, "*Reporting Procedures* were enforced only when it did not mention wrongdoing by a member of the upper management staff. Any wrongdoing by midlevel supervisors would result in that person(s) being thrown to the dogs. Upper-level supervisors do and did hide the evidence until the report died for lack of interest."

When questioned by a district official, no other INS officer besides Payan would corroborate seeing these kinds of abuses. Payan said, "I was never allowed to continue the investigation after I'd found out INS employees were involved and witnessed by Burns female guards. Ruiz wanted an outstanding work review every year, and any problems with the security companies would reflect on him. Any female complaints were filed and forgotten." Payan calculated that this was why the abuse continued. As the INS instructions for employees states, "Any officer that failed to report is just as guilty as the perpetrator" (no. 287-10). The rules make *witnessing* the abuse just as incriminating as *committing* it. So if nobody saw it, nobody could report it, and nobody was guilty. When I won my job back, Payan knew I understood the power plays involved. Our talks together gradually built trust, and he became my source for reliable inside information.

Payan gave me a copy of another letter he wrote on July 28, 1988, which he sent to an INS attorney. In it he named the five women who had made the joint sexual harassment complaint. The women had protested to Cecilio Ruiz that "some of the officers are stopping incoming mail and taking money that is sent to inmates.

They are also abusing the inmates, and are sexually abusing the women." They named two INS officers. Payan wanted the attorney to know that when the women were confronted by INS officers about their complaints, the officers threatened to deport them. Payan told the lawyer that he had released the women on their own recognizance, and that they were going to be witnesses for the FBI on the complaint.

Payan assured me that he was looking for ways to bypass the INS employees who were over him and bring the complaints to light, which gave me great relief. He wrote this in a memo he sent me:

> Most detainees agree that the first few days at the camp is a time to recuperate from their travels and feel safe from predators on the streets. It's only when they realize that the predators threatening their dignity and human rights are the ones keeping them detained that they start to panic. Neither the women nor the men can adjust to being detained when abuses by their keepers are threatening. All paperwork that a detainee signs advises him/her that they will be protected during their deportation process. But, the unofficial understanding informs them, you do what I tell you, or order you to do, and everything will be okay. The most common threat is, cooperate, or I will deport you. The detainee, unless he or she is a lawyer, does not know that only an Immigration judge has the authority to deport them.

■　■　■

Throughout my employment, tales of abuse circulated among the guards, but the blame was always placed on the detainees. They were the ones who caused this or that to happen. But the random abuse became so woven into our everyday work schedule that it was impossible for the perpetrators to keep it hidden for long. It seemed as though they were invincible, and the guards could do nothing to stop them.

In August 1988, I was on my rounds in the men's dorm. The loudspeaker blared the names of men being deported, and they rushed frantically for their belongings, then came to me with a million questions. Before long they were out the door, and I continued my walk. A strong smell of marijuana came seeping out of the bathroom. I pushed on the door, but someone was holding it shut. I commanded them to step back, and a few seconds later they opened the door.

Ten men stood inside, with the sweet, acrid smell of the drug heavy in the air. Five detainees held lit filter-tip cigarettes. The men milled about, avoiding eye contact with me. They started to split up and leave. I radioed Captain Rubio. He said to keep an eye on the detainees and call him if I smelled it again.

Later that day, I was approached by one of the men from the bathroom. A detainee named Jovanny told me that an immigration officer had sold him the marijuana. A Burns security guard was also selling it. They were charging three dollars a joint and two hundred for a baggie. I asked him to confirm that to my supervisor, but he strongly refused.

"If you tell anyone I told you this, I will lie," he replied. He said that the men selling the drugs would kill him if they found out he'd told. "Besides, I already gave the information to Mr. Payan, and I trust him," he said.

Payan sent a memorandum to his district director, Omar G. Sewell, on August 9, 1988, with Jovanny's information. Later, several Burns guards and one INS officer were arrested by the Justice Department's internal affairs division. A cook asked me on different occasions when I took my dorm to the mess hall if I knew where he could get some drugs. His behavior was odd to say the least. He was always joking with me, and now he was acting dopey, as if he were under the influence. At the time I had no idea he was trying to set me up—later on Payan told me that the cook was an undercover informant.

■　■　■

The abusive behavior seen on the job often followed us back to our homes. Occasionally people would have parties and invite people from work. One day in the late summer I was relieving a guard named Mary from Gate 3, so she could take a lunch break. She saw Rubio from a distance entering Building 3. Just about everyone knew Rubio and I were friends. She probably wanted me to know what kind of a guy Rubio was when I wasn't around, because she told me a story about what had happened just a few days before at a party she hosted.

Francis Carmona, in her late thirties and newly divorced, lived with her son and mother when she got a job at the camp with Burns. She had an easy, old-world way with people, drawing them to her with language sprinkled with "sweethearts" and "dears." Ecstatic over landing the job, she looked forward to meeting the other employees socially because her divorce had been nasty and long, and she was ready to have some fun.

Mary remembered that the night of the party was hot and humid, but it was held inside nevertheless. There was loud music, dancing, drinking, and conversation. As Francis stood with Mary, she noticed an older man leering at her. Mary said he was their supervisor, Captain Rubio, and that he had not been invited because he drank too much and behaved badly. Francis hadn't recognized him without his uniform cap because he was bald. Mary suggested she ignore him.

Francis turned her back to resume conversation, then felt a hand on her shoulder. She turned and found the balding, paunchy Rubio breathing alcohol into her face.

"You wanna dance?" he asked.

"No thanks, sweetie." She shook her head and tried to turned to the others, but he insisted. Again she told him no. When she turned away he grabbed her blouse and tore it. A struggle ensued. Rubio pushed her up against the living room wall where she lost her balance and fell to the floor beneath him. Francis slapped at him as his hand uncovered her breast. He threatened to rape her on the spot.

Three men finally pulled him off her as he yelled, "Stop fighting me, you bitch!"

An hour passed before Francis recovered enough to face her co-workers and leave the party. She worried all weekend whether Rubio would fire her on Monday.

But Rubio acted as if nothing had happened. Francis thought maybe he didn't remember. Even though the incident was embarrassing and painful, she was relieved to have her job and willing to forget about the whole thing.

■ ■ ■

Proper INS procedure mandates that when a child has a sexual complaint inside a government facility, the FBI must be called in. Minor detainees are supposed to be protected by the federal government.

In early September 1988, Payan notified the FBI about complaints he'd received from several boys, sixteen and seventeen years old. They were being kept in Building 308, a bungalow within a housing village of prefabricated homes just outside the entrance to the camp where many INS officers lived with their families. To hold juveniles with adults is illegal.

Several boys would share a bedroom, each one assigned to a freestanding bunk. An immigration officer or guard closely supervised them. The boys were far from home and emotionally lost. I was one of their babysitters.

According to the statements the boys gave Payan, when Juan, a seventeen-year-old from El Salvador, had first been apprehended and confined to Building 308 in late June, an immigration detention officer had molested him. The incident began when, late at night, the officer locked both doors to the house and walked into Juan's bedroom wearing only a cowboy hat and briefs. Juan woke up when he heard the doors slam shut, though the other two boys in the room remained asleep. The officer had a heavy black mustache. He walked over to Juan's bed and sat down at his feet. Then, with his back turned toward the boy, he started wiggling his buttocks.

Juan cried, "Man, what's your problem?"

The man told him he'd give him twenty dollars to make love to him. In Juan's country, a man could be killed for being homosexual.

The officer toyed with the boy's underwear then reached beneath it. He repeated his offer, saying, "I only want you for five minutes." He told Juan his replacement was due soon and he would throw in two packs of cigarettes. Juan continued to rebuff the man's advances until the new guard came.

Jorge, sixteen and also from El Salvador, had been deported once and reapprehended in April 1988, when he came under my supervision. Asked later about his involvement in the alleged sexual misconduct in Building 308, he identified the picture of the same mustached officer. He said the man wore only a cowboy hat and briefs, and approached him late at night. The man sat down next to him and started pulling on the boy's underwear, exposing his genitals. The officer told him, "I want you. Do you understand?" And offered him fifty dollars, saying he knew he needed the money.

Desperate, Jorge weighed the money against the shame and accepted, allowing his flesh to feed the vulture.

"Now, you won't tell anybody about this, will you?" the man asked.

Jorge also stated that the same officer had several sexual encounters with other detained juveniles. One of them, named Ricardo, used to grab the officer's rear end in front of the other juveniles to which the man would feign arousal and grin his approval.

When Juan and Jorge gave their statements in September 1988, the officer questioning them asked, "What prompted you to report these incidents after so much time has passed?" The molestations had occurred in the spring and early summer.

Juan replied vehemently, "Yesterday an INS officer came into our house and started calling us 'faggots' and 'queers.' I just couldn't take it, you know, so I stood up and yelled back, 'The only faggots and queers around here are the ones wearing green uniforms!' And I told him everything that guy was doing to us."

The boys gave the FBI the names of everyone they knew to be involved. Because the FBI had been called in, the man confessed, was convicted, and sent to jail for ten months. INS officers told me that if Jorge asked "for the moon," I was to get it for him or find someone who could. The INS was afraid there could be a lawsuit, and the boys got whatever they wanted.

When he received Juan's and Jorge's complaints, Payan discussed the matter with his supervisors, and they told him *not* to report it to the FBI. "We don't need an OIG [Office of the Inspector General] investigation," they said. He reported it anyway, against their wishes, and from that time on, Payan was not to be trusted.

■ ■ ■

The last several months of the year were relatively quiet as we rounded the corner into 1989 and another mild Texas winter. Assigned to be the day's runner, I thought the shift should be interesting. Runner duties included escorting detainees from different dorms to the processing building for meetings or court appointments, escorting them to work details, and relieving guards for their breaks. I'd get to talk to a lot of people and looked forward to the variety.

Five male detainees supervised by Burns guard Joe Vega cut the grass around the camp. My first order was to escort these men to the mess hall to eat with the women at an earlier hour. I stood guard as they sat on one side of the cafeteria and blew kisses to the women filing in.

Near me, INS Lieutenant Rosemary González stood watching the female detainees enter the mess hall, supervised by two female guards who escorted them. Usually languid, Rosemary's shoulders were rigid with tension and her eyebrows, raised practically to her hairline, expressed deep fatigue. By 1989, immigration had become a national problem. Immigrants streamed to every state in the country, seeking to be assimilated and find work. Meanwhile, our camp had grown into a gigantic overblown circus. Huge tents had been set up outside to accommodate the hoards of detainees. My contingent, which originally had a headcount of sixty-five, had grown to more than two hundred. All the INS officers were overworked, pulling double shifts and getting even surlier. Rosemary was one of them.

One of the women detainees was being helped into the mess hall by several others. She could barely walk. Her head bobbed up and down, and she grimaced.

I walked toward her to assist, but Rosemary held up her hand. She told me not to "get excited," as the woman had already seen the camp doctor and been pronounced well.

"She's just faking it, Hefner," Rosemary snapped, "trying to get attention."

I backed off. Rosemary had the authority. I watched as the woman was helped to a table. She sat with her head bowed and moaned while a friend brought her a tray and solicitously sat down beside her.

Then, all at once, her face fell forward into her plate and her torso slumped. She seemed to be unconscious. I left Rosemary and quickly went to her.

"She hasn't eaten in two days," said her young helper.

"You two!" I yelled across the hall to two grass cutters who had stood up to see. "Escort this woman to Processing so they can get her to a doctor." The rules were that all sick detainees had to report to Processing first. But surely the INS would make an exception for this poor woman.

Rosemary stood glaring at me, ticked off. I decided to follow through, feeling her eyes on me as I radioed the female runner in Processing about sending her a very sick woman. I told her to make sure the woman saw a doctor. At 11:45 a.m. I left the mess hall with my male grass cutters and went outside to the yard.

At 3:00 p.m. the afternoon guard relieved me from the yard. I was hoping to question the female runner I had radioed earlier, and as I walked past Processing, she came rushing toward me.

"Hey, Silvia," I said, "what happened to that sick woman I sent you?"

"God, Hefner," she said, rolling her hazel eyes, "it was a mess. They got her to stand up, but she passed out in front of Lieutenant González. She started yelling at her to get up, but the woman just lay there, out of it, so Rosemary starts kicking her. She kicked her around like a rubber ball in front of everyone."

"Where is she now?"

"As far as I know, she's still there. They put her on a cot. She was just laying there, kind of crying, last I saw her. She never said a word."

I sprang toward Processing. The door opened, and four female detainees came out carrying the sick woman on an army stretcher escorted by Lydia Dillard, a guard. Lydia told me the same thing, and from inside the building the venetian blinds bent open. It was Rosemary. She caught my eyes in a withering glare. I knew I was in trouble and that this could cost me my job.

The woman they carried past me was pale and breathed in wracked, uneven sighs. A froth of yellow bubbles foamed at the corners of her mouth.

The sick woman was named María, a thirty-nine-year-old from Guatemala. She had to be someone's mother, daughter, and wife, but by the end of the day, she was dead.

A week later I talked with Lydia Dillard. She said that the woman was not taken to see a doctor, but had instead been carried to a bed in the dorm office in Building 39. This was odd, as I knew the doctors and nurses were here until 5:00 p.m. every day (although not on weekends) and that Building 39—which had previously been used by medical staff only but was now used to house detainees due to overpopulation—was adjacent to the doctor's station.

"She was alive when they brought her in," Lydia said. "I checked on her all the time, but I'm not a doctor. I didn't know what to do for her." Dorm guards have no medical training. She described to me how the woman groaned then became silent, at which point a yellow liquid dribbled from her mouth, and she died.

Lydia called the acting security supervisor, Beatriz Huerta, to the dorm. Beatriz examined the woman and confirmed her passing.

Beatriz said she notified the INS immediately, but the body remained in the office from 4:00 p.m., when she died, until after midnight when she was finally transferred to a Harlingen hospital. No report had to be filed because no one came to examine the body.

A brainstem infarct was given on the death certificate as the cause of death. It had been caused by a cerebral aneurysm that in turn led to massive hemorrhaging. That explained her excruciating pain and loss of consciousness. Medical professionals outside the camp said that a burst spleen probably caused the yellow liquid that dribbled from her mouth.

María's body lay in the Harlingen Valley Baptist Hospital morgue for a week before immigration sent it to a funeral home. The immigration facility did not want to finance her funeral. When Payan heard that the hospital was requesting her body be transferred out of the morgue because it was decomposing, he gave them permission. The body was shipped back to Guatemala, but immigration did not want to cover the expense. When the bill for internment came, the INS balked at paying it. They wanted Payan to pay because he had authorized her burial. Eventually, they paid.

I had no reason prior to these events to speak with Beatriz Huerta, except to exchange hellos and commiserate briefly about the job. A beautiful Hispanic woman, tall with smooth skin and high cheekbones, Beatriz had a natural sense of authority. The detention officer Eloy Huerta was her brother-in-law and kept most of the men at bay. Because of my talks with other female guards, Beatriz began to seek me out about what she'd seen in the hope that I could do something about it.

In February 1989, she confided that she and other guards had observed medical staff giving white pills to some female detainees. This was something new, and the women would complain to guards that the pills caused severe cramps and heavy bleeding. Some detainees who had missed a period were given a white pill that would start hemorrhage-like bleeding. Others who had just had a period would bleed and cramp again after taking one. The guards talked about it among themselves, agreeing they had never come across such medication before. They didn't know what it was, but there was little they could do about it.

Soon after she learned of the white pill, Beatriz was called to Building 35, the female dorm. She found a group of detainees gathered around a bed attempting to comfort and care for a hysterical woman under the covers. The young woman beneath the blanket was bleeding copiously.

"She's been taking the white pills," another guard told Beatriz.

The distraught young detainee cried repeatedly that she did not want to lose her baby, but the others said, "The baby is already dead." As the guards took over she allowed them to remove the blanket but refused to move her tightly clenched legs, thinking, she said, that by holding them together the baby would not come out. Beatriz called for an ambulance to take her to the hospital.

"I wonder if the camp clinic is trying out some sort of abortion pill?" Beatriz asked me.

Soon after, Beatriz was demoted from supervisor to guard due to María's death, which had occurred during her shift. I no longer saw her on my shift.

The possibility of an abortion pill really haunted me. I knew that the guards were having sex with detainees and causing the pregnancies. I felt that the pregnant female detainees who were deported should have been brought back to America, and the government employees who were responsible for the pregnancies should have been forced to support their children.

■　■　■

In April 1989, I was working a weekend three-to-eleven shift in Building 32, a male dorm that was usually one of the cleaner, quieter ones. After evening mess hall, Control called to inform me they were going to show a movie.

The INS showed horror movies most of the time, usually in English. I often wondered at the recreation director's choices. Once they showed *The Texas Chainsaw Massacre*. The movie's violence put knots in my stomach. How would I protect myself if a riot broke out? As guards, we weren't trained to handle such a situation, and the INS hadn't clarified any procedure. They didn't even inform us if a detainee was HIV positive. We weren't given any precautionary equipment, such as surgical gloves or masks, to help us prevent contact with potentially infected blood or body waste. Inmates with tuberculosis were eventually segregated but were not identified immediately.

I could see the television area well from my desk, and to my surprise, the movie wasn't a horror movie—it was X-rated. The men started to whoop and holler as nude women appeared on the screen. As a precaution, I locked the door to my office in case a fight broke out.

A male INS officer in Control monitored the detainees by way of cameras positioned around the dorms. One camera in my dorm was not far from the television and was trained directly on the men watching. My phone rang. The officer in Control told me to go to the television area and check on my detainees. He was laughing.

I don't know what other guards felt, but the group of men out there frightened me. Locked up too closely together for months and desperate to get out, the men were now aroused as well.

"I can see them clearly enough from here," I said.

"Hefner, I order you to go in there and check on them." I was known to be an easygoing guy, and the INS officers loved it when they could get a reaction out of me with their silly head games. This was like walking into a lion's den and nothing to joke about.

Seventy-four men filled the small area and sat on wooden benches or leaned against the walls. As I gingerly walked toward them, the smell of their body sweat heavy in the air, I saw that their attention was focused on the passionate action on the screen. Several were masturbating, while others scrambled to get out of their way.

Back in my office, the phone was ringing. I could hear the INS officer from Control laughing before I even put the phone to my ear. The movie ran for about an hour.

Later that same night, Carlos, a young detainee with perfect English, and an older man, Samuel, rushed into the office.

"Señor Hefner!" Samuel shouted. "Come quickly!"

Samuel said, "Man and boy in shower. Sexual, sexual!" He was holding two fingers together.

From my air-conditioned office I ran to the bathroom, where the musty locker-room odor assaulted my senses. Six men, naked but for the towels hung around them, stood at a small shower stall entrance, heckling and craning their necks to see inside.

"What's going on here?" I tried to sound official and pushed them aside to see. In a shower stall two nude men were trying to rape a boy. The two men had the boy bent over. The one in the front was holding the boy's arms while the other was forcing him to the tile. Both nozzles were spewing hot water at full force in the dim stall.

I powered through the crowd, their wet bodies dampening my clean blue uniform. Shoved from behind, I thought I might get jumped. The naked boy was crying, "*Ayúdame, ayúdame*," help me, help me. I couldn't recognize the men with their long hair hanging in their faces, and they had no idea I was there. I reached through the shower and grabbed the boy away from them. They stood up with the water streaming down and looked at me as though I were from Mars. Then they released him quietly. I pulled him out of the stall. Everyone just stood there.

The boy was about fifteen. I threw him a towel and asked if he was okay.

His lips trembled as he wrapped the towel around his thin body. One of the spectators tugged at the towel to uncover him again, but the boy defiantly pulled away, his eyes lowered.

I commanded them to get out of my way and guided him out. Livid and shaking with adrenaline, I blamed the cruel choice of movie.

The boy came to the office to dry off and dress while I called Control for an escort to take him to Processing. Whoever processed him in the first place had to be blind not to see that he was underage. Poor kid. The horrors he had probably escaped in his own country, to come to this. My God, he was still so young. The next day he was sent to the IES (International Emergency Shelter) children's center in Los Fresnos. His name was Alejandro (or Alex, as we called him), and he was under the care of Homer Tamez, the IES administrator.

Payan gave me a copy of a report written about Alex three months later in July. It said that he had been in the Bayview *Corralón* for two months before the event that caused his transfer to the children's center. From there he had been sent to IES in Mission, also for juveniles. After a short time there he ran away and was missing for two weeks. When found, he was returned to the

Mission shelter, where his behavior became so aberrant that he was placed in counseling. The shelter's administrator followed up with a report about Alex that included the following account of one of his counseling sessions:

> During today's counseling session, the child was very uneasy, displayed some nervousness, made a sincere attempt to hold back tears, would refuse to make eye contact, and kept getting up from his chair in a very fidgety manner. Alex is not the same person I have known for the past two or three months. He is more quiet, less active, and appears to care less about hygiene, he is masking his emotions, and at times appears to have given up on himself. I asked if he had any sexual involvement with anybody during the time he had been on a runaway status. He became all but uncontrollable and confided that something had happened. Alex claims that upon returning to the shelter, he encountered a male adult staff person who almost immediately started to make sexual advances toward him. The staff person would tell Alex that he was his favorite person, would physically touch him to where Alex would feel very uncomfortable. He would rub his finger on Alex's lips and make nonverbal suggestions, would whisper in his ears, "I love you," and would gently bite Alex's ear, and hug him while running his hands all over the child. According to Alex, on one occasion this mysterious staff person went out and bought Alex some fried chicken and told him that soon they would be alone together. Alex said that he became somewhat scared when this person showed him a badge. He felt threatened that if he said anything to anyone . . . there would be repercussions.

Jesse Villarreal, director of programs for the International Emergency Shelter (IES), wrote a letter to Cecilio Ruiz dated August 2, 1989. In the communication he mentions a letter he received from Homer Tamez regarding Alex. The staff member Alex accused denied the allegations, and Child Protective Services of the Department of Human Services (DHS) concurred with IES that because they were conducting an internal investigation, no investigation by DHS was needed. "Mr. Homer Tamez will be arranging for a psychological evaluation."

The news of the abuse of children was especially alarming to me. The FBI was supposed to be notified, but they were rarely brought into the picture. Growing up, I felt like a prisoner in my own surroundings. I was trapped and abused. I understood what it was like to be forced to do what you didn't want to do, and I couldn't stop thinking about these children being trapped in this horrible place.

■　■　■

Carlos, an eighteen-year-old detained at the camp that spring, was nice looking, well groomed, had light brown hair, and a friendly disposition. He had been very helpful to me on several occasions. Everyone liked him.

His family had emigrated to the United States from El Salvador in 1974 when Carlos was three. Although he had a social security number and a green card, he was not a US citizen. In every other way he was American. He didn't even speak good Spanish. He told me that he had gotten into trouble with some other young people and would be at the camp until he was able to "prove his innocence." Every morning at 5:00 a.m. he faithfully reported to work in the mess hall to earn his one dollar a day. He liked to stay busy, he said, as he missed seeing his girlfriend and the work made time go by faster.

One night I was called in to work the graveyard shift as a runner. At 11:30 p.m. I was ordered to report to Processing. Barbara didn't like staying home alone, but her parents were visiting us for a few weeks, and I knew she looked forward to the time she was able to spend with them.

In early May, the nights never got cool unless you stood directly in the path of a Gulf breeze. Inside, the accumulated heat of the day raised the temperature another ten degrees. Some of the buildings didn't have air conditioning.

Over at Processing, I had some time to kill while the INS officer finished the forms I was to deliver. As I looked around I saw a naked man with his back to me trying to cover his genitals with his hands. A Control monitoring camera was pointed straight at him.

Everyone, including detainees, knew that women were in the Control room. They could obviously see him. Why was he being humiliated like this?

"I need those forms as soon as you're done with them," I said to the officer, wanting to get out. When I spoke, the naked man lifted his head and turned toward me. It was Carlos.

Raising my voice, I said, "I know this young man. Why is he being treated like this?" The more I talked the louder I became. "Why is he in there like that? What's going on here?"

"Settle down, Hefner," said the officer with the forms. "We're just trying to break his spirit."

With my mouth open, I looked at the officer and back at Carlos. "Break his spirit? Do you think he's a horse?"

I was overstepping my boundaries. Guards never questioned the officers. But instead of getting angry, he started to laugh. He thought my reaction was funny, and he explained that some officers told Carlos they were deporting him back to El Salvador, at which Carlos became upset. As far as I knew, he had no close relatives or friends there.

"Is he going to be deported?" I asked.

"I don't know. I think the officers were just teasing him."

Don't the officers have anything better to do, I thought to myself, than play games with these poor innocent people?

"Look, why don't you let him get dressed, and I'll take him back to his dorm."

"Can't do that."

"Why not?" I asked.

"Because *I'm* not in charge," he said. He stopped working and sat back, regarding me. "You have to get permission from the officer in charge."

Looking around, I asked, "Where is he?"

"Well, he's not here! He went into town with some other officers to get a pizza." Glancing at his watch, he said, "They should be on their way back now."

He handed me the forms. I stalled, looking them over, trying to think of some way to help Carlos.

The door opened, and an officer from Control burst into the room and strode over to Carlos. "Put your hands down," he ordered, and Carlos's hands dropped to his sides.

The cooler air from outside hit me in the face as I walked into it, closing the door on that pathetic scene. Four laughing officers were walking toward me from Control, carrying their pizza. They passed me on their way to Processing.

Now was my chance. They'd all be in there eating. But would they even listen to me? I knew what would happen. I'd be laughed out of the room and maybe even make things worse for Carlos. If it were just the officer in charge and me, maybe he would listen. But all the officers together formed a mob. I just gave up and went back to work.

It was after 3:00 a.m. before Carlos showed up at his dorm. Why hadn't they called me, the runner, to escort him back? It was a small thing, but ominous. I was trying not to make trouble but still do some good. It was getting harder to play both sides.

Three days later, when I was working as a guard in Carlos's dorm, I called his name over the intercom. When he came to the office I asked him what in the world had he done to get himself in that fix. He shook his head and started to talk. "Some officers came to the dorm and told me to bring all my belongings. They said they were going to deport me. I got real upset and wanted to call my attorney. They refused to let me use the phone, and then I really got mad."

I told Carlos that he would not be deported, that the officers were only teasing him. But he said it went beyond teasing. While he was standing naked in Processing, the officers used their batons to prod and poke him in the genitals and elsewhere, enough to cause welts and bruising.

"Mr. Hefner, they accused me of shaking my penis at the camera, but I wasn't," he said earnestly. "The officer told me to put my hands down, and I did. After he left, I covered myself again. I wasn't shaking my penis at no one."

After having their fun with him, Carlos was released from Bayview. I told him as I walked him to Processing the last time, "Don't you ever wind up here again." I felt like a big brother—responsible and guilty because I didn't fight for him. "You understand?"

Carlos stared at me momentarily with liquid eyes then nodded. As he walked away with his little satchel over his shoulder I thought about his parting glance. There was pity in it. He felt sorry for me.

I began to feel like a different person. Either I was a fake at Sunday school when I told the children to make the truth their friend, or I was a fake at work, guilty of allowing lies to stand and trying to stay on good terms with the liars. Either way, I was a fake. I was a child again, humoring Jim by agreeing with him even though I knew he was wrong. It felt like a tumor growing in my stomach. The thought of it made me sick.

When the INS donated two hundred old iron beds for use in my ranch ministry, I immediately thought it was a bribe. They were trying to buy my silence, to "take care of me" so I wouldn't turn on them. But words surged up within me, seeming to come directly from my bowels. I saw them in big black letters in my mind's eye, but they were wound with strings and sinews and strained upward but couldn't break through: truth and cowardice.

4
Horse Thieves Hit the Ranch

With enough money to go around and the ministry back in business during the summer 1989, I felt so good about our outward situation that I invited a lot of people we knew to share our prosperity. That's what we were here for in the first place—to be a blessing and good neighbors. I gave an open invitation to my friends at work to bring their families out to the ranch at a scheduled time. Some of the guards obliged and brought their children. Rubio's wife, Anna, was a nice woman trying hard to make their marriage work, and we had their whole family over. Rubio and I grew very close, and the two of us did some deep sea fishing together. Despite his behavior at work, he was well mannered and generous toward me off-hours.

The recently promoted Lieutenant Vicente Ramirez would occasionally drop by with his wife to look at the horses. I mentioned my surprise at his fast promotion to lieutenant at Burns. "It pays to have connections," he'd replied with no humor. "Get with it, Hefner, everyone likes you. Rubio would promote you at a drop of a hat." Barbara and I talked about the possibility, but we decided that it wasn't what we'd moved to Texas to do.

Ramirez and I had been on fairly good terms since we began working together, but I'd become uneasy around him because Payan told me he was having sex with the detainees.

One day at the ranch, he spotted a black bull calf that we had obtained in exchange for stud service from one of our stallions. Usually a calf would be fattened up and butchered for needy families within our church ministries. While his wife talked to Barbara, Ramirez studied the calf and said, "You know what, Hefner?"

"What's that?" I asked.

"I know that Rubio wants a horse for his kids."

I knew a little about Rubio's background. He was supporting five kids from an earlier marriage, and the money just wasn't there to buy a horse.

"We don't have any to give away," I answered. "Most of these have been donated strictly for the children's use."

"I have a horse Rubio would really like for his kids," Ramirez said. "She's well broke and real gentle."

I nodded. "Great. Why don't you give him that horse?"

"I think I will, Hefner." He paused thoughtfully, then looked at me with one of his slow blinks. "Just as soon as you give me that bull calf."

Ramirez had been my friend. I'd brought customers to him, he'd promoted my stallions. We'd had many talks. I knew his family was in the cheese business, and I wasn't sure if they used undocumented workers in the factory. "If you can't stand the heat, you can get out of the kitchen," he'd say. Although he was arrogant and manipulative, I'd still held out hope that he would respect our past relationship. I was wrong.

"After all, you know the pressure Rubio has been under lately." He stared at me with a force of will that made it hard to look into his eyes.

Rubio under pressure? What about the rest of us dealing with his chronic hangovers? He'd been impossible to please lately. He had cursed me out in front of my detainees and more than once wrote up complaints about the lack of neatness in my dorm, no matter how clean it was.

"This would be a good way to let up on the pressure at work, Hefner," Ramirez said, the hint of a smile beneath his dark mustache.

I was trapped. Ramirez was now my supervisor. I remembered the anguish of fighting Burns.

He waited with his hands on his hips and chest thrown out. I thought of the financial hardships Barbara and I had been through, and the back pay that had relieved us all at once. We did owe them some gratitude, but I didn't want Ramirez to know it. I'd make him think the calf didn't matter.

"Sure," I responded. "If you want the calf, take him."

He nodded at me before he left. "I'll be back in a few days. You can pick up Rubio's horse anytime."

"Fine." My insides were drying up.

Rubio's horse was skin and bones. Every rib showed. She was in such poor health, I thought for sure she'd die before we got her to the ranch. A month passed before she was strong enough for Rubio's children to ride.

In the meantime, Rubio asked me to get a group of guards together to put up fencing at his place for his new horse. No one but me showed up, so Rubio and I fenced the two acres ourselves.

Then before bringing the mare over, he wanted me to breed her with one of our stallions. "After all, Hefner. It won't cost you a cent," he said, using a line I'd heard before.

This wasn't the last of these demands. The previous November, an Ohio family had donated money for children's bicycles. Rubio heard about it and wanted me to give his son one of the bikes. He pressured me about it daily, reminding me what a good kid his son was.

My wife and I paid for his son's bike out of our own pocket. When would this end? How much gratitude was enough?

■　■　■

One hot August day at the camp, I knew something was wrong when Captain Rubio buzzed me to come to the office. He said to call my wife immediately. All kinds of thoughts flashed through my mind. She would never call me here unless it was urgent.

"Barbara, what's wrong?"

"Some people tried to steal our horses!" she blurted out.

Our neighbor Alice had called to tell her one of her ranch workers saw a truck with a horse trailer pull off the road onto the shoulder and stop adjacent to our barn. A man and two women jumped our fence with halters and lead ropes and were going through our stable, checking each horse as if looking for one in particular. When the ranch hand on the other side of the street yelled, they ran back to the pickup and took off. The ranch hand followed them in his truck and took down their plate number.

"Alice called the sheriff," Barbara said.

I was talking on the office phone within earshot of Rubio and Ramirez. When I mentioned horse stealing, Ramirez looked up from his papers and watched me. He lived only eight miles down the road, and I assumed he was afraid for his horses. He leaned forward with his eyebrows raised.

Barbara mentioned that Cameron County sheriff Alex Pérez wanted to talk to me so I left work. Pulling into the ranch's gravel driveway, I examined as much of the property as I could from the car, trying to take in any damage. Everything looked fine. The gate at the driveway entrance had still been locked. The only thing different was the news reporters standing around. They had learned of the complaint at the sheriff's office, where they often hung around looking for a story. I hurried to the stables and checked the horses. A quick tour of the property and the house determined nothing was missing.

I thanked Alice's ranch hand and asked him to go with me to the sheriff's office to file a report. As part of his statement to the deputy, he said the driver of the truck pulled the trailer up to what looked like a loading dock. Strange, I thought. Who would know it was there? It was well covered with brush and hidden from the road.

I realized who. Ramirez had recently come by the ranch to pick up the bull calf. I knew he was coming but wasn't there when he arrived. Noticing the calf was gone, I called him.

"How in the world did you get the calf out of here with the front gate locked?" I asked.

"I chopped down some brush and cactus and pulled him through the old loading dock," he replied.

After running the license plate we discovered the man suspected of jumping our fence had a son who worked at Bayview. The son and Ramirez were friends. They worked together and rode the same rodeo circuit.

Were they a team? Would they try it again? I made two trips to the sheriff's office to explain my situation at work and the probability of Ramirez's involvement, but the sheriff said he could do nothing more. Until they struck again, it was simply a circumstantial connection.

The next day the local paper ran the story: "Horse Thieves Hit Christian Ranch." Horses are serious business in Texas.

■ ■ ■

In September 1989, Ruiz was relocated to the Harlingen office. What a relief! This meant that he would spend less time at the camp, and we would no longer have to put up with his abuse. I wasn't the only one kicking up their heels. Ruiz's transfer made Payan the head honcho. It seemed too good to be true. And it was.

Ruiz made it a habit to surface unexpectedly, just like the back of my stepfather's hand. Payan was in charge, but Ruiz, who had a higher rank, maintained the upper hand.

■ ■ ■

Against INS policy, a white male security supervisor named Charles Gantt had developed a relationship with a pretty young female detainee named Santos. Female guards watching the affair develop wanted to report Gantt because the resentment he fostered among the women in the dorm could only boil over into trouble for them. The female guards called him Mr. Blue Eyes and swooned right and left. He smiled with his whole body. He had twinkling eyes, a soft expressive voice, and the gracefulness of a cat. The men knew him as a loose cannon because he did whatever he wanted right out in the open.

With impunity Gantt would slink into the female dorm, and the beautiful Santos, her hair dancing on her shoulders, would run to meet him. They would sit together in the television room. Cynthia Rodriguez, one of the guards, said that "they would talk in soft voices, pass notes, laugh, and whisper to one another. His eyes would rest steadily on her, flaunting the romance as onlookers grumbled. He gave her gifts, money, and visited her at night." Payan started to receive complaints from female detainees about Gantt and his detainee girlfriend. One detained woman told Payan that Gantt had physically shoved her. Female guards in Control complained that Gantt would call the camp and ask to speak with Santos. Female guards Cynthia Rodriguez and Beatriz Huerta supported the inmates' testimonies. After listening to the women's complaints, they discussed the matter among themselves and decided to file a Burns incident report, which they placed on Captain Rubio's desk. They were not surprised when, a few weeks later, they were summoned to Building 1 to discuss the report with Cecilio Ruiz. Cynthia was the first to arrive and gave her name to the woman at reception. Ruiz and several others were waiting to question her. Cynthia said she was nervous about Ruiz before she even knocked on the door. A twenty-five-year-old single woman, tall and large framed, she was afraid he would comment on her looks. She had heard stories about Ruiz and knew that he was mean and cruel.

He opened the door as soon as she knocked, smiling and smelling of expensive aftershave. Seated around the table inside were Captain Rubio, Lieutenant Ramirez, Eduardo Payan, and several other men.

"Wow!" Ruiz said, as his gaze traveled from Cynthia's feet up to her head. "You sure are a big one. How many orgies have you taken part in?" The others laughed, and Ruiz winked at her as he closed the door. "I don't know about any orgies," she'd told him warily. Stories had circulated around the camp about a sex party that had taken place on the premises during Hurricane Gilbert in September 1988. The detainees had been moved to El Paso as a precaution, but other volunteers and I had stayed behind to protect camp property. It had turned into a five-day sex and alcohol binge.

"I thought you wanted to talk about my report," Cynthia said.

Ruiz threw his head back and laughed, enjoying her discomfort. "Yes, I do. Come sit down." When he had her full attention he asked, "How would you like to be an INS officer?"

Cynthia was flabbergasted and fumbled for an answer. She smiled at the possibility and nodded. Ruiz dismissed Payan to get an application. As Cynthia looked over the application, Ruiz hovered behind her. After several critical sniffs, he exhaled at length into her long, dark hair, blowing the strays awry.

"Say, would you like to go out with me?"

Cynthia looked up at Ruiz's impeccable suit and flashing brown eyes.

"You mean like a date?" she asked. His smile deepened.

"You're old enough to be my father." She hesitated, and then looked him straight in the eye. "I don't think so."

Quiet mirth rippled through the room. Ruiz's face grew dark, and he took one step toward her and pointed, his diamond ring glittering. "Do you think you can take me on and beat me up?" he mocked. The rest of his words were drowned out by laughter.

Cynthia put the application on the table and walked out of the room. As she left the lobby, Beatriz Huerta was waiting for her turn. Beatriz said Ruiz was exceedingly polite when he asked her into the room. She was introduced and several men stood to offer her a chair. She answered their questions and left the room.

Rubio confronted Gantt the next day. Gantt admitted he was breaking regulations in courting Santos openly but denied making phone calls to her. After the interview, Captain Rubio wrote, "I believe he made the phone call, making the allegations true and correct at this time. I told him he was terminated as an employee for Burns International Security."

Later that day, Ruiz asked Captain Rubio to explain. Ruiz insisted that he "had nothing" and that the guards in Control who received the suspicious phone calls could not positively identify the voice on the phone as that of Charles Gantt. Ruiz told Rubio to meet privately with him again on Monday to discuss the issue. He reiterated his opinion that Rubio "had nothing on Gantt."

Their next conversation was short and to the point. Whatever his reasons or motivation, Ruiz wanted Charles Gantt back as a supervisor with Burns. Included in Gantt's sexual misconduct investigation is an affidavit Payan wrote stating that he was "approached by Ruiz and informed that he wanted Gantt assigned permanently to an evening shift." At the time, Burns did not have permanent shifts for supervisors; everyone rotated. Ruiz told him that he wanted "a shot at Gantt's wife and did not want Gantt around to ruin things."

■　■　■

On September 24, 1989, I got a call from Francis Carmona at home. She'd been attacked by Rubio again and was beside herself worrying what to do about it.

An employee birthday party had been thrown the night before by a Burns guard named Frank Herrera. Since it was a warm night,

Francis had changed from her uniform shirt to a T-shirt, but kept her uniform pants on. She left her car in the camp parking lot and drove to the party with a friend.

Around midnight Rubio showed up uninvited, already drunk, and spotted Francis. In front of the crowd, he demanded she have sex with him. She refused. Then he ordered her to comply because he was her boss. This time Rubio used obscenities and began dragging her to a shed nearby when Frank intervened. Rubio protested that he was simply taking Francis home. When she twisted out of his grasp, Rubio noticed her uniform pants. He demanded she remove them because they belonged to him.

Francis just looked at him with her mouth open. The crowd around them tried to diffuse the situation, but Rubio would not leave. Then another female guard approached Rubio and whispered something into his ear, to which he nodded. They staggered toward the road, the woman holding him up at the waist, and left together in his truck.

Francis's friend drove her back to the camp parking lot, where her car was. She was afraid that Rubio would somehow catch her unprotected. To her dismay, his truck was parked next to her car. Francis quietly got out of her friend's running car. She saw no movement in any direction. As she approached her car, she heard sounds from the truck and saw Rubio's bald head in the security lights, moving up and down rhythmically, while a pair of naked female legs stiffened against the driver's-side window.

Francis was certain she would be fired because she had publically refused to have sex with Rubio. However, he didn't remember the incident, as would often happen when he had been drinking.

■　■　■

When December rolled around a few months later, I struggled to get into the spirit of Christmas. Few possessed it here. I loved the weather—no coats, no scraping the walks—but the tension between brown and white never slackened, never took a vacation. Poverty and an excess of tequila formed veils around people, and not even Christmas could penetrate them.

Barbara and I concentrated on giving gifts to the children. Donations for the kids began to roll in around November and by Christmastime, she and I had distributed them with care, knowing some of the youngsters wouldn't receive anything else.

Barbara's employer owned a sports shop and donated a couple of bikes each year for our Sunday school kids. We had a contest to see who could bring the most people to church over the Christmas season, parents and family earning the most points, and whoever succeeded won the shiny bike displayed in front of the classroom. We were delighted to see the boys and girls work so hard. I know of no better image of pure, unhindered joy than a kid on a new bike, tearing down the road after church, multicolored streamers flowing in the wind. Such an uplifting sight to see after working in the sludge at the bottom of the barrel day after day.

5

One-Million-Dollar Lawsuit

The new year started out well. I was working forty hours a week at the camp and spent Saturdays visiting the children and their parents on the church's bus route. On Sundays Barbara and I taught the children Bible stories. We lived and worked for our time on the weekends when the children would refresh us.

During Sunday school, my favorite game was called "quiet seat." Only I knew who was sitting in that special chair. I gave the quiet-seat child a dollar after church if they had been still during the lesson. The youngsters stayed attentive the entire hour and were very excited to find out who had won the money.

Good reasons abounded to give away money and gifts to the kids. As in any poor area, gangs that sold drugs and bought expensive clothes, bikes, and cars were admired. Anytime we could afford to reward children with nice things as a result of living right, we did.

During prayer time one Sunday, I asked the kids if they wanted me to pray for someone who was sick or for a family member or friend with problems. The children were not usually open about their family life unless they were afraid and desperate to escape a horrible situation.

This time a twelve-year-old girl asked us to pray for her father. She said he had been drinking a lot and had beaten up her mother. The sadness in her eyes moved me. I had seen that look many times upon the faces of the families I visited and often wished I were a magician and could bring a smile to bad situations. I had seen that look upon my own mother's face. What could I do?

Pablo, another little boy in the group, raised his hand. He was a dark-eyed boy, a cute, skinny little guy about eight years old who loved church. He had a wide toothy smile that cracked me up. When I called on him, he bashfully asked me to pray for his cat because he was sick.

Absorbed by the girl's trouble, I said, "Sorry, Pablo. We don't pray for animals."

I hastily asked the children to bow their heads. The girl's face never left my mind that day as I remembered the soft sorrow held in those young eyes.

That night, Barbara and I lay in bed and discussed the day's events. She asked, "Did you see Pablo's face fall when you told him we don't pray for animals?"

It was like being hit on the head with a two-by-four. At that moment his stricken face appeared to me, and I jumped out of bed from the adrenaline rush. "I can't believe I told him that! Of course we pray for animals." What a blunder. An apology was in order.

The next day after school I pulled into Pablo's dirt driveway. He lived in a two-room patchwork house with a broken porch and cardboard on the windows. The fatty smell of bacon and refried beans drifted through the doorway along with soft Spanish. Pablo stood in the open door.

"Hi, Pablo. How are you doing?"

"I'm fine," he said without smiling.

"I bet you're wondering why I'm here, aren't you?"

He nodded.

"Yesterday, I made a mistake. I thought you should know, Pablo, even grown-ups make mistakes. Did you know that?"

Pablo frowned and chewed on his lip. He turned his head as if looking for a parent.

"Yesterday in Sunday school, I told you we don't pray for animals," I explained. "The real truth is, we *do* pray for animals."

His face lit up.

"Whenever God gives you an animal to watch over, if that pet is sick or hurt and needs prayer, then God wants you to pray for him. So I thought I better let you know. Will you show me your cat so we can pray for him?"

Eyes twinkling, Pablo took my hand. He led me around the house to a small broken-down shack. He pushed hard on the door. In a dusty corner, a gray tiger cat was curled up inside a cardboard box. I leaned over and patted the cat. It began to purr. I told Pablo his cat looked okay to me, but we'd pray for him anyway. This pleased Pablo, and we both closed our eyes.

The following Sunday when I stopped the bus at his house, he was already waiting outside. He gave me a teeth-too-big-for-his-mouth gigantic grin then grabbed me around the neck with a big hug.

"Well, thank you, Pablo," I said, laughing. "Say, how is your cat today?"

"He is fine, Mr. Hefner," he said and giggled. "The day after you prayed for him, he had five baby kittens!"

■　■　■

I had to jump over water puddles that were scattered around Gate 3, between the parking lot and the male dorms. Rain had fallen all night, but by 7:30 a.m. the sun had broken through the clouds and was powering through the wet air, making steam rise from the black asphalt.

I had gate duty, which was always an exceptionally busy post. Things were especially bad because it was Monday, and the camp was bloated beyond capacity with detainees. Border Patrol vans would come and go all day with new loads of immigrants apprehended over the weekend. Guards were stretched to the limit. Not only was I in charge of Gate 3, but also Gate 1 from the parking lot to the west perimeter road, Gate 2 from the parking lot to the auxiliary offices and laundry room, and Gate 4 across the parking lot to the mess hall and north perimeter road.

I was also responsible for male detainees who had been called to report to the bull pen, an area between the fences around Gate 3 where detainees waited for doctor's appointments or mail call. Their names were broadcast over the intercoms inside and out, and when they arrived at the bull pen I called Control to verify their names before allowing them to enter.

People were backed up already. Control was announcing names. Gate 1 had six vehicles ready to enter the camp and an INS van waiting to exit.

To complicate matters, I was the only one with a gate key. Master keys had been assigned to the runners, but too many were circulating, so they were recalled for fear a detainee would end up with one. So it was up to me to search each outgoing vehicle as it passed between the double gates, one at a time.

Horns were beeping, security guards and INS officers were yelling, wilted detainees milled about waiting to get into the bull pen, and the infernal intercoms created enough pandemonium for me to pull my hair out.

By 9:30 a.m. I had been running around for two hours without a drink of water. There was little air, only hot moisture, to breathe and no shade. The next vehicle to enter the camp was a dump truck with its empty receptacle high overhead. I unlocked and relocked the double gates one at a time then trotted past him across the parking lot toward Gate 3 and the bull pen. At least twenty-five male detainees had been waiting there since 7:00 a.m. I was wary of them as I unlocked the first gate and watched them closely for suspicious movement around the dump truck. I relocked and walked the thirty feet to the next gate and repeated the routine as the dump truck passed through the dorm area. All was in order. The truck would be back after picking up the dumpster next to Building 4.

Two detainees approached to ask if I would radio Control to remind them they had been waiting in the sun for several hours. I made the call, and Burns guard Yolanda Dragustisovis radioed back, "Stand by, Hefner."

An INS van waited to exit at Gate 1. I hurried toward it when a horn honked from Gate 4. Three guards began to talk to me at once on the radio, wanting a gate opened to escort their detainees. The dump truck was waiting for me to reopen Gate 3, papers and trash hanging from the closed dumpster above his cockpit. You're just going to have to wait, I thought, as sweat dripped into my eyes.

Fifteen minutes later I had reopened and relocked the four gates between the dump truck and the outside world and watched him drive off, knowing he'd be back in line again as soon as he had dumped his load less than a half-mile away.

Traffic grew worse. I fell further behind in opening the gates. I asked Lieutenant Ramirez for help when I saw him passing by. All the gates were full, horns were honking, and people were calling me. "Sorry, Hefner, we don't have anyone available." The dump truck was back in line outside Gate 1 and joined the honking.

Twenty-five minutes later, the dump truck driver motioned me to him. I ran over and stepped up on the running board. His voice was nearly drowned out by all the noise.

"Two illegals are at the dump," he said. "They fell out of the bottom of the dumpster when I opened it."

Aghast, I whipped out my radio. "Control, be advised!" I yelled. "Two Jack Rabbits at the dump!"

The alarm was broadcast to every radio. Everyone got very quiet. The guards dropped what they were doing and ran toward me asking questions. Rubio radioed. I looked up to see him sprinting toward me.

The truck driver repeated, "They just dropped out."

Rubio arrived breathlessly, demanding to know where the Jack Rabbits were. Guards and INS officers ran to their parked vans and screeched out toward the dump.

Why the driver came all the way back past the guard shack and waited in line half an hour before saying anything was a mystery.

Later a Burns supervisor said that in the ten o'clock headcount of the night before, two male detainees had been missing and unaccounted for during the night. Sometime during afternoon shift they had jumped into the dumpster and hid, knowing trash pickup was early the next morning. Checking dumpsters was not part of our protocol. Why hadn't they warned us?

Hours passed. When it grew too hot to continue, the searchers returned empty-handed. That evening Captain George Molinar and another supervisor took their horses to the area and found the dehydrated Jack Rabbits just before dark.

The next day, Captain Molinar wandered into the dorm where I was working. He was young, sharp, and disciplined—what I imagined a marine was like. I'd never seen him out of uniform. "Hefner, the government wants you to know we do not blame you for the escape yesterday." I appreciated his comment, although I hadn't considered taking the blame. He reassured me that nothing more would be said about it. Later, Payan shook my hand and said basically the same thing. Captain Rubio said from now on, guards would use a stepladder and a long stick to jab and check all dumpsters. I said that didn't make any sense, as we were not allowed to use force or any kind of weapon.

That evening, February 6, I was told to call Captain Rubio at his home. When I contacted him, he let me know that Burns was considering firing me again.

"Well, Hefner, Burns feels the two Jack Rabbits were your fault. It caused wear and tear on camp vehicles and lost man-hours to find them."

"That's impossible," I said. "George Molinar told me that the government did not blame me. Besides, why didn't you let us know at muster about the headcount being off by two? We could have been more prepared and had another guard helping me."

Silence at the other end. "Hefner, that's what the Burns district manager told me," Rubio retorted. "I'm just doing my job. I'll try to stop them if I can."

I couldn't believe it. I first met the district manager, James Austgen, when I returned to work in 1988. He wanted me to be a supervisor. "We need honest and respectable people," he had said. I declined his offer. The job was bad enough—why add more headache to a corrupt system that was only spiraling toward its own destruction? Was Austgen really sincere? Did he know what was going on? I had my doubts. Last Thanksgiving, I had seen Austgen in the mess hall while we were serving turkey and dressing for dinner. He had stood in one corner so drunk he could hardly stand up. Austgen awarded Rubio and the guards with a booze party every time they got a good grade from Ruiz.

Was Captain Rubio trying to squeeze me for another favor? Wasn't this the same approach they used to intimidate the women?

Six days later Rubio called me to his office to report that Austgen had indeed fired me, but that he, Rubio, would do what he could on my behalf. He made no promises that he would succeed, only that he would try.

Rubio, however, had been dropping hints about needing a saddle for his children's horse. It was clear that that was the price for keeping my job. "Why don't you take a few days off while this cools down," he said, "and I'll talk with Austgen again."

A few days passed. Hearing nothing, I called him twice at home on the fifteenth. His teenage daughter answered both calls and said he hadn't been home in several days, and when I called the camp the next morning they couldn't find him there either.

I called the EEOC in San Antonio and spoke with the attorney who had defended me in my first complaint against Burns. I reminded her of the agreement Burns signed not to retaliate against me. Though the special arrangement and back pay were supposed to be secret, every Burns supervisor seemed to know.

"Listen," I explained to her, "I'm fed up with supervisors blackmailing me and holding my job over my head."

I told her about the bicycle, the horse, the calf, and the weekend jobs. Rubio's wife had even asked me to take him on a fishing trip on Murphy's Charter Service in Port Isabel because he was under so much pressure at work. She said he would come home drunk after being gone for several days and take their newborn baby and throw her high over his head and catch her. When I called the boat's captain to make reservations, I told him I was taking my boss. While we were fishing in the Gulf of Mexico, along with about fifteen other men, the captain came down from his helm. He spotted me fishing between Rubio and an older, taller white man. The captain came over to the white man and started to chat with him, assuming that he was my boss. I tapped him on the shoulder and, pointing to Rubio, told him that he was my boss.

The captain took two steps backward and said, "Since when did a white man start working for a stupid Mexican?"

I started to laugh and asked him, "How long have you been out to sea? You need to come into port more often—times have changed."

Now they were laughing at me. They hounded me for favors, thinking I couldn't fight back.

My EEOC attorney agreed to call Austgen and discuss the matter. Later that same morning, she let me know I was to contact the camp and go back to work.

I was off for a week, unpaid.

Payan received a letter from Austgen on March 1 and gave me a copy. Austgen stated, in part:

> Officer Hefner was suspended on February 13, 1990 and returned to work on February 19, 1990. Our intention was to delay his return until February 27, 1990, but our immediate need for personnel to minimize unbilled overtime on post assignments, dictated our reassigning him to the schedule.

There was no mention of the call he received from the EEOC. Payan told Austgen over the phone that the government was not holding me to blame.

■   ■   ■

A few weeks later, as I walked through the gates into the camp parking lot, I noticed something unusual.

Cecilio Ruiz and Eduardo Payan were standing together talking. Physically, they were a study in contrasts. Ruiz was short and sinister with a dark complexion while Payan was tall and fair with a head full of white hair. The good guy–bad guy stereotype was as clear as in old Western movies. Ruiz was dressed up as if going to his own funeral. Payan, on the other hand, wore slacks with a striped shirt and tie, and always had a comfortable, casual look about him. I had never seen them together before.

Both men smiled and shook my hand. Weird. But that wasn't the only thing. It was 6:30 a.m., and a green INS bus was parked in front of Processing. I had seen buses loading up before in the late afternoon, as we prepared to transport detainees to Houston for deportation, but never this early in the morning. Several male detainees sat inside the bus. A group of INS officers in riot gear, with helmets and clubs, stood in a line alongside the bus. Captain Molinar faced them, his black billy club beating time in one hand.

I made small talk with Payan and Ruiz for a few minutes then continued to the Burns office. Something was up. I asked in the office but none of the guards knew.

As we stood outside for muster at 6:45 a.m., Rubio approached us with his morning report. He opened by saying that he assumed that we had already heard that some detainees had taken part in a hunger strike. He reported that when they refused to leave their dorm for the mess hall that morning, the riot team had been deployed. The demonstrators were now on the bus being persuaded to eat.

We were dismissed with the admonition not to give any information to the press if asked. As I walked toward my Four-Alpha post, the relief guard yelled, "Hey, Hefner, you're on first break."

"Oh, come on," I said, holding out my arms. "Can't you give someone else a break first?"

"Sorry, Hefner," he replied. "Rubio wants me to go down the line, and you're at the top of the list."

I shook my head. I'd have to wait until after my break to learn what I could about what had happened. So instead of taking my post, I turned and walked back to the Burns office and sat at one of the desks. Rubio looked up and lifted his eyebrows in question.

I shrugged and said, "I'm on break." He turned back to his paperwork.

Another Burns supervisor was in the office finishing some paperwork after pulling the graveyard shift. He got up and handed a report to Rubio just as Molinar opened the door, which then hid me from their collective view. Taking the report, Rubio asked the supervisor, "What's this?"

"It's about José, the detainee who was hurt when he got slammed into the door in his dorm."

Molinar, still wearing his black riot gear, interjected, laughing, "Yeah, next time we'll kill him."

Rubio chuckled and handed the report back to the graveyard supervisor. "Write that he tripped and fell against it."

The supervisor took back the report and sat down. It was time to announce my presence and get the heck out of there. I stepped out from behind the door into view. Molinar gulped. "You don't have to leave, Hefner," he said lamely.

"Nah, my break's over, and I have to get back to my dorm," I said. My heart sounded like the whole room could hear it. A startlingly clear picture of last night!

Five weeks later, on April 16, 1990, I cut out an article in the

Brownsville Herald that read, "Detainee Files $1 Million Suit Against Three INS Officers":

> An Immigration and Naturalization Service detainee this morning filed a $1 million lawsuit against three detention center officials, claiming they rammed his body into a door, and left him bleeding and unconscious on a bus.
>
> The suit, which complains of constitutional violations and failure to provide medical care, names "George Molinar," an INS supervising detention officer, and detention officers "Jose Perez" and "Eloy Huerta."
>
> Brownsville immigration attorney Linda Reyna Yañez filed the suit on behalf of a Dominican who was one of many detainees removed from the detention dormitories in anticipation of a hunger strike.
>
> At the time, INS officials said strike agitators spent the night on a bus because there was no room at the Cameron County Jail.
>
> They denied allegations of physical abuse, even in the case of a Nigerian citizen who was given a neck brace because of his injuries.
>
> On that night, about 16 INS officers wearing black riot gear and helmets entered his dormitory and started dragging detainees out, the lawsuit states.
>
> When [José] Checo sat up in bed and asked, "Why are you doing this in such a manner? We are human beings," he was grabbed by two detention officers, according to the lawsuit.
>
> "I then felt a knee jabbed into my back, my arms twisted behind my back; a club shoved between my elbows and my arms handcuffed behind my back," he states in a sworn affidavit to the suit.

"Officer[s] Huerta and Perez, clutching me by my arms, vaulted toward the barrack door," he writes. "[My] body violently collided against the door and upon collision with the barrack door, I lost consciousness."

Not long after the article came out, Rubio called me to his office.

"Just the preacher I want to see," he said as he tapped his pencil on the desk. "I have a job that only a preacher can do."

Puzzled, I waited for his orders. He'd never called me a preacher before.

"I need you to go to the visitation area and escort a female lawyer to her car. Her name is Linda Reyna Yañez. The INS wants her off the property. When you get there, tell her you are ordered to escort her to her car."

I nodded. Her name sounded familiar.

In all the years that I'd worked at the camp, I had never been asked to escort an attorney off the premises. I seldom saw the detainees' attorneys and wasn't sure what Ms. Yañez looked like.

Why wasn't an INS officer with greater authority called to do this? As I started out the door, Rubio said, "Hefner, if she asks for Ruiz, tell her he is in Harlingen."

Outside I saw an INS officer I knew well. I waved to him and asked, "Hey, do you know a lawyer named Linda Reyna Yañez?"

"Sure," he said as he led his five detainees toward the laundry room. He turned around and smiled as he cupped his hands in front of his chest. "She makes Dolly Parton look sick."

I reached Control. An INS officer was examining the personal belongings of visitors. He watched as each person walked through a metal detector. I asked him where I could find Ms. Yañez.

"She's on the phone," he said and pointed across the room to a short buxom woman.

I walked over and stood behind her. She was speaking fluent Spanish to someone on the other end. She glared back at me through the fringe of her russet-dyed hair, as if to say, "back off." Finally, she hung up. Her mouth was a grim line, her eyes fiery.

"Ms. Yañez?" I asked.

"Yes?" she responded indignantly.

"I was sent over to escort you to your car. INS wants you to leave the property."

"Why those dirty bastards!" She drew herself up to her full height and raised her voice. "What the hell is going on?" People stared at us and backed away as she slammed her briefcase down. "I'm going to make another call first." She looked me in the eye as she started to pick up the phone.

"I'm sorry, ma'am. I have orders to escort you to your car."

Her eyes narrowed, and she slammed down the receiver. "I want to see Ruiz!" she demanded in a loud voice. Her cheeks were now bright red.

"I'm sorry. He's in Harlingen at the district office." I apologized again as she picked up her paperwork. "I'm only following orders."

She walked briskly with me to her car. I opened the door for her, and she got in. I watched her drive away toward the guard shack.

On the way back to my post I quizzed an INS officer. He said her clearance was lifted because she was the lawyer who had filed José's lawsuit. Yañez was at the camp trying to arrange depositions.

I stewed over whether to call and tell her about the report being falsified. But, as always, it was my word against theirs. The graveyard supervisor who initially filled out the report would lie to keep his job because of his pregnant wife and four young children. It would be me against Rubio and Molinar.

About two weeks later I was relieving a guard, Joe Rodriguez, in Building 34. Through the dorm office window I saw Molinar talking privately to José. He was still talking to José when Joe returned from his fifteen-minute break. I noticed Joe did not log

Molinar's dorm visit in the daily logbook. Before I left, I asked him what Molinar was doing there. He said, "Captain Molinar told José he'd have to stay confined here for the length of the lawsuit, and it might take years before it got to court. He told him he couldn't promise him safety during his stay. I think Molinar is scaring him."

On May 3, 1990, several weeks after filing the suit, José told Payan he was desperate to leave and wanted to drop it.

I immediately called Yañez at her Brownsville office and expressed my willingness to be a witness to keep José from being bullied. After all, she had the right to visit her client, and Molinar had no right using scare tactics on him. When she moved to a new office out of state, I again made the offer, but she never called me back.

■　■　■

Alejandro, twenty, from Mexico, came in with a new group one day, assigned to my dorm in Four-Alpha. He was a little slow to respond to orders and just a bit peculiar.

A loner, Alejandro stayed off by himself or curled up on his bed, muttering. He seemed oblivious to his whereabouts, often masturbating at will. Over the length of his incarceration he showed more and more signs of mental illness. It was hard to reason with him. Guards punished him for disobedience and inmates mocked him until he became violent and dangerous. He could no longer function in the dorms.

Because of his increasingly odd behavior, no other guards wanted to work his dorm. Rubio knew I wouldn't complain so I was there every day. Some weeks into his detention I came in to find him locked away in a segregation cell. I had to check on his condition every fifteen minutes and report.

I told Rubio that the man needed professional help.

"He's only putting on a show," Rubio said. "The less you pay attention to him, the less he'll act that way."

Day after day I hustled back to segregation every fifteen minutes and looked at him through the bars of the steel door's small square window. His behavior deteriorated rapidly after he was separated from the others. I'd write in the logbook, "Detainee in segregation is okay." I would cover my mouth with a napkin to block out the putrid stench from the cell, which still made my eyes smart. The toilet inside was plugged, and an inch of foul sewer water puddled the floor. The cell was furnished with a bare plastic mattress lying in the water and a sink. Dirty paper plates and flies floated in the filth. Alejandro was completely naked. His clothing and bedding had been removed as a suicide precaution.

Two open windows let in some fresh air and daylight but were never closed during the cold nights. In the mornings, I would find him rolled up like a ball trying to get warm. And when the wind blew, the nauseating smell filled the entire dorm.

Once, he climbed up the steel wires that covered the windows. He worked his way to the ceiling, holding on with his fingers and toes. Hanging there nude, clamped to the steel wires and covered with flies, he dangled by his fingers and swayed back and forth like a chimpanzee. I wasn't going to write that he was "okay" anymore.

Fifteen minutes later I looked in on him again. He was now squatting on the floor relieving his bowels. He took the feces in his hands and examined it carefully like a child with a new toy, then tasted it and smeared it on the walls.

Just then the male runner came to the dorm with a paper plate of food. "How in the world are we going to feed him?" he asked.

"I was instructed not to open his cell door unless an INS officer is present," I told him.

We looked at the pitiful scene but knew the consequence if we disobeyed orders. The cell should have been sandblasted. The runner said he wasn't going inside unless he had backup, which was procedure in cases of segregation.

I called Control over the dorm phone and asked them to send over an INS officer. "This has to change. The man's condition is worse, and his cell is unbearable."

The runner contacted me a few hours later and said that Processing didn't have an INS officer to spare. I set the food down outside the door and shook my head.

The next day I was relieved to see Alejandro's cell had been cleaned. He was still naked and had no bedding, but the water was gone, the toilet was fixed, debris had been removed, and the smell reduced to a musty odor. I was pleasantly surprised that INS had responded so swiftly.

A woman in Control called and said, "Hefner, we have some visitors on tour. When they arrive at your dorm they are not to go into the segregation area. Orders are to keep that door closed."

Their quick response now made perfect sense. The INS officer Jesse Rosales who led the tour group told them we had people with contagious diseases in that area, so it was off limits.

After Alejandro had been in solitary for a month, Payan was summoned to Ruiz's office. Molinar was also there. Ruiz said he'd spoken to Alejandro and thought the man was a "psycho." He ordered Payan and Molinar to get rid of him as soon as possible.

Payan began the paperwork to deliver Alejandro back to Mexico and contacted the Mexican consulate. He then scheduled a psychiatric evaluation for the next day.

But Ruiz took matters into his own hands. That afternoon he ordered the detainee taken to the border where he was deposited without ceremony or provision. They just left him there. We never heard what became of him. Payan fumed when he found out. "They treated him like an unwanted dog!"

While Alejandro was still in segregation another inmate was sent to a solitary cell for fighting in one of the dorms. He would howl through the wire-screened window and yell that he was innocent and wanted out. He would shake the door handle and kick the door with his foot for minutes at a time and generally make a big ruckus. This went on for several days.

Then one day four INS officers came into my office. One of them opened my desk drawer and withdrew a brown paper bag. He threw it at another officer named Rocha. The officer, who recoiled, let the bag fall to the floor saying, "Don't throw that thing at me, it's got shit on it."

I had had the misfortune to look into that bag earlier when searching for a bar of soap to give to a detainee. I thought it was someone's forgotten lunch, but inside I found a rubber penis.

Another officer picked up the bag, and the four started for the loud detainee's cell. I began to follow, but an officer told me to stay there and not come in.

Five minutes later I got a call from a female officer in Control asking for one of the officers. She said to go tell him to turn on his radio because they were trying to call him.

When I opened the cell door, three officers stood inside watching the bed. One officer stepped toward me to block my vision as I entered, then guided me back outside the door and closed it behind us.

After they left, there was no more noise.

■   ■   ■

In May 1990, at the same time Alejandro and that unfortunate man were being held, some female guards passed me the information that a very attractive underage girl from El Salvador was being kept at the camp against her will. INS was aware of it yet made no effort to remove her. I wrote a short letter to Rubio. The situation was illegal, and I feared what might happen to the girl.

Rubio was out of the building so I placed the letter on his desk and told the supervisor there about it.

I bumped into Rubio several times that day, but we didn't discuss the letter. I figured he hadn't seen it yet. Still, I reminded him of it at the end of the day.

At seven the next morning I was helping the runner escort male detainees from the recreation area to Processing and back again. A few clouds could be seen on the horizon, and it promised to be a hot day.

At eight o'clock, Lieutenant Ramirez approached me purposefully and asked, "Have you had an outside post yet this week?"

"Yes," I told him.

The common rule was that outside posts were assigned only when a guard had returned from two days off, unless notified ahead of time and given a chance to prepare. An eight-hour shift in hundred-degree heat and high humidity required at least a thermos of cold water to maintain hydration.

"I need you posted at Building 11," Ramirez ordered.

I protested that I'd already done my outside duty and that that particular post had no shade. Ramirez told me that I was needed only until he could get a replacement.

Right. I'd be burned in about ten minutes.

Ramirez and I hadn't been getting along. I had lost a lot of respect for him and his uniform. The idea of the underage girl was pushing me over the edge.

I reported to the Building 11 area as ordered and stood there. I began to count the seconds. Guards generally dislike outside posts anyway because there's nobody to talk to and time drags. I could already feel my arms soaking up the sun.

At one o'clock, five searing hours later, I was desperate for a drink. I radioed Ramirez.

"I need a 10-100, sir." This was the code for a bathroom break. I was getting light-headed.

"Stand by, Hefner."

Half an hour later, Ramirez's voice came over the radio, "Security guard Barela, what is your twenty?" He was asking where he was.

Barela replied, "Helping the runner in Processing." My job.

"Barela, go to Building 11 and give Hefner a break," Ramirez told him.

"Ten-four," Barela said.

Five minutes later Barela ambled along the fence toward me in slow motion. He was like a mirage. I finally headed for a long, cold drink inside. After lapping up a quart of cold water, I still felt woozy.

I spotted Ramirez, who was watching me, and complained of dizziness and a headache.

"I can't spare another guard right now," he said.

I bought a soda to take back outside. Only one more hour. It seemed like forever.

That evening at home I became so violently nauseated that Barbara called our doctor. I had a severe case of sunburn and was flat on my back for two days. My arms looked like I'd stuck them in open flames. I sent the doctor's bill to Burns for some satisfaction, but they wouldn't pay it. Knowing their vindictiveness, I believe Rubio and Ramirez put me out there because of my "meddling" letter about the minor and my short temper toward Ramirez.

When I returned to work, I was scheduled for afternoons. I was ordered by Rubio to "Keep out of the sun. It's for your own good, Hefner."

I had been working strictly days, and my network of informants were used to seeing me in certain places to trade information. One afternoon and all that was foiled. What had happened with the girl? Did Payan know about her? Maybe all of it was just my misunderstanding, maybe her being there was all an innocent mistake, maybe the camp had been short on guards that day, and I should have been posted in the sun. Maybe it was all coincidental. To quiet my doubts, I called the FBI in McAllen with the girl's name, alpha number, and age. FBI agent Luis Vásquez took the report.

I often remember the abuse I witnessed and try to understand how it was permitted. It wasn't as if I were the only one in the camp with any sense of decency. Some women guards had compassion for their inmates, and this girl in particular, but were distracted from banding together by quarrels with one another. No one trusted anyone. The atmosphere was tense. More female guards and detainees complained about sexual abuse. The detainees characterized the facility not as a detention center, but as a jail for prostitution. Female guards constantly argued with each other over rocking the boat, upsetting the fragile balance of their job security, when a little "playfulness" was all it took to maintain the status quo. The midlevel supervisors enjoyed and fueled their bickering. It kept the women from uniting.

On May 22 I reported for my afternoon shift. My post was to relieve the guard watching detainees at court hearings inside the camp. Coming on late in the day, I only expected a few cases to remain. Outside the waiting room I was stopped by the female guard I was to replace, Cynthia Rodriguez.

"Hefner," she whispered, "come and see!" She gesticulated toward the waiting room doors and simultaneously motioned me to be quiet. She was usually so businesslike. She told me about a juvenile girl that the camp was keeping, who was, as we spoke, inside the double doors of the courtroom waiting area.

Cynthia stood in front of the doors and slowly inched one open. A very pretty, if thin, young woman sat by herself on a chair. She had long dark hair and looked almost sophisticated except for her knobby, bare ankles and scuffed high heels. She turned a soft face toward us when she heard the door open and smoothed her skirt self-consciously. Cynthia closed the door with satisfaction.

She pointed to the court docket with names, ages, and alpha numbers. "She's the last one to see the judge today." It was the same girl I had reported.

Her presence in the camp was entirely mysterious. According to the information I had been given, the girl had an aunt in

Brownsville who wanted her. That should have gotten her released some time ago. And at seventeen, why wasn't she at one of the children's centers?

"Last week I escorted this girl five times to Molinar's office in Processing," Cynthia told me. "Every two hours I was ordered to escort her there. I tried to go in with her, but he wouldn't let me." She continued furtively, "She would be there about forty-five minutes, then I was called to pick her up again. She'd come out all hot and sweaty. I asked her, 'What in the world are you doing, girl?'"

The girl told her that she was "performing" for the INS brass. "They like me to dance the lambada for them." She was told that if she did what they asked, she would be released. Cynthia asked her about the handful of candy bars she came out with. She replied, "I did other things for the men," but she wouldn't say what.

I took the court docket from Cynthia as she left and promised to pass on any information I received. I intended to talk to the girl's dorm guard, Juanita Flores.

But on May 24, two days later, a Burns guard named Rudy Cantu was fired after his clearance was lifted by Molinar. When a decent employee was fired it usually meant someone higher up wanted to hide something.

I was very suspicious. Rudy was a good worker. He always went the extra mile for his job. He was my friend, and more importantly, he was the brother of Danny Santana, a Border Patrol agent, and Mario Santana, an INS officer. Both men came highly recommended by Cecilio Ruiz. Rudy was the youngest of the three men. Surely he had to have some pull with two brothers working for the INS.

By coincidence I ran into Rudy in downtown San Benito and asked him what had happened.

"It's simple," he said. Molinar wanted him out of the camp because he had talked with the juvenile girl they were holding. Rudy said she told him that she was being sent back to the children's center but needed a ride back to camp for her court date the next day. Rudy offered her a lift. This was not unusual; I saw guards and INS officers give rides to detainees just released. When the INS officer in the guard shack observed him with the girl, he apparently called Molinar.

"I got fired because while we were driving, the girl told me what she had to do for Molinar and the others."

I told him I knew she had to dance for them.

He shook his head. "Nude, like a striptease. Every time she took off a piece of clothing they'd give her a candy bar." She told Rudy that in the beginning she tried to maintain limits, saying, "No sexual, no sexual." But as she stripped down, on more than one occasion, Molinar pulled her toward him and put his hands on her, and she slapped him. "Anyway, they got her out, before she filed a complaint."

We stood staring at the cracks in the sidewalk. I asked Rudy if he would try to win his job back.

"Heck no." He shook his head. "I'm outta that place. I can't take the chance that my wife will find out I drove the detainee home, and if I fight them, they will make sure she finds out."

A few days after I spoke to Rudy, I saw Juanita Flores when I went to relieve her from foot patrol. I asked for a minute of her time as she handed me the radio. In her usual peppery mood she said she didn't have a minute. I told her I wanted to talk about the juvenile. "Boy, Hefner," she burst out. "You never miss a stroke do you?" She scribbled down her phone number and said to call her at home.

Over the phone she related to me how Molinar had learned about this girl from the supervisors at the children's center, who had seen her dance. They shared stories about the girl's prowess. Molinar had her transferred to the camp for the express purpose of having her perform for the officers.

"While she's here," Juanita went on, "Molinar, but sometimes Ruiz, too, is asking for her every two hours. No sooner did she take a shower and change than they'd be on the damned phone calling for her again."

She told me not to worry about it, though, because she had recorded each request, and from whom, in the daily logbook. It was all down in black and white.

When I finally contacted Payan, he too knew about the girl. He told me that Ruiz wanted to turn her over to Humberto Manazares, a paralegal that worked for Roberto Arias, an attorney that often represented detainees. Payan said, "Humberto has offered me women and the use of his condominium on South Padre Island if I would do certain favors for him." What kind of favors? According to Payan, reducing bonds and releasing females under orders of recognizance.

When the FBI investigated, they'd find plenty.

■ ■ ■

The things I heard and saw were obviously illegal. But in the daily plodding from home to workplace it was easy to deny the abuses one day and investigate (as best I could) every hint of impropriety the next, depending on my energy level or other distractions. We were all just going to work. But the thought of those officers debauching a young lady, making her think that this was what she had to do to make her way in life—it went against every ethical instinct in me. I felt I had to do something, and I was determined to do it. But what?

The whole of Bayview was worse than any individual event I can relate. It was all happening simultaneously, from the first deliberate distortion of US law to the purposeful mistranslation of detainee testimony before English-speaking judges. The shakedowns, the thievery, the beatings, sexual abuses, and petty power trips were like threads of yarn woven together into the dark shroud that lay over the camp and cast evil shadows on every act. I didn't hear everything that went on. But nothing would have surprised me.

6

Firings at the Camp

Vicente Ramirez was a man who outwardly maintained the virtues of hard work and open-mindedness. He had a sharklike predatory nature that worked only for self-interest and used knowledge as a weapon against those with less. The women liked his looks and his body, which had been hardened in the rodeo ring riding Brahma bulls. He dominated everyone not ranked above him or useful to him. Rank and superiority were everything. Anger and punishment followed disrespect.

During my tenure at Bayview, he was caught fondling a detainee in an empty building, sleeping on the job, having sex with multiple detainees, blackmailing female employees with dismissal for refusing him sex, phoning detainees, and countless infractions that went unpunished because he was discreet, and was protected and promoted by his crony Ernesto Rubio.

I had long ago given up believing that any shred of friendship remained between us and worked to stay out of his way. Even so, I had to put up with lots of his efforts to belittle me, which had the effect of Chinese water torture, no doubt designed to make me want to quit.

■   ■   ■

Maria Perales, a Burns supervisor, asked me late in the spring of 1990 if I'd heard the latest—a rumor about a female guard named Jovita Urrutia and Vicente Ramirez.

Jovita was *not* the type around whom rumors easily circulated. She wasn't loose or flamboyant, but reserved. Though she was Hispanic, I use to picture her as that delicate china doll in the Ricky Nelson song "Travelin' Man."

Perales told me Jovita had been attacked by Ramirez, and that she had run away crying, begging another officer for help.

I had a bit of history with Jovita. Once, her supervisor had overloaded her with the work of two guards because he needed the other guard at a card game. She was swamped, so I pitched in and also corroborated her complaint against that supervisor, who was eventually fired. Jovita trusted me, and I felt protective of her. I called the supervisor Perales said Jovita had confided in after the assault, Sergeant Jesse Castillo.

Jesse said it was true. (He was also surprised by the speed and accuracy of my information.) Jovita had been distraught afterward, so he had gone to Ramirez to confront him. Ramirez became angry and asked what business it was of his but told Jesse he would apologize to her.

"He admitted it, then?"

"Sure seemed like it."

When the first opportunity presented itself I asked Jovita if she wanted to talk about it. I explained what she could do legally. Her soft chin dropped onto her chest and her long brown braids fell over her shoulder. "I hate this," she said. "I'm so embarrassed. Everyone looks at me like I'm different. Can't we just forget it?"

I asked if Ramirez had indeed apologized as he promised, and she said that he had, but her smoldering eyes and disquiet led me to believe she was not satisfied. She thanked me for caring but wouldn't say more. I offered an ear if she wanted to talk later.

She was different somehow, not the delicate and naïve girl I had known.

■   ■   ■

During the first week of June 1990, the camp was so hot and crowded I was called in on my day off. Given a list of guards to relieve for breaks, I was otherwise on my own.

Around noon I gave myself a lunch break. Halfway through my sandwich the radio blared my name and pleaded for me to come to the mess hall as soon as possible and help the guards there that were shorthanded.

Many guards are needed at the mess hall to be posted at doors, supervise food lines, and stand around tables to keep order. Inmates liked to sneak back into the food line and each one had to be searched for utensils as they were leaving, which required more manpower.

I answered Joe Vega with my mouth full. He insisted I cut short my lunch and beat it over there. So I wolfed down the rest of my sandwich and headed for the door.

I hit the pavement trotting and almost didn't hear Lieutenant Ramirez call to me from the doorway of Building 32.

"Come here, Hefner," he ordered.

"Sorry, Ramirez, you heard Joe call me on the radio." Everyone with a radio hears all broadcasts.

"No. You come here. I have something to show you."

I could see the detainees two buildings away waiting to enter the mess hall. They couldn't go in until all the guards were in place. What could be so important? I followed Ramirez into the empty dorm.

Ramirez was as tense as a jaguar ready to pounce. He slowly circled the bunks, eyeing me.

"These beds are badly made, Hefner," he said, pointing at them then yanking a blanket off. "You know INS wants a six-inch collar on each bed, not a four-inch, or a five-inch, but only a six-inch."

I was baffled. I told him some of the men didn't even know how to spell their names, let alone gauge six inches of sheet.

"That's it right there," he said. "It's your refusal to enforce military rules that allows for this mess. You are supposed to, why don't you?"

"Hey," I reminded him, "this isn't my dorm or my job today, Ramirez. I'm here on my day off. I've got to go, they need me in the mess hall."

Ramirez started toward the exit, then turned, pushed open the latrine door and went in. I was walking past him when his muffled voice called from inside, "Tony, come here." He hadn't called me Tony in a long time. What now?

I opened the bathroom door and stood just outside, with my hand on the frame. Ramirez was in front of a toilet stall, pointing at a few pieces of paper on the tile floor.

In his thoughtful manner, as if each phrase were a translation into a foreign tongue, "Come over here and see this mess, Hefner." My antennas went crazy. What was this guy up to?

The air was thick with the smell of mildew from the showers. I was beginning to feel like a child without any control over a bad situation. I thought about what those four officers did to the detainee in segregation and didn't want to leave the safety of the door.

"I can see it fine from here," I said.

Again, Joe Vega's tinny, irritated voice blasted at me from the radio, "Hefner, we need you now!"

"I am en route," I answered. I looked at Ramirez. "Have to go."

Bristling, Ramirez walked toward me. He pointed at my chest and then pointed to the shower. "I only want to show you one more thing," he insisted.

Was he trying to keep me from doing my job? What would happen if I walked into that room and allowed the door to close? We were the only ones in there.

Then he yelled at me, "I told you to come here! Look how dirty the tile is in this shower!"

I had learned never to go into an uncertain situation with this man, or any of them, without a witness. Otherwise, it was my word against his. He motioned impatiently for me to come closer, but this time I was white-knuckled at the door, flashing uncontrollably on images of Jim angry and beckoning me to receive my punishment. The smell of the mildew triggered my subconscious. The night I had rescued Alex from this very shower stall I had been afraid for my life, and that smell and the fear I felt now brought back the memory of that night until my stomach went sour and the room began to spin.

"Hefner! You're pale as a ghost. Are you having a heart attack?" Ramirez yelled.

My lunch pushed against my throat. I ran out of the building.

When the door opened and latched shut again, I was leaning against the outside wall, my head pressed up against my arm. I'd just vomited and was coughing so hard I had tears in my eyes. Ramirez laughed as he walked away.

Another few minutes elapsed before I was composed enough to report to the mess hall. The men were already in and being served. Vega just scowled when I approached. "You sure took your good sweet time getting here. Report to the serving line." He tilted his head and looked away.

Joe Vega, an older and demanding guard, always looked out for Rubio's best interest. He always got the easier jobs. Whenever Ruiz gave the Burns district manager, James Austgen, a good job performance report, he gave Rubio the money to buy beer for a guard party, and Vega furnished his place for the parties. He even had a special room adjacent to his house where Rubio could stay so he wouldn't have to drive home drunk. I knew he would report me.

But to my surprise Joe Vega was fired on June 11, 1990. Rubio had no choice in the matter as Ruiz gave the order to take Vega off the payroll. This was puzzling. Vega started to work at the camp back in August 1985. Always on time, he never missed work and took his job seriously. Ruiz even made him security guard of the month when he and the five grass cutters cleaned up the yard and flower beds around Building 1.

So I was all ears when Joe Vega showed up at the ranch shortly thereafter. "Ruiz told Rubio to fire me because I have a DWI on my record. I told Ruiz about the DWI when I was hired, and it was not placed on my record. Ruiz told me not to worry about it because it happened months before I was hired."

"Come on, Joe! There has to be more to this story than that," I said. "Rubio would do anything to protect you."

Joe looked downward as he sat across from me at the picnic table. "Well, there is more, I guess. Once when I had the grass cutter at Building 1, Ramirez came out of the building and was boasting to me about having had sex with a female detainee inside. He even told me about Ruiz having sex with a young Honduran woman named Berta. The woman got pregnant by Ruiz, and she was deported." I showed Joe a picture of Berta that Payan had given me along with the same story. "Yes, yes! That's her."

All the laws being broken bewildered me. I was now so involved and mad, so ashamed of myself for being so blind and so quiet. Asking myself why was not going to do me any good. I had to decide what I was going to do about it.

Vega went on to compare his DWI to Rubio's DWI and to the DWI of David Rodriguez, another guard. "Ruiz knows about the nights these men spent in jail because of their drunk driving. Maybe Ruiz saw Ramirez talking to me when he came out of the building that day."

"Maybe. Whatever reason, Ruiz doesn't want you working there."

■　■　■

The bonding out of detainees was a confusing business that offered an open door to thieves and scoundrels at the camp. The bond amount was set by the INS anywhere from one thousand to ten thousand dollars, depending on how risky the detainee was. A detainee being released from prison and sent to the detention center had to pay a higher bond in most cases. Cases for asylum or immigration stretched into weeks or months, sometimes even years. Once detainees paid their bond and supplied their attorney or the INS with an address where they could be notified of court dates, they would be released.

Payan stated in a letter to the district director that an attorney named Roberto Arias, who was a close friend of Ruiz's, had been given a batch of bond reduction forms, which were used by lawyers to make requests for reduced bonds. Ruiz sent Arias the forms from the day before. Payan knew it was a conflict of interest. Assistant Chief Detention Enforcement Officer Jesse Rosales and Payan were told by George Molinar that Ruiz was personally handing Arias a list of newly arrived detainees, which Arias used to solicit new clients. Molinar witnessed this himself. Ruiz gave orders on weekends to have the list of the new arrivals delivered to his home.

Rosie Pérez, an employee of the Aaron Federal Bonding Agency, asked to speak to Payan in the lobby of Building 9. She said she was afraid that neither she nor her supervisor would be allowed to enter the camp after an encounter she had had with Ruiz. Payan describes their conversation in his letter:

> Rosie Pérez informed and showed me her requested list of twenty (20) detainees submitted at 12:15 p.m. By 3:00 p.m. she had seen only five detainees. She stated that she never complains, and she doesn't, but had then been informed that she had already seen her clients. I informed her that I was no longer in charge of visitation. Instead of waiting for the detention supervisor, I compared her list to the escort list and the list in Control. The escort list showed that she had

seen all her clients. I made a copy of her list and called for the last two people on the list to be taken to the office. I spoke with detainee[s] Hector . . . and Hemecio . . . and asked them if they had been summoned for visitation. Both replied that they had and had been interviewed by Attorney Roberto Arias.

When Pérez had been told that she had already seen her clients, she asked to speak with Ruiz. In response to her questioning, Ruiz hollered at Pérez for being a troublemaker and said that he was the only one who had the right to make demands at the camp.

Arias caused problems for the detention enforcement officers on June 12, 1990, as he did not supply the Visit Request Form as required but had instead written all the names of the detainees he wished to meet with on a sheet of paper and turned that in. Arias refused to follow the rules, and minutes later Ruiz ordered everyone to accept the list. To further complicate matters, Arias was upset because the detainees were not responding to his page. They were attending the Orantes presentation, which offered detainees from El Salvador information regarding their legal rights, and were unable to respond.

Arias would interview a detainee and then immediately ask for a bond reduction. This was at times difficult, as the detainees had been in detention for only a couple of days, and files had not yet been created for their case. Ruiz admitted to Payan that he gave Arias a list of newly arrived detainees on a daily basis. According to Ruiz, it was payment for inside information that Arias had that enabled the detention center to exist without problems. Payan wrote, "I don't understand why the US Immigration Service has to depend on one attorney to be able to perform and exist."

■ ■ ■

One infernal afternoon that August 1990 my home phone rang. A woman's breathy voice said, "Hello, Hefner. This is Anna María García."

Anna María, a guard at the camp, had been recently laid off. She was gorgeous, the kind of girl the officers loved to keep around.

She asked if I would be willing to come to Brownsville in half an hour to talk about her and her boyfriend getting their jobs back. I sighed inwardly. I looked over at Barbara and asked if she could go with me. She raised her eyebrows.

On the border, Brownsville was a sad, crime-ridden town, and Barbara didn't like to go there. So much was going on at work that we feared this meeting was a trap to discredit me in some way. But I was eager to hear Anna María's story.

Fifteen minutes later we pulled into the Whataburger parking lot. Barbara wanted to wait in the truck and read. I assured her I'd keep my eye on her.

All dressed up, Anna María wore a white blouse with a ruffled collar, a short pink skirt, and matching pink high heels. I tried not to stare, though every other man in the place did.

"Thanks for coming," she said and smiled, showing her perfect white teeth. She went to find a booth for us as I stood in line to buy a soda for Barbara.

I yelled over the heads of others in line as she walked away, "Get the booth next to the window. My wife is waiting in the truck." I heard soft laughter around me.

"So," I asked, trying to sound casual, "what can I do to help you?"

Anna María sighed and stretched her manicured fingers. She said she'd heard that I lost my job once and got help from somewhere to get it back. I nodded and told her about the EEOC. This troubled her because she'd heard they needed positive proof of discrimination before they would act. I wanted to encourage her and invited her to tell me her story. I glanced out at Barbara, buried in her book.

"I started work at the camp in February 1989. I'd just gone through a bad marriage and my ex-husband was very jealous. We fought all the time."

She met Lieutenant Ramirez shortly after being hired by Burns. Ramirez had asked her personal questions: Are you married? How many children do you have? Are you dating anyone?

Ramirez seemed interested in her life. He thought she should start dating again and asked if she'd go out with him. His question was so unexpected that she said yes, then demurred, realizing she wasn't ready yet. Ramirez sympathized and told her he knew just how she felt because he, too, was in a bad marriage. He told her his wife was a lesbian, didn't want him, and that he would soon be divorced as well. He said that to find the strength to date was hard for him, but he encouraged Anna María to go out again, even if it wasn't with him.

Anna María learned in the following days that Ramirez was admired by most female guards and was flattered when he scheduled her on easy jobs with plenty of free time to spend with him.

The two would talk for hours in his office, and she eventually grew to like and trust him. She looked forward to going to work each day and began to fall in love. When he asked her out again, she did not hesitate to accept.

Ramirez asked her, for the sake of discretion, to keep their new love a secret. Anna María agreed. Most of the female guards knew anyway, because when she sat in the office with him, and he was radioed by a supervisor to ask her to come back to work, Ramirez would send another guard in her place. She felt the other guards' resentment but didn't care.

One day in the female dorm office, she decided to confide her feelings for Ramirez to Juanita Flores. Juanita happened to live down the road from Ramirez and told her that far from nearing divorce, the Ramirez family was expecting a child. Anna María refused to believe her until Juanita explained how long she'd known him and how many hearts she'd watched him break. Anna María was devastated.

When the inevitable confrontation came, Ramirez neither acknowledged nor apologized and demanded only to know who had told her.

Anna María attempted to change her schedule so she wouldn't work with him anymore, but Rubio controlled scheduling and wouldn't do it. Ramirez continued to pursue her, scheduling her on special jobs and badgering her about reconciliation. She asked him not to call her at home anymore. He reminded her that as her supervisor, he had the right not only to call her into work, but to call anytime during the day or night. No phone, no job.

He harassed her for months. She now feared that if she didn't at least talk to him, she would be fired.

One day, Anna María was walking with a supervisor, Howard Bergendahl, and confided that Ramirez's conversations with her had turned ugly. He was openly crude and sexually explicit. "I can't take it anymore," she told him.

Bergendahl loathed Ramirez and his tight relationship with Rubio but never had the backbone to stand up to them or follow through on a complaint. He was sympathetic to her plight and tried to schedule Anna María with another guard where the harassment would not be so blatant. Ramirez would change her schedule at the last minute and continue to force himself on her, groping her and attempting sex in his office. Anna María was run ragged by the constant threat.

About that time, Anna María began to date another guard, Hector Leal. Anna María told Ramirez about her feelings for Hector, thinking it would put an end to his harassment, but Ramirez became more persistent. He called her frequently at home. Hector would answer the phone, but Ramirez would insist he called about camp business. When Anna María got on the phone, she was plagued with questions about whom she preferred in bed. Worried about her job, she felt compelled to listen.

One day, Hector was ordered into Rubio's office where both he and Ramirez confronted him over dating Anna María and pressured him to stop. Rubio made it clear that if Hector wanted to keep his job, he would have to let her go. Rubio did the talking while Ramirez watched, his feet on the desk and his hands behind his head.

But Hector told them that he would continue to date Anna María as long as she wanted to see him. From that time forward, Hector was assigned all outside posts. When that did not prevent them from being together, his shift was changed.

Anna María saw Rubio at a Brownsville nightclub and asked him to put Hector back on her shift. Rubio replied that he would be happy to put Hector wherever she wanted him. "All you have to do is come out to my truck and have sex with me."

Getting no sympathy from anyone but Bergendahl, Anna María bore the daily onslaught of sexual pressure and innuendo with no apparent relief in sight.

Then, out of the blue, Rubio told her that beginning the next day she would be reporting to work at the INS office instead of Burns. "Dress up. You'll be working for Ruiz. The secretary at Building 1 is on vacation."

Anna María felt protected by her new situation. She did secretarial work and a few odd jobs for Ruiz.

Then one day as Anna María was attending to her paperwork and answering the phones, Payan approached her at her desk.

"How do you like your new job?" he asked.

"It's a good change," she answered, smiling.

"And what do you think of Mr. Ruiz?"

"Oh, he's nice," she hedged, not fully understanding the implication.

"Mr. Ruiz thinks you are doing a good job and was wondering if you would like to go out with him. Would you be interested?"

Anna María shook her head. "I don't think so. I have a boyfriend, and I don't think it's a good idea."

A few days later, she was back at her regular Burns job as guard and back to the old routine. Anna María decided she'd had enough. She had been called into Ramirez's office, where he'd cornered her and pinned her on his desk with his full weight, kissing her neck and bosom until she managed to wriggle free and run out. When she confided it tearfully to Bergendahl, he told her she had to face him, and that he would stand with her.

As Anna María told Ramirez off, alternately raging and crying, Bergendahl sat in a corner working on a schedule. When the time came to stand beside Anna María in agreement, however, Bergendahl remained withdrawn and oblivious. In the face of Ramirez's cold silence and Bergendahl's cowardice, Anna María realized she was on her own. Not surprisingly, several days later she and Hector Leal were fired.

Anna called Ramirez to apologize, hoping he would rehire them. But he chillingly reminded her, "You could have kept your job if we had gotten back together again."

I was suddenly back in the present. "Is that your wife?" Anna María asked. "Hefner, is that your wife?"

"What?" Looking out the window, I saw Barbara pointing to her watch. I had been listening for an hour. I waved back and nodded.

"Do you think the Equal Employment Opportunity Commission could help me?" Anna María asked as we stood.

"I don't know, but I would surely try," I said, and agreed to help her write to them.

Anna María and Hector Leal weren't the only ones laid off that July. Frank Herrera, another "troublemaker," had complained about wrongdoing at the camp. I had heard a supervisor was gunning for him. Frank made the mistake of going over the heads of camp supervisors to a Burns district officer in San Antonio to make his complaint. He found that Burns District Manager James Austgen and the government enforced the unspoken rule that if you ever complained outside the camp, you lost your job.

But Frank also felt that his layoff was primarily retaliation for the time he threw Rubio off his property for trying to molest Francis Carmona.

■ ■ ■

Toward the end of that summer, I was working foot patrol on the east side of the camp. It was going smoothly, not too bad for a weekend. I ambled on the footpath from the north corner to the south corner of the camp perimeter, back and forth all day, watching. From where I stopped to rest, I saw the mess hall to the north on my right. In front of me sat the recreation area, then Building 4 to my left.

Antonio, a Salvadoran about twenty-one years old, came out of Building 4. Antonio had once helped on clean-up when it was not his turn. I thought it poignant that this helpful young man, educated and fluent in English, would find himself in this detention camp about to be deported to a war-torn country.

Antonio walked toward the storage area on the dorm wall. I thought he was collecting a broom or something. I wasn't concerned that he'd left the dorm and was expecting a call from the guard in Four-Alpha to inform me a detainee would be outside unattended. About forty feet away, Antonio stood at the shed looking at the brooms and mops. Then he carefully stole glances in all directions. I knew those looks.

Antonio dashed then leaped toward the fences. I felt a simultaneous explosion of adrenaline and a sensation of slow motion. By the time I fumbled the radio off my belt, he was already halfway up the first fence and climbing for his life.

"Break! Break!" I cut through all radio conversation. "We have a Jack Rabbit coming over the fence at Building 4 and foot patrol. Repeat! Jack Rabbit at foot patrol!"

Guards started running to the scene. Antonio jumped to the

ground between the fences and within two steps bounded up the second. Guards nearest the fence inside yelled at him to stop. At the top, Antonio carefully positioned himself on the barbed wire, trying not to get cut as he maneuvered over.

"Hold it right there!" I yelled up at him.

He froze as he heard my voice. "What are you doing out here?" he asked, his mouth open and breathing hard.

"Just stay where you are, Antonio!" I ordered.

He looked down at me and back at the guards streaming in on the other side. I was the only thing standing in the way of his freedom. Between us was a two-foot ditch paralleling the fence. If he jumped straight across, he would have to land on top of me.

"Let him jump, Hefner," several guards at the fence bellowed.

"He'll break your neck if he jumps on you!" another said.

The guards wanted me to move so that Antonio would have a good start ahead of them. These INS employees and guards looked for any reason to be brutal to the detainees. If the employee had had a bad night and had fought with his wife or had a hangover, he took it out on the detainees.

Antonio looked down, his moment slipping away. "If I knew you were out here, I wouldn't have tried it!" he yelled down at me in frustration.

Too late now.

"Please move, Hefner. I don't want to hurt you." His voice was shaky and his arms quivering as he tried to hold himself off the sharp metal barbs.

He was so much safer up there on top of the fence. Once he reached the ground the INS officers would beat him. If he ran and made it to the cover of the wildlife refuge beyond, they might try to run him over with the van.

"Let him jump, Hefner!" one officer yelled. "Let us have some fun." A voice came over the radio, "Hefner, this is Control. Get the hell out of the way. That is an order."

The green van came barreling around the corner, its tires screeching. I started to back off, keeping my gaze on Antonio. I'd leap on him as soon as he hit the ground.

Then he jumped. When he hit the ground, I lunged forward and threw my arms around him. But he bounced up with such force, I was thrown off balance and tumbled into the ditch.

Antonio sprinted for the refuge, his orange shirt flapping like flayed skin behind him. The van sped after him in pursuit. Two INS officers crouched in the van's open side door like cowboys ready to spring on a wild steer. They closed the gap and threw themselves on the running man, bringing him down in a cloud of dust, his orange figure smothered beneath sagebrush and khaki.

I slowly climbed back out of the ditch. "Hey, Hefner, you okay?" a guard yelled from the other side. I felt a jab in my right elbow. "Looks like you're bleeding."

In the distance, the officers dragged Antonio's limp body into the van.

Afterward, they all slapped me on the back and congratulated me for what I'd done. One officer said, "We knew what you were up to, trying to slow him down. You know, if we treated these dumb illegals as good as you do, they would make this their vacation resort."

Antonio was in a segregation cell for two weeks. His bruises faded, his cuts healed. Each time he saw me he apologized, without fail.

The Blacklist

On August 6, 1990 at 9:00 p.m. I was headed from the Burns office to the dorms. I walked up to Gate 2 and saw Jovita Urrutia. She was tending gates that evening in the parking area on the other side of the fence. The day was winding down. Once the dorm cleaners finished, the only thing left would be to get the detainees ready for headcount and bed.

I stood there feeling the breeze, waiting for Jovita to come unlock the gate, but she hadn't noticed me. I clanged the lock up against the latch, and her head jerked up with a start as if from a daydream. She walked toward me slowly, the keys jingling on her ring. I hadn't talked to Jovita since questioning her about the Ramirez incident.

As she approached, I didn't see a hint of her normal pleasantness. She was distracted, her face a blank mask.

Francis Carmona rode in Jovita's car pool and told me they all wondered what was up with her. I could see why. Francis said Jovita cried on the way to work because she hated the place.

I asked why she was carrying the weight of the world on her shoulders. Jovita looked uneasily down at the ground as she twisted the key to secure Gate 2 again. We started walking toward Gate 3. I turned to say something again and saw her upper lip trembling and her dark brown eyes full. I stopped her.

"Jovita?"

"I need my job, but I hate this place so much. I'm afraid I'm going to get fired, but I wish I could just leave it, go, get out of here."

"Whoa! Jovita, why would you get fired?"

"I heard Captain Rubio and Lieutenant Ramirez have a blacklist going around. I think Lieutenant Ramirez will put my name on it."

I asked if she thought so because she rebuffed Ramirez's advances, but she said she wasn't sure. Tears welled up in her eyes and fell. She moved to start walking again, but I touched her arm.

"Then why should he fire you?"

"I wish I could tell you. Or someone."

"Jovita," I said quietly, "try, maybe I can help. After all, I helped you once before. You do remember, don't you?"

"Not this time you can't," she said with a hint of humor far, far away. She sighed as she finally made eye contact and wiped the tears. "No one can help me."

"Look," I said, "Ramirez can't fire you or anyone else for seeking help." Hollow words. We both knew Rubio and Ramirez were protected by Ruiz and had free rein.

Jovita asked where I was headed. I had half an hour until I was to help with ten o'clock headcount in Building 4. I could see she wanted to tell me something.

"You know," I said, "lots of people confide in me, Jovita, because it makes them feel better. Most of them I hardly know. But I'm your friend. You can tell me what happened, and I promise I'll do everything I can to help you, and I won't quit until the problem is fixed. Is that fair?"

Jovita looked off into the distance and struggled for words. The corners of her mouth trembled. "That night Lieutenant Ramirez called me to his office he told me to come in and close the door, that he had something to tell me. I turned and closed it. Then he ordered me to lock it. I wondered if I'd done something wrong. He was probably going to chew me out for something. When I turned around, he was in front of me and grabbed my wrists and pulled me toward him. He squeezed my wrists and twisted them really hard until my arm hurt, and then tried to kiss me on the lips."

A new tear had squeezed out of her eye and fell from her down-turned face into the darkness. "Hefner, he's so strong! I tried to get loose, but he held on. I tried to pry his fingers away, but whatever I did, he twisted harder. He wouldn't let go.

"He knew he was hurting me. I didn't want to, but I had to kiss him so he would stop. After I did, he let go of my wrists and tried to put his arms around me. That's when I got away and ran to unlock the door."

"This is what he apologized to you for?"

"Yes, about a week later. He said he was sorry and told me that he couldn't help himself because I was so pretty. But he swore it wouldn't happen again."

"Well, he knows you're not afraid to get help. You have Sergeant Jesse Castillo to back you up if he ever does try it again," I said, referring to the officer she had confided in before.

"Hefner, Jesse doesn't work here anymore."

I felt an electric chill. "What happened to Jesse?"

"I don't know." She started to cry again.

Helpless, I suggested that perhaps Payan could help her, since he was building a case of complaints against Ramirez.

She turned toward me, highly agitated. "He tried it again."

"Lieutenant Ramirez did something again?" I asked. Now we were down to it. "When?"

Jovita sobbed openly now in large choking spasms. "A week ago. He called me into the office again. I went in but stayed pretty far away. He told me to go into the uniform closet and hang up the uniforms that were on the floor."

"The closet in the hallway by the bathroom?"

"Yes. I was in the closet, and you know how small it is. I was in there, and he comes in behind me and pushes me to the wall. I hear the door close and then he locked it. He was in there with me. If my boyfriend ever finds out, he'll kill him."

Maybe I didn't want to hear what happened next. I told Jovita she didn't have to tell me more as long as she told someone with authority.

"What am I going to do? I can't lose my job!" she cried.

"It'll be okay, Jovita, he won't get away with it."

"He showed me his private parts. He unzipped his pants and tried to make me touch it. He had an erection, and I couldn't stop him. I was begging and crying for him to stop, but he jerked me back and forth. I was hiding my face with one hand. He had knocked my glasses off, and I was holding them in my other hand, trying not to lose them. But he was prying my fingers open to put them around him, begging me to touch him. He unbuttoned my shirt and put his hands all over me and was kissing me."

Jovita's shoulders collapsed and she cried. I wanted to comfort her but I couldn't.

"I wanted to kill him," she said finally as her convulsions eased. "I wasn't going to do what he wanted, no matter how much he hurt me. He was crazy. I kept saying over and over, 'please don't do this to me, please don't do this.' Finally, he just stopped. He zipped his pants up and left. I could tell he was mad, but it didn't matter anymore. I locked the door and stayed in the closet for a long time."

Howard Bergendahl seemed weak when he did nothing to help Anna María. Now I knew how he must have felt. I didn't know what to do.

I said gently, "Jovita, you need to report this, and it has to come from you."

"I can't. It's too embarrassing. Anyway, who am I going to tell, Captain Rubio?" She wiped furiously at her wet cheeks and nose. "It's just so hard to come to work each day. I'm scared to death of him. When will he try it again? I see him watching me all the time."

■ ■ ■

We'd just gotten home from church on Sunday, August 12. I changed and headed for the barn, looking forward to spending time with the horses in the balmy weather.

A car turned through the gate and headed for the barn. Squinting, I made out Howard Bergendahl and his family inside. He'd asked me Friday about buying a horse, so I wasn't surprised to see him. His wife carried their newborn in her arms, and I saw his two boys in the back seat. Their heads popped up and down.

Bergendahl looked at the horses and decided to buy a gentle older mare. We discussed the price. An upcoming children's retreat would cost us around three hundred dollars, so we agreed that this sale would finance that activity. Bergendahl knew about our mission work and that the money was needed before the retreat within ten days. He promised he would pay for the mare when he picked her up.

I had the horse ready to go, with her papers and transfers made out in Bergendahl's name when he came a few days later with his trailer. After we loaded her on the trailer he took me by surprise when he said he didn't have the money with him. At least I hadn't signed the papers yet.

"Can I pay you within a few more days?" he asked.

I was quiet for a moment, then reminded him we needed the money before the retreat. He said he understood.

"By the way, Hefner, did you hear that Burns lost their contract at the camp?"

I turned sharply.

"Not only that, but Rubio and Ramirez are making up a list of the guards they don't want working for the new security company."

The blacklist Jovita had heard about was no longer just a rumor.

"Any complaints from those two and phew," he made a whistling sound through his teeth, "your name goes on that list."

I asked him if my name was on it.

"Heck no, Hefner. Look at all the stuff you've done for Rubio.

You think he'd put your name on the list after all the things you gave him?" He said they kept the blacklist in the Burns office in the upper filing cabinet behind Rubio's chair.

I studied him. How did he know I gave gifts to Rubio? Then I wondered if he planned to keep this horse as a gift. I waved good-bye as he took the mare and drove away.

Bergendahl gave me one excuse after another. Finally, I told him he had to pay for the horse or I would call Ruiz. Bergendahl had applied for an INS position and didn't want any obstacles to get in the way. He blew his top when I demanded payment, but he finally brought the horse back.

I knew there would be a reprisal. When I came back to work, Bergendahl's mind was made up about whose side he was on.

I had hoped to win him over, and now all that came crashing down with my determination not to be taken advantage of. We financed the retreat with the selling of another horse.

■ ■ ■

Before District Director Omar G. Sewell and Deputy District Director George T. Somerville Jr. retired, they were quoted in the morning paper as saying that this was "perhaps one of the smoothest running and least controversial times for the local office." A quiet time? Were they serious? No, it wasn't quiet as far as the influx of Central American immigrants, thousands of whom cross the US-Mexico border each week. What about the continuing complaints that hounded the camp's administration on a daily basis? Payan told me, "The act of forcing a detained female to have sex in any form is considered the same as rape." The blacklist threat had circulated throughout the camp. Guards were openly intimidated by Ramirez. He outright told them that if they didn't do as he ordered, their names would go on the list. Rubio and Ramirez held a regular reign of terror over the guards.

Rubio was seen repeatedly coming out of the uniform closet with different female guards, and once in the afternoon I saw four female guards waiting at the women's bathroom wanting to get in. "What's the problem?" I asked.

One of the guards said, "It's Ramirez and Juanita Treviño. We have to wait here until they tell us it's okay to come in. They said they had to inspect the bathroom to make sure that the detainee who had cleaned it had done a good job."

Before I had a chance to ask another question, Treviño and Ramirez walked out. As I walked toward the door to leave, I heard one of the women say, "They sure took their time, didn't they?" Ramirez wasn't worried about being discovered.

Guards took the threat seriously and came bearing gifts of cakes, tamales, and other goodies to Rubio and Ramirez. One of the female guards even showed me a letter Ruiz gave her recommending her for the job. She sat at the table in the entranceway to the Burns office, wanting to show the letter to Rubio. I looked into her deep brown eyes. I can't even imagine what the letter cost her. We all took the blacklist seriously. I needed to get my hands on it.

Rubio, in the meantime, had been badgering me about using our motor home. At first I just put him off. The motor home wasn't new, and we never used it. It was just a place for missionaries to stay when they came to the US from Mexico to renew their visas. Rubio wanted it to take his family on vacation.

"When can I pick it up?" he finally asked me.

"You can't. We can't loan it to you or to anyone else."

Rubio strode away, grim faced. If he was drinking and driving, and had an accident, what excuse would I have to offer, knowing he had a drinking problem and a DWI on his record?

Captain Rubio told us at muster that another security company was taking over the new contract, and we needed to have our clearances updated by both sheriff and police law enforcement. "Take your diplomas and police clearances to the Sheraton Hotel on the expressway. There you will complete their application and be interviewed."

At four o'clock I reached the hotel and was directed to the conference room. Most of the guards were leaving but a few sat at tables, still working on their applications.

A tall dark-haired man in his early forties with a southern accent asked if I was there to apply for work. His name was Russell Pierce, and he was the vice president of United International Investigative Services. I told him I had worked at the camp since 1983 and understood that I had to complete an application and supply him with all my diplomas. He seemed to like me and told me he was from Kentucky, just across the border from Portsmouth, Ohio. I told him I had been there many times. Mr. Pierce was a likeable man, and I thought this would be a piece of cake. He was hoping I was applying for a supervisor's position, and probably because of my last name and the color of my skin, he was not shy about what he thought of Mexicans.

He said, "I can talk to you, we are of the same blood. To be honest with you, I don't know how you can stand working with these stupid Mexicans. I thought niggers were dumb and stupid, but these dumb idiots are far worse." He hired me on the spot and wrote down my uniform size, and I filled out a W-4 form. We shook hands, and he returned my paperwork. He told me to give everything to Rubio, that he would send my paperwork along with everyone else's to California, where their main headquarters are located. He asked once more before we parted, "Are you sure I can't talk you into being a supervisor?"

I said, "No, not today."

The stress of knowing what I knew grew day by day. Why did I stay quiet? When I was young I learned that staying quiet was to my advantage. My stepfather wanted me to agree with him, and by doing so, I lessened the beatings. If I rose up in defiance, it would have been worse. Now the vice president's approval made me sick.

He was willing to judge me on the color of my skin. I wanted to look him straight in the eye (something I wasn't able to do with Jim) and tell him that my real father was a wetback from Mexico and that I wasn't better than anyone else. I wanted to see the look on his face as I shoved my diplomas and my years of experience down his throat. For all these years I carried that chip on my shoulder and was mad at myself for not standing up once.

■ ■ ■

In February of 1990, the INS had contacted me and the churches in the area to let us know that the government had scrap metal it wanted to donate. I was given steel beds and mattresses for my ministry, as were other local churches in the Rio Grande Valley. I had to personally sign for these items. INS officer Joe Ortiz, who was in charge of the donations, told me that nothing was allowed to leave the government facility on the weekends. Then, one weekend, Ramirez and Sergeant Ignacio Salinas came to the facility and took fencing and fence posts for Ramirez's ranch. They used their pickups and empty trailers to transport the stolen government property. I was contacted and told that the government had put a hold on all donations. The foot patrol security guard who was working that weekend, Ralph Garza, told me he witnessed the property being stolen. The first thing I thought was that my name and the name of other preachers were being forged on government documents to make it seem as if we were the ones who had taken the property. This was not the first time property was stolen at the camp. Later on, Salinas admitted he helped Ramirez, but only to save his job. "All the material was taken to Ramirez's ranch." He added, "Hefner, it's a good thing you didn't let Rubio use your motor home. Rubio has been arrested two times, once in 1987 for DWI and again in 1991 for the same thing. His driver's license has been taken away, and he can only drive from work to home."

A few days later Sergeant Perales slipped me a folded sheet of paper.

"What's this?" I asked.

"Heard you wanted it," the sergeant said. "I got it from Rubio's cabinet."

I turned my back to the room and looked at the paper. The infamous blacklist. It had about forty names. "Is this a copy?" I asked.

"No. It's the original."

"Good Lord, let's make a copy and put this back."

"Not me. My nerves are shot, can't take the chance."

My name was written at the bottom. Would it matter that the United International vice president had hired me? What if Rubio didn't send my paperwork? Good grief.

When United International posted their list of new hires, we eagerly, fearfully lined up to read it. My name was not there. I was not surprised.

I headed to the office to ask about the roster. I arrived at the same time as Cynthia Rodriguez, who went in just ahead of me. Rubio looked up at her and flashed a toothy grin.

"Hi. What do you need, Cynthia?"

"I need a fresh battery," she said holding up her radio. "Mine went dead."

"Look here, Cynthia!" Rubio pointed between his legs while leaning back in his chair. "Here's a good battery."

Ramirez laughed and jumped up from his chair. He grabbed his crotch and bellowed, "I have a bigger one! And it's guaranteed not to go dead!" Both men chortled.

Cynthia stormed out of the office, brushing me to the side on her way out.

Rubio was still chuckling. "What do you want, Hefner?"

"My name is not on the new-hire list," I said, my jaw clenched. "Will another one be posted?"

"I don't know, Hefner. You'll just have to wait and see."

Ramirez had shaved off his mustache, and I didn't even notice until he said, "Hey, Hefner! Just in case you don't get hired, remember to send some of your horse customers my way."

"You know, Ramirez, you may know a lot about horses, but you don't know anything about how to treat people. One of these days, by the time I get done with you, you're going to wish you had that mustache to hide behind."

I had finally talked back to Ramirez because this was probably my last chance to really express my disgust and frustration. He was always on top and protected by Ruiz and Rubio. He could never do anything wrong. It was obvious my name would never be put on the list of hires.

Ramirez was so shocked that anyone would stand up to him that he stood there with his mouth open. I remember Rubio looking over at Ramirez to see how he would react. Ramirez didn't take any action because I think for once he realized I was right. Soon I would no longer be under his thumb. I can't explain the satisfaction I felt just looking at his blank face, as I tightened my fists and walked out.

■   ■   ■

About a week into September 1990, a call went out over the radio from the dorm in Building 32, requesting help. A fight was in progress between two detainees. Personality conflicts, different ideologies, women—whatever. In those close quarters fights erupted but were most often over as soon as they started.

When I arrived the worst was past. The men still glared daggers at each other but were easily separated. We checked them for injuries but found only scrapes and a few bruises. It didn't seem as if they'd been in mortal combat. I lectured them as we escorted them to Processing.

Back in position at Gate 3 about an hour later, I saw the same two men being escorted from Processing to an INS van in the parking lot. This time, their heads were wrapped in blood-flecked white towels, and their orange uniforms were bloodstained and torn. The van took off toward the guard shack and out of the camp.

When the escorting guards returned, I asked where they had taken the men. "The hospital," the beefy one answered and rushed away to his post. I figured they'd found some internal injury or something, as they seemed to be all right after the fight. But, all the blood made me suspicious, and I was convinced something else had happened.

Later that day the runner stopped by during his rounds. "Did you hear what happened to those guys who were fighting?"

"I know they were covered in blood and taken to the hospital, but I want to hear it from you. What happened?"

"The officers handcuffed them together."

I asked why they would do that when they were still angry at each other. The runner said it was on purpose, left hand to left hand. One officer said if they weren't right-handed, that was too bad. The runner said they handcuffed the men and put them inside the wire pen in Processing. To get them going again, an officer pushed one into the other and said things meant to inflame them against each other. By the time they began to fight again, the officers were loudly goading them on. The runner said, "It was gory. Blood was flying everywhere. They beat the crap out of each other. The INS officers were putting bets on who would win."

He asked if I'd ever been to a real dogfight, and I shook my head no.

I quickly asked, "Where was Russell?"

"Hefner, Russell was there . . ."

Russell was the officer in charge that day. Once a security guard, he now worked for the INS. The man in green. Would he stoop this low?

About a week later I reported to the same dorm in Building 32 in time for headcount. The count was off by one, but the guard told me a detainee was in segregation.

I went to the wire glass window and looked in. A detainee lay on the bed swathed in white bandages. The left side of his face was mostly bandaged, with the visible parts swollen and bruised.

David Rodriquez, the guard I was relieving, hustled toward the exit door.

I asked, "What happened to him?"

David yelled back, "He's one of the men who got in the fight at Processing."

I hadn't recognized him. "Where's the other one?"

"He's still in the hospital," David said and pushed on the outside door. "The one in the hospital is in even worse shape—he lost the fight." He pointed to the man on the bed. "This guy was the winner."

Back in the office, I pulled the *Burns Handbook for Security Officers* out of my back pocket (we were required to carry it at all times). I wrote down the man's name and alpha number, and planned to get information on the other fighter when he returned, but to my knowledge he never did.

Later I learned that the man who lost the fight had also lost his eye.

■　■　■

My name was never added to the new hiring list. Neither was Cynthia Rodriguez's nor Jovita Urrutia's. We were disheartened and angry, but the last weeks there gave us time to adjust and band together.

A moment of rebellion came when United International's owner William Gudice pulled into the parking lot in his rental car with boxes of new uniforms. He told Lieutenant Oziel Puente, who was on duty, to have me and a few other guards coming on duty help carry the boxes to the Burns office in Building 36. With the three of us standing there, I told Lieutenant Puente to kindly tell Mr. Gudice to get somebody else to carry his boxes, because I didn't work for him. If Gudice knew anything about the rules anyway, he would have known that nothing came into the camp until it had been inspected for explosives and contraband. As I walked away, I heard him ask Lieutenant Puente, "Is that Hefner, the preacher?"

In those last days Cynthia gave me a letter that Consuelo, a female detainee from Colombia, had written:

> I will direct my comments particularly to V. Ramirez, some officers in green uniforms, and some in blue uniforms. Aside from moral insinuations after they learn that some of us have served sentences of up to three years, they make lewd invitations and lowly comments.
>
> P.S. I hear the following statement on a daily basis: "when are you going to leave here? Let me know. I will find out when you are leaving. Colombian women are good with their tongues." When I arrived at this institution on July 8, 1990, the official that received us told me, "I will marry you. Do you like to do everything?" I asked him, what everything? He responded by stating that he would like to go down on me, and asked if I would like it? I told him that he was not precisely the one whom I should discuss this point, and that I would reserve my response, and to limit his questions to his work.

■ ■ ■

The Saturday before my final week, I was at the church cleaning the Sunday school room when our pastor Jerry Smith stopped by.

He knew I would soon be laid off. He handed me a nice letter of recommendation to help in my job hunt and said that the church had pledged twenty-five dollars a month to help our ministry.

Now twenty-five dollars may not sound like much, but it was a lot coming from a poor church. We felt that we were finally part of the community, that our ministry was judged worthy of support. Moreover, other churches had promised help in the past that had never materialized. Though small, this monthly gift was proof that we were now accepted.

■ ■ ■

My last day was to be September 21, 1990. I'd lost my job, but soon it appeared that those blacklisted were not the only ones. I had just arrived in the camp parking lot on a Wednesday when I saw Rubio and Ramirez. Angry and defiant, they walked from the Burns office through Gate 2, across the lot to their cars, got in, and drove off the property. I ran to the office for some kind of explanation. Walking off the job was too obvious a violation to be ignored. My heart raced at the possibilities! It looked like a freakish victory. Had they been given an ultimatum and been fired? Had United International refused to hire them? Was this too good to be true?

According to Burns security supervisor Adán González, Rubio and Ramirez were as good as gone. No one knew the particulars, but Lieutenant González had been promoted to captain in Rubio's place. We guards were slapping each other on the back in celebration. Even with this good news, we still had to swallow our pride having unfairly lost our jobs. It didn't really help ease the pain and hurt these men had inflicted upon detainees and good hard-working guards. We took our jobs seriously and cared for the misfortune of others.

González had a professional attitude about his job, an untarnished record, and was well qualified. Did this mean that things would finally change at the camp? I had to find out what had happened or my curiosity would kill me. We all thanked God that Rubio and Ramirez were gone. We were only sorry that it hadn't happened before we'd been sacked.

Though no longer at the camp, I stayed in close contact with many there. The Monday after Rubio and Ramirez left, a friend called and sadly reported that the relief we had all felt when they left was short lived. They were back on Monday morning as if nothing had happened. It seemed they had to quit or be fired from Burns before United International could hire them officially. So they took the opportunity to get themselves fired with a couple of extra days off in the bargain. González was demoted back to lieutenant, and Rubio and Ramirez were again in charge.

In my forced absence I alternately stewed and became depressed. I felt such a churning frustration inside. I could not relax. Memories surfaced that should have been forgotten. It was as if I were six years old again and trapped. I remembered once at a carnival in Warren, Ohio, Jim took me to the bathroom. He left me alone in the dark, and I was to stay until he returned with my mother. But they didn't come, and people walked by laughing until one curious man asked if I was lost and if he could help me find my parents. I could only cry because Jim said he would beat me if I weren't right where he left me when he returned. My mother finally came, and I tried to tell her what happened but Jim backhanded me in the mouth. I was beaten anyway, because Jim told her I had run away from him.

I felt buried alive and fighting through the blackness to get a breath of fresh air. I wanted to get on a rooftop and shout about what they were doing over there. The eyes of the young dancer, and Alex, and those two boys in the bungalow. I can't express in words the outrage I felt down to my very bones.

I never knew that one talked about abuse; I didn't when I was young. I accepted it as a way of life. I hated it now with unfathomable determination, and no one was going to silence me. I was an adult and could fight. My anger was a ticking bomb, and I was ready to explode.

When following up on my original complaint to the FBI, I could now use my real name without fear of retaliation. When I mentioned the young dancer, I was met with stonewalling. I called the investigator with whom I'd first spoken to ask what had been done. Five calls later, I had no information and was told to direct any further inquiries to the Office of the Inspector General in McAllen. These people wouldn't talk to me anymore. No investigation was planned.

The McAllen office told me they couldn't reveal whether or not they'd even received a complaint about a female juvenile who had been forced to dance nude for immigration officials. There was no protection for children. Nothing had been done. I felt as if there was no way for me to help.

Or was there?

■ ■ ■

The new district director of immigration, E. Michael Trominski, was transferred from Mexico City to the Harlingen INS office. Trominski was taking the place of Omar Sewell, who had just retired—at a "quiet time," according to the newspapers. Would Sewell explain to Trominski how things were in this very quiet and orderly district? No. But I would.

I called the *Brownsville Herald*, the *Harlingen Valley Morning Star*, and two local television stations and told them about the abuses at the camp in light of Sewell's retirement. They sent reporters to accompany me to the INS office in Harlingen to give my "report," in the form of complaints and affidavits, to Mr. Trominski on his first day of work.

Standing on the steps of the district office with a bunch of reporters with cameras and microphones hovering behind me, I didn't feel very brave and righteous anymore. More like queasy. My hands perspired as I tightly held the stack of complaints. This was like storming a police station; all those uniforms deserved respect, not criticism. What was I doing? I knocked on the door. Each moment I waited was torture.

Finally, a secretary opened the door. The cameras rolled. I took a breath and asked to see Mr. Trominski; I had some papers of importance for him. She replied that he was too busy to see me at this time and assured me she would deliver the papers to him. "Thank you," I said politely. I showed her a letter I had written to Trominski that I wanted her to give him first. The microphone was about three inches from my mouth. I could have bitten it. "Certainly," she said, as the cameras recorded her receiving the complaints with a smile. It was all so nice. Then she closed the door, and the electronic whirring clicked, clacked, and thudded off. I breathed a sigh of relief.

Like it or not, I was now a crusader.

8

The Cover-Up

Just a week after my last day, on September 27, *The Brownsville Herald* carried the story of my visit to Trominski and made our allegations public: "INS Investigates Alleged Sexual Harassment." The article stated that the INS had sent reports to the US Office of the Inspector General (OIG) complaining that security guards at Bayview sexually harassed inmates and other guards, and named United International as the contractor of those guards. It said that guards were allegedly dismissed for objecting to sexual advances from superiors. When the *Herald*'s city editor, Robert Kahn, asked the deputy director of the Harlingen INS district office to comment, he said he couldn't, but that he had indeed received the allegations, which he would pass on to the OIG.

When the EEOC in San Antonio was contacted about complaints filed with their office, they didn't release any information nor did the OIG in Washington return "repeated phone calls."

Kahn did get a comment from Ramirez, however. He said, "It's all news to me," and went on to blame the ex-employees. "A lot of people are getting laid off. All I know is that we have a lot of tension down here right now because of the new company. All I know is they're blaming it on the supervisors."

The *Herald* reported, "However, another female guard [Marta Oviedo], who did not file a complaint with the EEOC, said that the same midlevel supervisor and his superior officer use the camp as 'their own supermarket for sex, from detainees and guards.'"

I had described the Salvadoran who danced the lambada for

supervisors in exchange for a no-strings-attached release and showed the court docket and several affidavits regarding her case to the editor. He followed it up and then announced that "a spokesman for the Executive Office of Immigration Review in Falls Church, VA, said the Salvadoran girl's case was closed on May 31, 1990."

"I don't see where there's any indication an asylum application was filed in the case," said Jerry Hurwitz, spokesman for the Executive Office of Immigration Review, in Falls Church, Virginia. Robert Kahn got another quote from the Harlingen director about it. "I received Mr. Hefner's allegations about the woman being told to dance the lambada, and that the allegation was being investigated." He added, "I have no idea why the case was closed."

"Cecilio Ruiz, INS deputy district director for deportation and the officer in charge of the Bayview Camp, said the incident has been referred to the internal investigations division of INS."

The article got attention. The woman who accused the supervisors of using the camp as their "supermarket for sex," Marta Oviedo, had already been blacklisted and fired. She gave me the names and numbers of the two detainees who had been forced to provide "cleaning services" to Rubio and Ramirez. The two detainees, Dina and Marin, were even escorted to the Burns office *during the day.* The guards were told to wait outside the closed office door as Rubio and Ramirez stayed inside with the two detainees while they "cleaned."

Lydia Dillard said when she had to get the two detainees up in the morning, they would call the female guards bitches and threaten them, saying that if they didn't stop bothering them, they were going to tell Rubio and Ramirez and get them fired. The two main supervisors backed up the detainees on their threats.

After the article appeared, Marta and several other women who had also been fired were summoned to Rubio's office. They were all given the opportunity to win their jobs back if they would sign a statement saying that the information they had given "Reverend

Hefner" was false. Marta did not sign the statement, but she knew one woman who did and was rehired.

The next day, September 28, the paper printed another story dealing with allegations surrounding the International Emergency Shelter for Children in Los Fresnos, where young Alex and the Salvadoran girl had reported abuse: "Sexual Harassment Alleged At Immigration Shelter." The article stated that according to a Los Angeles lawyer, federally funded nonprofit children's centers in Los Fresnos and Mission, Texas, were violating the rights of Central American children. These rights—access to political asylum, legal counsel, legal materials, and telephones for private calls—were insured by a 1988 ruling, *Orantes-Hernandez v. Thornburgh*, and were being denied.

The International Emergency Shelter (IES) director Jesse Villarreal angrily denied the charges. He explained, for example, that staffers would make phone calls for the children to insure that they would not contact someone that they shouldn't. He pointed out that he was also responsible for protecting them.

A paralegal from Proyecto Libertad, a Harlingen-based alien rights law office, however, was denied access to the children when she began to investigate complaints from them that an official and other detainees at the Los Fresnos shelter were sexually harassing them. A fifteen-year-old stated in an affidavit, "I feel I have no one I can trust here in the shelter."

Villarreal then said at the end of the article, "I haven't heard anything about anybody being sexually harassed."

The upshot is that before this article with Villarreal's denial appeared, I saw his signature on letters that described the sexual harassment mentioned by the reporter, showing he had indeed heard about it. And if he were so righteously protective, why did he allow the seventeen-year-old girl to spend five days at an adult detention camp, then be returned to him?

The media was our means for being heard. Reporters were

always on the lookout for stories, and we had stories to tell. Payan continued to deliver complaints to the INS through the proper channels, and those complaints regularly disappeared. We decided that we would fight them with the light of media attention and let the public judge how their tax dollars were being spent. Payan told me he needed to remain anonymous to avoid suspicion and stay within the information loop, and I agreed. I would be the lighting rod. Payan passed everything he discovered to me. And I made sure the newspapers got it.

Over the next two months I often appeared on the six o'clock local news. People started to recognize me on the street. It was disconcerting because I'd always felt invisible before.

One young man approached me after a broadcast. He grabbed my hand and started to shake it and thanked me over and over for trying to stop the abuse. He explained that now he was a citizen, but at one time he and his family had come illegally to the United States from El Salvador. His sister had been caught and sent to Bayview.

While there, she had become pregnant and reported it to the INS. They asked her to name the father of her child. She told them that she didn't know; there had been three officers in green uniforms and two in blue. Any one of them could be the father.

I called Payan to confirm this story. According to him, whenever an officer got a detainee pregnant, she reported it and identified the man responsible. He was then transferred to another post outside the facility, and the detainee was told that the man had been fired. When the woman was deported, the officer was brought back to his original post. This was not uncommon.

■   ■   ■

As kids, when we were sick, my mother would make a mustard plaster on a sanitary napkin and tie it around our necks. I assumed until I was thirteen that that's what a sanitary napkin was for. But one evening on my way home I was set straight. A car with two teenage boys and a girl circled our block, and when a bloody sanitary napkin was thrown out of the car in front of me, I ran screaming murder. I thought the boys had slit the girl's throat.

Maybe I was that ignorant again, but I honestly thought that once those in higher positions in the government were informed about the reprehensible acts of the camp supervisors, they would be grateful to find out and would put an end to it. I was puzzled when, in article after article, INS brass "looked into" or simply ignored what we said. I had aligned myself with the church and thought everyone saw things as I did, namely, that we stood for the truth and wouldn't lie. But top INS brass simply did not believe the complaints or didn't care. Others said the situation had been blown out of proportion. Camp officers smooth talked and spun the predicament to their advantage, making me and the others seem like ex-employee bellyachers. It was a quick education. I felt like a gnat buzzing around the generalissimo's head.

The men we fought against were highly respected in our community for their positions and for the power they wielded over people's lives. They had authority over who could keep their jobs and who couldn't, and all the possessions to awe poor people. Those beneath them tended to protect these men rather than squeal because they would be rewarded for their loyalty. These rich men were the nobles in our humble serfdom.

■   ■   ■

Barbara and I were at the kitchen table with our coffee cups, reading in Ecclesiastes for some perspective on our troubles. "There is a just man that perisheth in his righteousness, and there is a wicked man that prolongeth his life in his wickedness" (7:15). So don't expect justice in this world. "For there is not a just man upon earth that doeth good, and sinneth not" (7:20). Yes, we all have a dark side; I'm not perfect either.

The phone rang.

"Is this Hefner?" a man asked. It sounded like Payan.

"Yes, it is."

"This is a good friend of yours. I have some information that may be of help to you."

Looking at Barbara, I raised my eyebrows and reached for a pen. She frowned back. The caller asked if I knew George Molinar.

"Molinar came into the camp a short time ago and told us that Cecilio Ruiz has been arrested in Mexico. He's in the Matamoros jail." Matamoros lay just across the border from Brownsville.

He continued, "Molinar was mocking Ruiz because Ruiz had been caught in a hotel room Friday night with several women in the act of snorting cocaine. This was funny to Molinar. He said the Mexican police were hard on Ruiz and did not look kindly on a US government employee using an illegal substance in their country. Molinar said they beat him and put a loaded gun in his mouth, threatening to blow his brains out, then took him to prison."

I swallowed hard. Barbara must have had a good time watching my face.

"Molinar is picking up Mike Trominski, and together they are en route to Mexico to negotiate his release. It will not be easy, but it is assumed that the government will intervene to ensure that it is done and done quietly. We are under oath to keep it out of the news. We will deny the reason for his arrest."

He went on to say that it was up to me to report the arrest because I wasn't afraid of Ruiz. I guffawed but told him I'd start calling around with the news.

"What?" Barbara asked in a deadpan voice, though her eyes were like silver dollars. As I started to tell her, the phone rang again. It was a Brownsville police officer with the same news, then another anonymous caller after that. The date was Tuesday, October 2, 1990.

I started dialing every newspaper and television news station I could think of and laid it all out before them. Barbara was astonished as she heard secondhand what had happened.

After I got off the phone, we talked and made some fresh coffee, then settled down to finish our study. Barbara pointed out the final verse in Ecclesiastes: "For God shall bring every work into judgment, with every secret thing, whether it be good, or evil." Yes, God will see to it that justice is done.

■   ■   ■

Later that Tuesday a local anchorwoman called and confirmed the information I'd given her about Ruiz's arrest. She described the scene as she and her broadcast team and several other reporters waited in front of the Matamoros jailhouse that morning to see if the story materialized. When Trominski and Molinar drove up she knew it was true. She said they were shocked to see the news people run to them with microphones and cameras rolling.

"We were all asking the same questions about Ruiz. We knew he was in there," the reporter said.

Mike Trominski was about to enter the Federal Judicial Police headquarters when the anchor woman asked him if they could talk to Ruiz. Trominski replied, "Ruiz is not here. He's on his way back to Harlingen."

Then she said, '"Well, sir, if Ruiz is not here, then why are you here?"

Trominski had no answer. Ruiz didn't leave until all the reporters had gone away. The anchorwoman said, "I found out later that Ruiz was very upset with me as I was the last to leave. Apparently, the longer I stayed, the longer he had to put up with the Matamoros police."

In the next few days I received many phone calls from government employees thanking me for calling in the news hounds. They were relieved that this time, the government was exposed and could not cover up the events. The public would now demand that something be done about Ruiz and the corruption at the camp. Payan said that INS employees were hopeful that Ruiz would be transferred or fired. "We all knew a cover-up would take place," Payan told me. "We just did not know how it would be accomplished."

Ruiz immediately took sick leave to have his teeth fixed after receiving a few well-aimed slaps by the Mexican police. Payan said that there was no urine analysis or blood testing. Weeks later, a supervisory Border Patrol agent with collateral duties as an investigator looked into the incident. Payan continued explaining to me:

> Before the investigation, Ruiz had a meeting with all his supervisor personnel, including me. He advised everyone he was innocent and that we were not to help any investigator that might ask about him. At the time of the investigation, I did not have the information that I have now. I obtained copies of the newspapers, and names of the Mexican police officers who were present during Ruiz's arrest. The investigation fizzled because everyone that was questioned had almost nothing to say because the district office carefully controlled any and all information. The Cecilio Ruiz spy network, which is a route to promotion, informed Ruiz as to who had spoken to the investigator.

When Molinar showed up at the camp, he said Ruiz was guilty, and if not for Trominski, Ruiz would still be there. Not until later did Payan inform me that one of the women who had been in Ruiz's company at the time of his arrest now worked at the Fort Brown Hotel and Resort on East Elizabeth Street. She said she had to pay $65,000 and spent four months in jail before being released.

The other man who was arrested—who had been in the lobby and was caught with a small dose of drugs—worked for an insurance company.

That night I felt some satisfaction as I saw Ruiz's picture plastered all over the local television news.

On October 3, 1990, the *Brownsville Herald* ran a story in which the commander of Mexico's Federal Judicial Police, Ramón Uriarte Solis, claimed that "Ruiz was arrested with others in the bar at Hotel Del Prado Sunday night" because he "happened to be at that particular place."

A week and a half later I received another anonymous phone call. The male voice identified himself only as a friend. These unknown callers were supervisors or officers still working at the camp concerned that the phone on either side of our conversation was tapped. They were always just "friends."

The man asked for my address. I gave it to him.

An envelope arrived a few days later with a clipping from an October 2 Matamoros newspaper, *El Popular*, inside. Following is a translation of the article:

"US INS Official Jailed"

Cecilio Ruiz, chief of the force of the Immigration Service of the United States in charge of detention in Bayview, was detained this past Friday in this city by Federal Judicial Police with a quantity of drugs, supposedly cocaine.

El Popular was officially informed that this high official in our neighbor city was arrested Friday, but kept secret by the police agency.

La Fuente (police spokesman) stated that Ruiz, veteran of many years of service with the stated agency, was arrested by Federal Judicial Police led by Commander Ramón Uriarte Friday night, in the company of several women.

According to the same spokesman, the immigration official was beaten by our federal agency and detained at the PGR holding area (office cell).

During the day, PGR is expected to release information on the case, including the identities of the women arrested with the official and the amount of drugs confiscated.

It seemed that Ruiz had few friends on the other side of the border as well. Apparently, someone had tipped the police about his activities, and he'd been arrested on Friday, not Sunday. He'd actually been incarcerated four nights and a day. When Ruiz went back to work, Payan reported that he still had some slight bruising on his face. Who knows how bad he looked when he left the jail?

When Payan called to talk over the Ruiz fiasco, he did so after fully identifying himself. Then he abruptly stopped and told me that if the Office of the Inspector General contacted me as part of this Ruiz investigation, I was to give them his name as a witness and as my source of information.

"Are you sure?" I asked. "You're going on record against Ruiz?"

"Yes, I'm sure," he said. He thought his credibility would lend weight to our accusations, and since he was close to retirement, he felt they wouldn't dare touch him.

I guessed that just like everyone else, he had a personal reason to bring Ruiz down.

"What can they do to me?" he asked philosophically. "Ruiz is the one who broke the law."

When I saw the discrepancies between the US and the Mexican reports of Ruiz's arrest in black and white, I knew our government had lied. They might call it diplomacy or political expedience to preserve public confidence, but it's still just lying. I had always respected our government. It was like a great officer in uniform: educated, full of honor and moral authority, and always sure of the right thing to do. For the first time I realized that maybe it wasn't like that at all.

If the truth had been allowed to surface, public confidence *would* have been shaken. Outrage and well-deserved government embarrassment would have fueled the engine of change. The corrupt detention facility would have been busted. What's wrong with the truth?

I began to call every church in the area, and everyone I'd ever been affiliated with outside of Texas. I told them what had happened in Matamoros and how bad things were at the camp. The pastors agreed to form a coalition for a letter-writing campaign.

I used one of Ruiz's pictures from the local newspaper and put the whole story together, addressing each copy to the attention of Gene McNary, Commissioner of the US Immigration and Naturalization Service in Washington, DC. Each petition held twenty-four signatures of concerned citizens, and I sent nine of them out on October 18, 1990. Throughout San Benito and Harlingen, I knocked on every door. Churches as far away as Michigan began to send their signed petitions. We sent them all in to the INS—and got zip in response.

Someone suggested I write to my senator, so on October 22, I sent the first of many letters to Texas Senator Phil Gramm. I told him about the corruption at the camp, naming Rubio and Ramirez, and how I lost my job taking a stand against it. I thought Senator Gramm would also want to know that my job there had supported a very worthy ministry of which he would approve. He held the same goals of teaching productive, drug-free living. I explained my compassion for the detainees at the camp and how they benefited from the Spanish New Testaments I still delivered there.

I protested the lack of response from Trominski and the Washington INS office despite my legwork and told him our government had performed a cover-up on Cecilio Ruiz's drug-related arrest. I asked him why our government couldn't do the same for other US citizens who claimed that they, too, were innocent and locked up in foreign countries.

The next morning, the telephone rang.

"This is Cecilio Ruiz. I don't want you coming to the camp anymore." He was forcing his voice to be calm. The phone line crackled with high tension.

I hemmed and hawed, calmer than I expected under surprise attack, and informed him that I didn't actually come into the camp but dropped off the Bibles at the guard shack. I asked politely if I could perhaps send the Bibles with another church group.

"I don't want you, or any of your groups, at the camp!" he bellowed and slammed down the phone.

Ruiz, of course, could not forbid any preachers from visiting the camp. The detainees were entitled to religious services, and someone had to lead them. I decided that tomorrow I would send more letters to churches, saying that Ruiz had denied us access to the camp. I would ask them to continue the letter campaign to pressure Washington.

"Barbara? Did I sound nervous on the phone just now?"

"Nervous? No."

9
High Hopes

We had known for weeks that Senator Phil Gramm and Clayton Williams were going to make a personal appearance at the Harlingen Community Center on November 3, 1990. Clayton Williams was on the Republican ticket for governor of Texas, and the election was the following week. Ann Richards was the Democratic candidate. The election looked close.

We had lots of children in our Sunday school who wanted to see the politicians. The children knew about the letter I had written to Senator Gramm, and they had even requested prayer for him. I promised to take them to see him.

The community center was crowded with an even mixture of brown and white faces. Organizers, press, and local politicians filled the hall, so we waited outside. Banners of all sizes flashed in our faces. The children were shined up in their Sunday-best outfits, and I had on my pinstriped suit. They beamed with the anticipation of meeting someone famous. Maybe I did, too.

The first car to pull up carried Mr. Williams, who waved and walked briskly by us to the double doors as the crowd cheered. The children smiled broadly and fidgeted with excitement. Then Senator Gramm arrived. He got out of his car and looked down at the kids standing in a straight line before me, and surprised us all by proceeding to shake each little hand in the line. The children were thrilled. I was impressed that such an important man would take the time out for the kids.

Afterward, the youngsters urged me to write another letter to

Senator Gramm. They thought he could help clean up the bad things at the camp and help me get my job back.

Four days after seeing him I received my first reply from Gramm, stating, "I have contacted the INS . . . and I will write you again as soon as I receive a reply." Good. He'd get some answers. In the meantime, other churches had agreed to send more signatures to INS Commissioner Gene McNary.

On November 19, I wrote another letter to the senator, thanking him for his response and detailing the firing of two security supervisors for trivial reasons, compared to Rubio and Ramirez who, despite all of their outrageous offences, were still employed. And I asked him "for help in our government to place someone at the camp to oversee these complaints and many more."

I felt progress except in one area—I needed to learn how to type. In the midst of campaigning for truth and justice, I had to hunt and peck at letters on Barbara's old typewriter. So, I practiced for hours every day after my ranch work was done and waited for Barbara to proofread my letters when she got home.

Typing out a professional letter was harder than anything in Bible school. I must be the world's worst speller.

In late November, nine female guards including Cynthia Rodriguez, Jovita Urrutia, and Juanita Flores, who had filed sexual harassment complaints with the Equal Employment Opportunity Commission when they were fired from Bayview, were informed that their complaints would be investigated. The Texas Commission on Human Rights said they, too, would perform an investigation.

In early December, I persuaded Joe Vega and Juan Martínez to write to Senator Gramm about their dismissals. Juan was a supervisor at the camp and a good one too. He had written earlier letters to Senator Gramm about complaints regarding Rubio and Ramirez while still employed. He was fired by George Molinar for sitting in the control room watching and monitoring the television cameras.

As a supervisor, monitoring things in the control room was part of his job.

Joe was the diligent guard who had reported me for being late to the mess hall when Ramirez waylaid me. He believed that Ruiz fired him—in spite of five years of perfect work attendance—because Ramirez had bragged to Joe about having sex with detainees in Ruiz's office and told him that Ruiz had gotten Berta, a young woman from Honduras, pregnant and then deported her.

Martínez wrote, protesting his unethical firing, and asked, "If I could be fired so easily, why couldn't the two corrupt supervisors [Rubio and Ramirez] be fired for their great offenses?" He asked, "Was it possible that the two supervisors knew something and could spill the beans on a higher-ranking government employee?"

Lydia Dillard, a guard and one of the nine who wrote to the EEOC, named Rubio and Ramirez as perpetrators of sexual harassment and abuse toward her. Rubio would call her into the office and try to persuade her to do him favors and get under his desk. "Don't worry," he would laugh. "If anyone comes in they wouldn't see you under there." She quoted this to the EEOC.

Ramirez hounded her for sex and would run his hands up and down her arms, asking if it turned her on. This was always in the presence of two or three witnesses.

Lydia also corroborated other complaints of sexual misconduct against Rubio and Ramirez that were already before the commission. She could speak to many cases of female guards who had entered the uniform closet to have sex and who still had their jobs. Lydia was the guard who had told me about the sick woman detainee who had been kicked on the ground and later died a slow death in the dorm.

■ ■ ■

On December 10, 1990, the winter sun was shining, but the air was brisk as I hustled back to the house after feeding the horses. Once inside, I was taking off my boots when the phone rang.

A man asked for Reverend Anthony Hefner. He said his name was Dwayne Jones from the Office of the Inspector General in San Antonio, and that he'd just checked into a hotel in Harlingen in preparation for his investigation of the complaints I'd sent to the Washington OIG. He wanted to meet.

After I had spoken with him, Barbara called, as she did every day around that time, to let me know she had gotten to work all right. Since taking a public stand against the local big shots, I had begun to receive anonymous threats. One caller said, "You're a damn dead man," and hung up. I got that message three other times. Another said, "Watch your back, stupid," and, "Your doomsday is coming, big-mouth." Then there were those times when the person wouldn't say anything. Answering the phone had become a battle of nerves. Barbara wouldn't do it anymore.

I didn't really think anyone would harm my wife, but you never knew. Besides, if she didn't call within thirty minutes of leaving the house, she might be having car trouble.

I told Barbara about the investigator's call and that I would be meeting him in half an hour at the La Quinta Inn.

"Be careful, Tony," Barbara said. "This could be a trap."

Barbara didn't like any of this business. At first she thought we were living a television script, but once she realized the nature of what I was up against, she saw infinite possibilities for my destruction. I reassured her and promised that after this investigation I would drop it, and we would put our lives back together.

"Call me as soon as your meeting is over," she said. "I'll be worried until I hear from you."

I promised to stop by her office and tell her firsthand what we had discussed.

"I'll still be worried until I see you face to face," she added.

Standing before room 802 on the walkway by the parking lot of the La Quinta Inn, I surveyed the scene. Cold and gray. Not a soul in sight. I stepped up and knocked on the door. The knob began to turn. Slowly revealed in the doorway was a tall cowboy in his late forties. He had a bushy mustache, a tan Stetson, a brown sport jacket, and alligator boots. He looked like a Texas Ranger.

He stuck his hand out. "Hi, I'm Dwayne Jones," he drawled. "Come on in."

I gingerly sat in a chair next to the door.

An old brown striped suitcase lay open on the bed, still full of folded clothes and lumps. He took off his hat, which left a barely visible impression in his hair. When his jacket was half off, I saw he was wearing a shoulder holster. Then his gun became visible. Was I in the movies or what? My heart started to pound.

Nonchalantly, he took a coat hanger and hung up his jacket. Then he reached—almost in slow motion—for his gun. Do investigators carry guns?

My blood pressure skyrocketed. Jones put the gun down on the bed and searched his pockets, withdrawing a wallet. He opened it and showed me his identification and his picture with a badge. It confirmed what he had told me, that he was from the San Antonio Office of the Inspector General. It looked real, but what did I know?

From his briefcase he withdrew a sheaf of papers that he handed to me. They were the complaints I had delivered to Mike Trominski on the INS office steps.

"I was sent here to investigate each of these complaints. I know you've put a lot of work into this, but I can't promise we'll be able to get your job back."

I said I understood, and he asked if I'd help him get in touch with the witnesses. I had promised Barbara to get out of it. I asked if I had to be at their meetings, too.

"No," he said. "I just need to talk with each one."

Nodding my flustered head, I pointed to the bottom of the first page.

"As you can see, their names and phone numbers are written on each complaint." Then I gave him an envelope with another list of names and numbers, and a brief description of the testimony each provided.

Jones looked over the list and gave a low whistle. "You sure been busy."

He questioned me for over two hours. We talked about what exactly had been witnessed, the juvenile abuse, and which supervisors (such as Payan) were willing to talk. I poured it all out, and he seemed to listen. Jones said he had three days to investigate, as he'd be leaving on the fourteenth. He thanked me, and I reassured him that he could call me anytime if anything needed clarification.

Walking toward my truck, I felt perceptively lighter and relieved, finally confident that at last someone in authority was paying attention. All he had to do was call the witnesses on the list, and Payan would explain things when he got to the camp. Maybe the light at the end of that dark tunnel was sunshine instead of a roaring train.

When I met Barbara at her office, the relief spread over her face like sunbeams. She hugged me hard.

"Tony, I've been so worried."

"You're not crying are you?"

"Heck no," she lied. "You know I never cry." She smiled. "Only when you make me mad."

I gave her my handkerchief, and we sat and talked about the whole thing. It gave her great comfort to know that the official investigation had finally begun, and I was done.

That evening the phone started ringing. Four of the listed women asked me if Jones was for real. I assured them he was there to help and urged them to tell him the honest truth so he could do his job.

The next call was Jovita Urrutia. "I'm afraid," she said. "Can you be at the meeting with me tomorrow? I don't even know this man . . ." Jovita hated to talk about this, even with people she knew.

To Barbara's chagrin, I drove to the Whataburger on Boca Chica for Jovita's ten o'clock meeting. I planned to just sit there, support Jovita and Cynthia, who would also speak, and leave it all to the trained professional government investigator. My job was done.

Jones and Cynthia were seated at a round booth in the restaurant. An attractive woman sat with them. I thought I knew her from somewhere but couldn't place the face. As Jones explained that the woman was from the Office of the Inspector General in McAllen, I suddenly remembered—I'd seen her around Bayview!

"Your husband works at the camp for INS. He's an INS officer," I exclaimed.

"That's right," she said coolly.

"I just thought her being here might make the women feel a little more comfortable, Mr. Hefner," said Jones.

I appreciated his sensitivity, but her husband was an officer working under Cecilio Ruiz! Wasn't that a conflict of interest?

Cynthia began to tell her story as Jones asked questions and took notes. She told about Ramirez taking credit for her not being laid off at an earlier point, and that he expected a sexual favor in return, and how he attacked her from behind after multiple unwelcome propositions and jumped on her back. She said, "He acted liked a horny dog."

As Cynthia finished, Jovita came and sat down. Very tense, she eyed the two strangers warily. Then Jones asked her to tell her story. All eyes went to Jovita.

Her head dropped to her chest and silent tears began to flow. "Do I have to tell you everything?" she asked softly.

"Well, if you want to help me stop this man, I need all the information you have," said Jones.

Jovita described in grisly detail the whole episode with Ramirez. She was crying hard now and fumbling for words. Her poise evaporated. We all looked away, then back again, trying to help her on, everyone uncomfortable and self-conscious. Jones finally asked if she would feel better talking in private to the woman investigator. Jovita nodded without looking up. Jones offered them his car outside.

When the ladies had slipped out and we saw them resume Jovita's statement in Jones's car, he shook his head. "Something's got to be done with this man," he said. "I'm gonna do whatever I can to make sure he doesn't do this again."

During the next two days of the investigation, I received calls from guards on my list that an investigator was at the camp asking questions. They asked when he would contact them. I told them it should be very soon since he had a deadline. Then Payan called. "Did you give the investigator my name?" he asked.

"Yes," I answered, perplexed. "He's going to contact you. I told Mr. Jones that you're an eyewitness who can prove complaints about sexual abuse from female detainees."

"Well, here it is Wednesday, and so far this Jones fellow hasn't contacted me yet."

"Don't worry. I gave him your phone number and beeper number," I said. "Maybe he doesn't want to make personal contact at the camp. After all, he may be concerned about retaliation against you."

Payan was excited. A lot of people believed that the government was finally doing something. We were hopeful that none of the big-wigs could cut the teeth out of this investigation, as they had with other ones.

A female guard at the camp told me that when Jones questioned the female detainees who had volunteered as witnesses, they asked for protection. Consuelo, the Colombian who had written to me on my last day of work, was especially worried. She asked if our government would protect them while they were detained because "there are many things that go on here, and we don't want to meet with an accident."

But when Jones couldn't promise protection for the female detainees, the women stepped back and refused to talk, fearing for their lives.

Within three days of Jones's investigation, Consuelo was deported.

On the last night of Jones's investigation, before he was to leave early the next morning, I couldn't stop thinking about it. Around 8:30 p.m. I called Jesse Castillo, the ex-supervisor whose testimony was crucial to verify Jovita's complaint against Ramirez. After Jesse stood up for her, he was laid off and was out of the camp loop. Barbara followed me and watched suspiciously as I made the call.

I told Jesse about the investigator and that I had included his name on my list as he could corroborate Jovita's testimony. I wanted to make sure he had been contacted.

"Nope. Nobody's contacted me about Jovita or any complaints," he said.

I told him to sit tight while I called Jones.

"Tony, you said you were done with all this," Barbara said.

"Well, almost, Barbara. I just have to make sure of this one thing—"

"You're obsessed, you know," she said, leaving.

At 8:35 p.m. Jones picked up the phone in his hotel room. After identifying myself I asked him how the investigation was going.

"Real well," he said.

"Were you able to talk to all the people on the list?"

"Yes, everyone whose name you gave me."

"What about Jesse Castillo?" I asked. "Did you talk with him?"

"Sure did," Jones said. "I talked with everyone."

"Did Castillo tell you about Jovita's coming to him seeking help?"

"Yes," he said. "I got his story."

My jaws clenched into a vise. I told him he was a liar and that Castillo was waiting for his call even as we spoke.

Jones didn't attempt to squirm out of it, but after some sighing said he'd call Jesse right then, and did.

I was beside myself. Was this another show? He had seemed so concerned. Were they only giving the appearance of an investigation? Maybe he just missed Castillo's name on the list?

The next morning I called Beatriz Huerta. She had a catalog of sexual harassment complaints from witnesses who were not willing to go to the EEOC or the Human Rights Commission because of Ruiz's stranglehold on them. I asked her, "Has anyone from the OIG contacted you about your complaints?"

Beatriz paused for a moment then said, "I heard there was an investigator at the camp during the day. But as far as I know, he didn't stay to question any guards on the afternoon swing shift or graveyard shift."

I told her if she had anything to say she'd better call him this morning because he was packing up to leave.

"Well . . . I don't know. I have two kids. I don't know if it's worth it."

This didn't sound like her. "What do you mean?"

"I was told that if I talked to him about my complaints, my clearance would be lifted. The others were told the same thing."

"Who told you that?"

"Just an INS officer who secretly advised us. I can't say who."

I called Jones again. He was getting ready to check out. I confronted him about not talking to half the guards and told him they had been threatened. Then I threatened to call his supervisor in Washington.

"Now wait a minute, Hefner," he said, exasperated at last. "Wait just a doggone minute. What if I just go on back to the camp and get this straightened out, and then you don't have to go calling anyone's boss."

Later that evening Jones called, telling me once again that he had talked to everyone. He said he would call me "when he'd finished dotting the i's and crossing all the t's."

I, for one, never heard from him again. Nobody I talked to did either.

Two days after Jones went back to San Antonio I got a call from Payan.

"What happened to that investigator who was going to call me?" he asked.

I was aghast. Jones never contacted him. It was heartbreaking. After telling Payan the whole wretched story, I said I thought the entire investigation was a sham, just to shut us up. Though disappointed, he was not surprised. Something similar had been done before. I promised to call if I heard anything. I sensed that Payan was more concerned about his status at the camp now.

After that phone call, the morning stretched out in front of me like an empty highway in the cold of winter. I had been so hopeful. My mind wandered back to my childhood, when I wanted to be Pancho, the cowboy, or Zorro saving the señorita from the bad guys, riding my horse over an interminable Texas plain. I remembered the Halloween when I was seven and asked to be a cowboy like Gene Autry or Roy Rogers. Instead, Jim dressed me up like a Mexican woman, with lipstick and a black wig, and sent me out, the butt of his joke. I felt like that again. But it was different now. If I had to be a fool in a wig and lipstick and walk the whole road myself, I would do it if it ended with the guilty being brought to justice.

10

New Investigation

The Office of the Inspector General in McAllen contacted me. I was to address all further complaints to Mr. Perry Suitt. I sat down and began a letter.

The problem with OIG's internal investigation was that all the guards and officers who had complaints or had witnessed wrong-doings were afraid of losing their jobs. So they didn't report trouble, and OIG, another branch of the government, wouldn't dig into its own looking for it. If Ruiz said that you didn't see lawlessness, then you didn't see lawlessness. You played along or you were out of the best job in a poor town. The whole mess boiled down to guards telling the truth versus protecting their own interests.

Five days before Christmas 1990, the Texas Commission on Human Rights asked me to participate in a discrimination suit against United International Investigative Services, the new contract guard company. I would be joining others who had been unfairly laid off in the transition—all younger, with less training, education, and experience than I.

The suit couldn't hurt, but it was surely just a shot in the dark. I had also pretty much given up on the EEOC helping anyone at this point. They hadn't even talked to Jesse Castillo or any of the female guards who had filed grievances with them. The big agencies seemed to be hamstrung.

■   ■   ■

On December 23, 1990, the *Brownsville Herald* ran a story that revealed that United was not licensed to provide security guards in Texas. I thought about all the good guards who had tried to do their jobs and had been given the ax by a company that didn't even have the legal right to employ them as guards.

Holiday celebrations couldn't distract me from my campaign nearly as well as fifty brown-skinned, shiny-eyed, jumping, fidgety, noisy, innocent, and impressionable kids sitting in the Sunday school room. After children's church, they'd come skipping and laughing from the beautiful new church building out across the yard to the old yellow bus where I stood waiting to drive them home.

After meeting for some years, mission-style, in a leased one-room building on a used car lot, our congregation was given enough money to build a sanctuary. In characteristically Texas fashion, the pastor's son wooed his widowed aunt, who was the beneficiary of a sizeable insurance settlement from his uncle's death, into loaning the money for the sanctuary. The kids, however, still met in the portable building out back, which the pastor and I had constructed.

After church, the children would go to the new building to get a drink of water and use the restroom. They looked in awe at the sanctuary. Then they'd fly out the front door toward the bus.

One Sunday I stood waiting beside the bus, talking with Brother Mike, the church treasurer. Some boys came out teasing and chasing the girls. I hollered at them to stop running before someone fell down. As they climbed rambunctiously up the bus steps, Mike looked at the darkening sky. "Looks like rain," he said.

"If it decides to," I said, glancing up. "I hope to get these kids home first."

I felt Mike's gaze on me. "So, how's your fight with the government coming?"

Because I'd mentioned my connection with the church in television news broadcasts about Bayview, the church had unfortunately received some anonymous threats. The threats themselves had then become stories on television as well. Everyone knew about us.

I rubbed the back of my neck. "You know, Mike, it's crazy, but I can't help but think about it most of the time." Like an open floodgate, I began to gush. I told him how I felt I should be content with the success of my ministry and the children's church, and the fact that I had gotten my first unemployment check in December, but I wasn't. Despite my best efforts and two hundred dollars in phone calls last month (which should have been spent on retreats), it seemed like no one was listening to the women's complaints. I was frustrated.

Mike folded his arms and nodded silently. The clouds were billowing darkly above us.

"Even though I've done everything I can think of, I'm still haunted by the thought that there's someone out there who has the power to stop the abuse of the women and children—I just haven't found that person yet."

I helped the last of the kids onto the bus. Mike stared down at the ground between us. I apologized for dumping the whole thing in his lap.

He frowned. "Tony, do you really think someone is going to listen to you?"

I realized that Mike was addressing more than just my personal confidence. He was talking about how we, the less powerful, viewed our chances of being taken seriously.

"Brother, I sure hope someone, somewhere will. Senator Gramm was very encouraging."

"But Tony, those men you're fighting have a lot of power around here." Mike looked me straight in the eyes. "Aren't you a little concerned they might try to retaliate against you by, say, burning down our new church, or some such thing?"

We both looked at the church. What he said was true. "Think for a minute," he continued. "Those are strong allegations you're making against them. What about your wife and your own safety? Anyone can pay an assassin from Mexico fifty dollars to kill both of you without any trouble, have you thought about that?"

"Of course I've thought about it," I said, remembering the spate of new death threats no one else knew about. "But we can't live scared. That's exactly what they want."

"Brother," he said, "we love you and appreciate all the work you've put into this church and the children. But just think how it would look if someone tried to hide some drugs at your ranch or here at the church. That's how these men work. They tip off the police, and the next morning all our names are in the newspapers."

Mike looked at me with forced patience, like a stern father admonishing his naughty boy, and asked me how that would look to our community.

"What do you think I should do?" I asked sincerely. "What does Pastor Smith think?"

"Well, Pastor is concerned that attendance is down. He hears that the people are afraid to come to our church because they think one morning a car will drive by and shoot it up. It could happen, it happens every day around these parts."

"Brother, that never crossed my mind." I thanked Mike for his concern and told him I'd think about what he said. I climbed the steps into the bus, and Mike leaned in after me.

"You know, they have all our names on that list of signatures we sent to Washington. This Ruiz probably has our names and addresses at this very moment. He knows exactly where we all live. Tony"—he took a step up—"you're wasting your time. Nothing will be done about the complaints because they don't care. In the meantime, you've put a lot of pressure on the members. The pastor is very concerned."

I looked down at him from the top step, feigning an ease I didn't feel. "I'm sure the pastor is overreacting."

"Maybe *you're* the one who's overreacting."

My jaw dropped. Mike thought I shouldn't fight the abuse?

"Please understand," I told him. "I have to do what I can." Mike's face settled grimly against me. "It'll be okay," I pleaded. "I'm just trying to find a lawyer for the women."

As he descended into the street, Mike lifted his hands as if to wash them of my stubbornness.

"Yeah, I think you're right," I said as I closed the bus door. "It sure looks like rain." Now it seemed as if I was getting it from both sides. Going up against the government is not an easy task, and the more publicity I got, the more obscene phone calls I got, each one hoping to scare me and Barbara to death. If these men are innocent, then why are they trying to scare me with death threats?

I couldn't bear the thought of someone hurting Barbara. Mike's words kept coming back—a fifty-dollar assassin, that's all it took. She had gotten two threatening calls at her office. One male voice said, "I'm an old friend of your husband's. I'm looking for him." Then the line went dead. Another man called and asked, "Do you know where your husband is right now?" and hung up. Petrified, Barbara stopped answering the office phone, too.

Once, three Hispanic men dressed in expensive suits and driving a late-model Chrysler stopped by the ranch while I was feeding the horses. They wanted me to go with them to look at their horses. Not once did they get out of their light brown car, but they tried to persuade me through the open window that I could make a lot of money on the breeding fees. From that time on, I avoided visiting other ranches.

Not a Sunday went by that someone from the congregation didn't mention the safety of the church. Members told me of their fear of retaliation by the officials I was accusing. It became harder and harder not to give up.

■　■　■

In January 1991, my safety concerns took on new meaning. By phone I heard from an anonymous security supervisor at the camp that someone had started a fire in the filing room of Building 9. This was the INS records room. The supervisor said, "Government employees deported our witnesses and tried to cover their tracks by starting a fire." Records and files on numerous detainees were destroyed by smoke, fire, and water. Firefighters ruled out faulty electricity as a cause.

My source told me that the INS then paid male detainees their dollar a day to clean up the mess. The next day, when higher authorities questioned why so many files had been lost, the detainees answered that they were instructed to throw away anything that was smoke or water damaged, as well as burned.

I shook my head. What a convenient time for a fire to occur.

The very next day, Senator Gramm sent me a short letter and enclosed a response he'd received from Bonnie Derwinski, the director for congressional and public affairs under the United States Commissioner. She told him that "an investigation of the allegations was being conducted, and as soon as the report was complete, they would forward the information needed to respond to our constituents." Had Senator Gramm urged Washington to initiate another investigation? Was this a follow-up on the complaints not investigated? Maybe they were finally hearing me!

■ ■ ■

On January 18, I got a surprising phone call from a man named Jud Springs, identifying himself as another investigator from the Office of the Inspector General (OIG) in McAllen. He wanted to come out to the ranch to talk. I told him what a sloppy job Jones had done.

Springs was slightly younger than I was, maybe thirty-five, with black hair and a well-groomed mustache. He was all business and came carrying a notebook and a perfectly sharpened pencil.

After giving him the same list of names and phone numbers I had given Jones, I said, "You know, this Jones was supposed to talk to Eduardo Payan, our government witness. He never did and lied to me about it. Do you know Jones?"

Springs hesitated then said, "No." Then he told me that Jones had no "right" to do an investigation here in this area, and that from now on, the investigation would be handled only through his department.

I was confused. Jones's assistant at the Whataburger meeting, the attractive woman dressed in black slacks, was an investigator from the McAllen OIG, the same office for which Springs worked. If a problem existed with Jones's authority, why didn't their OIG office do something about it?

Springs replied that he was assigned this investigation solely because of my letter to his supervisor, Perry Suitt, on December 17 of last year, when I complained about Jones.

I didn't have much contact after that with Springs. He'd asked specifically about Beatriz Huerta, so the next day I called her. She said that she had indeed talked to Springs about the harassment and blackmail, and had directed him to other female guards who had been threatened. She then told me she thought she'd met Mr. Springs before.

"Where?" I asked. "Do you remember?"

"Yes," she said. She was sure that she had seen him in Ruiz's office when she'd been called in to answer questions about the incident report which involved Charles Gantt.

Was he one of the men who had jumped to get her a chair or had laughed when Ruiz propositioned Cynthia Rodriguez minutes before? It was possible. He knew exactly what went on at Bayview. An uneasy feeling grew in my gut for Beatriz.

Payan told me later that, once again, he had not been contacted.

On January 25 I sent a third letter to Senator Gramm. I wanted him to be aware of the sorry state of the investigation and let him know that I was broadcasting his replies to churches in other states.

I told him about Payan being ignored by both investigations, about the theft of government property, and the recent fire that had destroyed evidence of wrongdoings. I asked why the government was protecting these men when they were undermining the government.

At the time, President Bush had just ordered US troops into the Persian Gulf for Operation Desert Storm. I made the point to Senator Gramm that although we hated to endanger our troops, we realized that Iraq's president, Saddam Hussein, had to be stopped. I said that the situation in South Texas demanded the same kind of treatment for the "little Saddam" running Bayview.

I made dozens of calls to Washington. I spoke with director for congressional and public affairs Bonnie Derwinski, who was interested in our complaints and asked me to send her copies. I notified Perry Suitt, my local liaison, that I was doing this since his office had not given satisfactory responses.

I sent the packet of complaints to Washington by certified mail, requesting a signature as proof of delivery and notification of the packet's arrival. I received confirmation that her office had received the packet on February 4. About a week later I called again to make sure she had personally reviewed the information.

"No," she said. "My office has not received your envelope. But we'll look around. Maybe it's here somewhere."

After about fifteen minutes she returned to the phone. "No. No one can say they've received or seen a brown envelope like you described."

"That's funny," I said. "I have a signed return right here in my hand." Of course, I couldn't begin to read the signature. It was totally illegible.

Derwinski asked if I would fax the information to her. I did—thirty or more pages of complaints.

How had my envelope been intercepted, though? The only one who knew what I was doing was Perry Suitt at the McAllen OIG. I went back over our last conversation.

To bolster our case about rampant corruption, I had given Suitt incriminating information about a former government employee who had once worked at the camp directly over Ruiz. Payan had been my source for this information. Within the hour of my telling Suitt about this fellow, who is now working in Washington, he called me. He said he heard I had some incriminating information about him and kept me on the phone for an hour trying to find out what I had told Suitt. He called me a liar and said three times that I didn't "have anything" on him. He made a point of saying he knew where I'd gotten the information.

I also remembered an encounter I had with someone while working the outside gate to mess hall. He was a tall, dark-haired white man who drove up to the gate in a government car. I opened the gate as he entered. He suspiciously asked if I knew who he was. I had no clue. So off the top of my head, I said, "Your name is Ruiz." He became so angry, he started to yell, "Do I look like a dumb nigger?" When I told Payan about him, he laughed and said that the man hated Ruiz. Obviously, I had not made a good impression.

I called Bonnie Derwinski back and asked if she knew him.

"Yes. He works in an office on our floor."

I told her to check with him. He probably had her brown envelope.

■　■　■

Abel Zavala was a kind supervisor who had written a letter on my behalf explaining to the EEOC that my first firing from Bayview was racially motivated. Zavala had since left the camp and taken a job at a rival security company, T.I.S. Security, where he was a supervisor. At the beginning of February 1991, he heard that I had been sacked for good and offered me a job with his company. I leaped at it, and the income was a huge help to Barbara and me. One requirement was that I learn how to use a handgun. Barbara surprised me by coming out to my makeshift range on the property and practicing target shooting with me. She was becoming quite a frontier woman.

■   ■   ■

Home again after a relatively quiet Wednesday-night church service, I strolled out to the barn to check on our four-year-old mare Blessing, who was expecting her first foal. The father was Faith, our gentle stallion, and we had high hopes for a sweet-tempered baby. I hadn't had the heart to ride Faith much lately.

I was a little troubled about some recent retreat cancellations. We had by now been averaging maybe two retreats a month on the weekends, with an occasional request to bring horses for a church party on ministry promotions. In one sense, cancellations helped because money was tight with all I was spending on phone calls and mailings, but on the other hand, fear had provoked the cancellations. I could hear it in the parents' voices. They worried that the government might retaliate against me by threatening their children at a retreat.

I went back into the house with that thought, took off my boots, and put my feet up to watch television with Barbara for the rest of the evening. The blasted phone rang.

"Do you have any idea what you've *done?*" our pastor barked.

"Uh, no, what did I do, Pastor Smith?"

"You undermined my authority, that's what. You put me down in front of my family and other church members."

The gist of his complaint, to my astonished ears, was that in talking with Brother Mike that day by the bus, my comment that maybe our pastor was overreacting had been interpreted as making him out to be a coward. We had an awful confrontation. He was infuriated as I protested that we prayed for him, and that Barbara, especially, would never, ever remotely criticize him.

But he just laughed. "Y'all called me a coward and don't think that's disrespect?" His wife and her family were most concerned about safety. The upshot was that he was taking the children's church and bus ministry away from Barbara and me, and pitching us out on our ears.

I argued, "The Bible says we're to bring our accusers before the church. Let's all go before the congregation and talk about it openly. Barbara and I don't want to lose the children."

He yelled that they had already had a meeting. Complaints were coming at him from all sides, and he believed what our detractors said. We were removed from all responsibility. I began to defend myself, but he was more than firm.

"I won't listen to any more, and if you persist in this matter, I'll make sure no church in the Rio Grande Valley accepts you as a member. Now, do you understand?"

Pastor Smith was so loud over the phone that Barbara could hear almost every word. Her eyes filled with tears. He was still raving when I hung up on him. I rushed to Barbara and held her as she started to sob against my neck.

I could not remember ever feeling such anguish. The children were our lives. Barbara's ties to them were maternal; it was like taking away our own children. The phone rang again. The answering machine recorded Pastor Smith's voice saying, "Don't expect any more money for retreats. Bring everything back that belongs to the church . . ."

I broke away from her embrace and headed for the phone.

"Don't answer it, Tony," Barbara said quietly. I reached for the cord and yanked the plug out of the wall.

The rest of the night we just sat there together, our arms around each other, thinking black thoughts. It was final, like the death of someone you loved and cared for. I had been trying to protect my wife. I never dreamed an attack would come from her most vulnerable side. Who would take charge of the kids? How would they feel when we didn't pick them up on Sunday? Would they wait for an hour? Would someone else do it? What would Pastor Smith tell them about us? I saw all our work turn cynical in the children's eyes.

That night, after much tossing and turning, I finally fell asleep. Apparently, I slept fitfully, because Barbara nudged me into consciousness a short time later.

"Are you all right?" she asked.

"I had a bad dream." I was only half awake and clammy and still felt the abysmal darkness of it.

"What about?"

"I saw myself trapped between two tall fences, just like the detainees," I said. "The government was on one side of the fence, and they had all of our children. I was scared to death they were going to hurt or take them away.

"On the other side were a group of preachers and our church members. They were laughing at me. I kept begging them to help me stop the government from taking the children."

I reached for the comfort of Barbara's hand. "The preachers wouldn't help. They told me God didn't care. They said he didn't love me either."

The two of us lay like wide-awake corpses until dawn. As the security of daylight surrounded us and the howling of coyotes faded in the distance, we finally fell asleep. I asked myself over and over again, would God hate me? Had I somehow broken with him?

■ ■ ■

By March, I had closed up the ranch. We were under the authority of a few other supporting churches, but retreats waned because of the fear. I had begun to do security work around Harlingen, night-time stakeouts at warehouses and shopping centers. But during the day what took up all my waking thoughts was the "fight," so that's what I did. I talked to several attorneys on behalf of Jovita Urrutia and Cynthia Rodriguez, and was directed to one in Brownsville who might take their case on a contingency basis. The attorney, Barry R. Benton, listened to the facts and asked his associate, John F. Hood, to join him in pursuing it. The two women signed a contract with them on March 20. Soon afterward, I received a letter from the Equal Employment Opportunity Commission, advising me of my "right to pursue a lawsuit under the Age Discrimination in Employment Act." I showed the letter to the two attorneys, and they agreed to represent me as well. I was hopeful.

A reporter with the *Brownsville Herald* called to do a follow-up story on what the Office of the Inspector General had determined after their investigations of Bayview. She asked if the OIG had contacted me since then. I said no.

The story, "Investigation Of Bayview Harassment Charges Stalls," appeared in the *Herald* on April 15. The slant was how long (seven months) I had been waiting for action in response to my complaints and how disillusioned I was becoming that the government could police itself. It repeated that the INS had sent my information to the Office of the Inspector General, and that I had complained to Senator Gramm and area churches about their sluggishness.

The article stated that "a female guard who spoke to the newspaper on conditions of anonymity said little has changed. The sexual harassment between detainees and some officers is still going on."

Neither our local OIG agent Perry Suitt nor the Washington office would comment.

■　■　■

In mid-April I got a tip from United supervisor Miguel Zamarrón that Ramirez was the subject of a new official complaint by a young guard named Laura Zuniga and that Ramirez was looking for a way to fire her. The supervisor gave me her number.

I remembered Laura because I had written in my notebook about her being hired. She was young, blond, and underage when she applied for the position. Ramirez had told her to say she was twenty-one on her application, that it would be their "little secret."

Laura still lived with her mother. When I called and identified myself on the phone, her mother knew me from the six o'clock news. She was outraged at the treatment "those women" received from their supervisors at the camp. Apparently Laura hadn't told her that she was now one of "those women."

Laura confirmed that she had filed a harassment complaint against Ramirez with an INS official. I asked which official, but she said he was new and I didn't know him. His name was Roel Delgado. I asked her to describe her complaint, hoping she had a case to add to ours.

"I just got fed up with Lieutenant Ramirez coming on to me at work. He wouldn't keep his hands off of me," she said. "He felt that I owed him something because he hired me."

"When you were underage?"

"Yes." She said Ramirez thought because he did her a favor, she owed him one, too. She reported to Delgado that Ramirez implied he would fire her if she didn't go out with him. Delgado told her to go back to work and not to worry because he would make sure that didn't happen. Then Delgado himself began making sexual advances, saying they "should do some hanky panky," and asking her out. Laura was disgusted because he was "an old man" and married besides.

When Ramirez asked for a date with her in exchange for

granting a request she had made for certain days off, Laura went to Rubio instead of Delgado to complain. "Lieutenant Ramirez came up to me the next day and said that complaining was useless, that he'd just deny everything, call me a liar, and nobody would care. Then I'd get fired."

I offered to give her the names of our attorneys. Laura, however, didn't think an attorney would do her much good because she had signed a retraction of her complaint to keep her job.

"But I won't sleep with him, never, never, never."

The retraction sunk her legally. I told her I understood, and if she thought I could help her with anything, to call. I also told her to tell her mother.

Since Laura was still under the threat of losing her job, I decided to write to Perry Suitt at the OIG again on her behalf. His "help" didn't inspire confidence, but at least the problem would be documented if she were to get frivolously fired. I was not convinced that the OIG even believed these abuses were occurring.

Ironically, at this time, Roel Delgado was arranging a seminar on the Whistleblower Protection Act for INS employees at the camp. The act was designed to prevent retaliation against employees who reported wrongdoings. The seminar, however, was only for paid government employees, as they were the only ones protected by the act. The memorandum announcing the seminar was addressed to Jan Hernández, the acting administrative officer, and the list of invited employees included Cecilio L. Ruiz Jr., Roel M. Delgado, David M. Greene, Peter W. Niezborski, Eduardo Payan, Juan Castro, George Molinar, Jesse Rosales, George González, Rosemary González, Rolando Gómez, Leo Yzaguirre, and Ramiro Salinas. (Although some of these officers have yet to come into play in this account, that will soon change.) The training seminar was scheduled for April 23, 1991, at the Harlingen district office, but due to flooding, it was moved to McAllen Border Patrol sector headquarters and scheduled for 1:00 p.m.

Within two months Laura received her letter of dismissal from United International Investigative Services for poor job performance.

■   ■   ■

Barbara was putting up a fuss about teaching me to type, though I was begging her to. Sometimes I had to type a letter three or four times before it was good enough to send. When she came home from work, I would ask her to look at my latest effort, which would inevitably have many errors. I'd become frustrated and angry, so she would tell me to hush up, sit down, and retype the whole thing. "Why don't you take a class and learn to do it yourself?" she would say. I didn't think I could. She was the smart one, not me.

■   ■   ■

Between April 23 and May 1, I received letters from both our attorneys stating that because they "disagreed on some things" they were no longer able to work together and could therefore no longer represent the women and me. It had something to do with including Ruiz, a government employee, in the suit. One thought that suing the government or its employees was impossible and would most likely get the case thrown out of court. The other wanted to plunge ahead. Neither saw an easy out-of-court settlement. They suggested we find another lawyer without delay, as the statute of limitations would expire September 21.

September 21 was four months away, but it felt like tomorrow.

On May 29, Jovita Urrutia's complaint with the Equal Employment Opportunity Commission was dismissed after their investigation. They reported that "the witnesses did not see or hear of her being subjected to sexual advances."

The EEOC made no mention of the fact that the two female

guards who had witnessed Jovita's harassment had signed statements immediately following the investigation saying that they had been instructed not to cooperate with the EEOC investigation.

In one affidavit, Francis Carmona stated:

> The supervisors knew when there was going to be an investigation, and they would warn us not to say anything. Once, when an investigator visited the camp, we were told this at muster, and while I was going to my post, Lieutenant Ramirez approached me. He told me I was going to be the first one. He again warned me not to give out information.
>
> In the room where we met, there was only a booth that lawyers used to visit with their clients. I was afraid Rubio or Ramirez might be listening in, and I had to be careful. The EEOC investigator asked questions about Jovita. After the meeting was over, Ramirez came up to me and asked me if I told the investigator anything. I told him, no. He patted me on the back and said, Good, we knew you wouldn't. I felt bad. I had wanted to give more information, but was afraid I would lose my job if I did.

Another guard, Juanita Reséndez, reported that she was stopped by an investigator and questioned in front of Charles Gantt. She told the investigator she had no information. Afterward, she said, "You think I was going to make a statement right in front of Gantt?"

I contacted another attorney, R. W. Armstrong, immediately. Several weeks passed before he turned us down via letter. "Not," he stated, "to say your suit is without merit or that it should not be pursued," but that his firm didn't have expertise in this area. I called him to ask if he could recommend an employment law attorney, and he graciously did: Denis Downey.

I called Downey, who said, "It [harassment] is a hard thing to prove. But keep me informed on what is developing with the government's investigation."

The intimidation at the camp was getting worse. Beatriz Huerta had been told before the investigations that the INS knew she had a lot of damaging information. She was warned that if she revealed what she knew to an investigator, she was out.

Though she hadn't talked to Jones, she told Springs everything she had seen and been subjected to. And true to their word, in June 1991, Rubio fired Beatriz. She was four months pregnant, and the INS said she might "lose her baby" if she continued to work. Payan labeled this as nonsense. Desk jobs were available for pregnant women, but she was laid off just the same.

On June 27, I received a letter from the Texas Commission on Human Rights regarding my age discrimination complaint. After the investigator talked with the security company, they determined that I was not hired because of absenteeism, which resulted in a poor work record. "The evidence indicates your record and past work performance were less satisfactory compared to the individuals that were hired by the respondent."

Unbelievable. They had written whatever they wanted in my file. How pointless to argue that I had been well respected at Bayview, consulted on policy, responsible, relied upon. I no longer expected justice from any agency. It seemed that every time I moved forward a step, I was pushed back two.

Just before she was fired, Beatriz reported to me that Ramirez, who knew she had testified against him, had stopped her in the hall. He bragged to her that he was so protected by the government that God *himself* could not touch him.

I was beginning to believe it.

11

The Abuse Continues

Battle lines were drawn, and the soldiers were choosing sides. Mike Trominski, INS district director at the Harlingen office, had maneuvered into the no-man's-land between public advocacy and loyalty to his INS officers. He had a longstanding friendship with Cecilio Ruiz. Trominski, Ruiz, and George Molinar were all ex-marines. Molinar used to tell everyone that he and Ruiz could do nothing wrong because Trominski could and would cover up anything they did. He would say that nothing could come between them. In earlier years, they had worked together in the Krome Avenue detention center in Miami, Florida, and the Marine Corps motto, *semper fidelis* (always faithful), kept them unified. Now it seemed Trominski had decided that this motto was more binding than his public oath.

In mid-August 1991, the *Harlingen Morning Star* ran a story suggesting that many others were interested in righting the abuses at Bayview. The article, "Release Of Beaten Honduran Sought," states that "a refugee rights group called for the release Wednesday of a Honduran it claims was physically abused at the Immigration and Naturalization Service detention center last week." Trominski declined to comment.

Besides protesting to Trominski, a refugee rights organization based in Harlingen called Proyecto Libertad sent copies of its objections to Gene McNary, commissioner of the Immigration and Naturalization Service; Senator Phil Gramm; Senator Lloyd Bentsen of Texas; as well as twelve other national and local human and refugee rights groups, calling for the alleged perpetrator to be suspended pending the OIG investigation.

Trominski, however, chose to side with his officers, like the loyal fraternity man he was, and let stand the official explanation that the detainee made the whole thing up.

I thought about the Guatemalan woman who was kicked as she lay on the floor. It wasn't hard for the INS to find a detainee willing to be a witness on their behalf. He could be promised something in return, and chances are, he was from a different country and would eventually be deported. There was no way to hold a witness accountable behind the closed doors of the detention center. No action was taken against the accused officer.

■　■　■

Several months went by very quietly. Public interest waned with the stalled judgments, and I wasn't on newscasts or in the newspapers anymore. We didn't have many retreats. I was able to continue on a small scale but felt as though I did nothing. Life settled into a horse breeding routine by day and work as a security guard by night, which I frankly didn't mind, though a dull sameness pervaded, with certainly no sense of mission.

On a mild and beautiful October day, I was unloading bales of alfalfa as our blacksmith, Sam, trimmed the horse's hooves in the barn. The fresh alfalfa aroma was heavy as Sam battled a young filly named Angel Te Spears, who was leaning on him to show her displeasure. He mentioned that people were starting to think "those government men" had scared me or something, because they didn't see me in the news anymore. I told him I had nothing new to report, that the agencies were in charge now, and hopefully, I was out of it.

A red car swung through our front gate, came up the driveway, and parked at the house. The door opened, and the tall, dark figure of Pastor Smith emerged. I gave a short hello. His head snapped around, then he started toward me.

"What does he want?" I wondered out loud. We hadn't spoken to him or seen him since that horrible phone conversation eight months before.

As I walked to meet him halfway, I sucked in my gut and fought unsuccessfully to drop the chip on my shoulder.

He reached out his hand. "Hello, Brother Tony," he said in his Texas drawl as we shook. "I suppose you're wondering why I'm here."

"I didn't expect a social visit, no."

The preacher looked out to the pasture and down to the ground, anywhere but into my eyes. He said it wasn't easy for him to come over after what had happened, but he'd appreciate it if I heard him out. I folded my arms.

"It looks like we might have been wrong taking the children's church away from you. Plain and simple, I'm asking you to forgive me."

Pastor Smith even wrung his hands a little. He wanted us to take it on again, if we would, including the bus ministry.

I actually began to tear up, so I turned away and leaned with both hands over the corral railing to collect myself. The pastor admitted he was wrong and said it wouldn't happen again. "We just want you both to come back and take care of the children." He said they missed us.

"What more can I say?" Pastor stammered to my back.

Suspicious, I didn't know what to think. In the barn, Sam was clipping Fresco, our big bay. The children had loved to pamper her and brush her long black mane and tail. Smith had separated all of us. Turning to face him, I asked if he changed his mind because he thought the fight was over. As Sam said, I hadn't been in the news in months. Things were quiet now, but . . . "What if things heat up again? Will I be a threat to your church?" I asked him. I told him how crushed Barbara had been by the whole experience. That's what stuck in my craw.

He nodded. "I know you struggled through this, Brother, we all did. All I'm asking is if you'll help us out." I told him we'd pray about it.

He drove off. Could I ever trust him again? It was becoming harder and harder to take anyone seriously.

Barbara was not quick to jump back in either. I could see caution and fear in her eyes. She reminded me that this wasn't the first time a preacher had used and then mistreated us. (She was referring to a former pastor at Central Baptist Church on Filmore Street in Harlingen. He had participated in our retreats until I sold a horse to Gig Maples, a Hugh Hefner playmate, at which point he denounced me, thinking I was somehow related, because of my last name, to the "smut business.")

I put my arms around her. "Sometimes we've just got to take a big deep breath and go on," I said. "Are we doing it for ourselves?"

Barbara took my hand and led me over to the sofa, where we sat down and bowed our heads to pray.

■　■　■

I received a letter from Jovita Urrutia dated December 4, 1991. Strange. Why didn't she just call? The tone of the letter was discouraging, and no wonder, she had been in discussions with Rubio and Ramirez about her rehiring. Jovita had approached Rubio in October. He told her that she had to talk with Ramirez first as he was in charge of hiring. She told Ramirez that she knew he was hiring some old employees, so why not her? She reminded him that she had already taken the required four-day class, but was never called to work. The last day of the class, Rubio told Jovita to "go with" Sergeant Salinas, another United supervisor. Jovita didn't know for sure what he meant by "go with." She thought she was going to be rehired, so she left the classroom with the supervisor out of obedience to Rubio's orders. Once in his car she was driven to the main gate. She said Sergeant Salinas tried to touch her and asked her out on a date. She rebuffed the supervisor, who then became flustered and dropped her off. Salinas had told me on several occasions that he sometimes did things against his will in order to keep his job and that this was one of them. Ramirez and Rubio wanted Jovita to file a report against another supervisor, which, when taken together with her original complaint, would make it appear that she had a habit of making things up when she didn't get her way. Within a few days Jovita called Ramirez and asked when she could report to work. Ramirez told her, "No, I don't want you here."

This encounter devastated Jovita, who was pressured by circumstances on every side. She said in her letter, "Ramirez will never hire me as long as I have a lawsuit against him. I don't know what I'm going to do." She asked me to send all her statements and court papers back to her. She also said her phone had been disconnected. Jovita was broke. Would she sacrifice herself to get the job back?

She said I could make copies of her papers before mailing them to her.

■ ■ ■

After three visits and six phone calls between October and Christmas, Pastor Smith convinced Barbara and me to take on the children's church again. The pastor asked us not to hold this mistake against him. The church members, and I think his wife in particular, were frightened of the government men who had power and influence in the Valley. He implied that the church might have to change its name.

We didn't need convincing about his reasons, but about whether his family and other members would accept us again without lingering mistrust. We told him we wanted what was best for the children. We didn't want to come back into their lives only to abandon them again if new disputes arose.

He suggested we begin visiting the church on Sunday evenings to get reacquainted and start teaching in January.

Our first Sunday night back, we were warmly welcomed. One member told us it was not his idea that we leave, and others agreed. Barbara was happy again.

Driving home that night, all we could talk about was the children. How tall were they now? How were they doing in school? After almost a year, we wondered how the kids would react when they saw us again. We prattled on like a couple of delighted third graders.

With great anticipation that first Sunday, we went early to inspect the classroom and set up the chairs. The morning was cool and damp and the church parking lot deserted. I unlocked and turned the classroom doorknob and was greeted by an unfamiliar musty odor. When I opened the door I gasped.

Barbara's hand flew up to her mouth. "Oh, Tony."

I rubbed the back of my neck as we looked at the clutter and debris inside. The carpet was grubby with mildew and tracked-in mud. Pews were covered with stacked plywood and sawdust. Bricks and cement blocks, shovels, rakes, and other tools were stacked and leaning about the walls. A rusty wheelbarrow sat between the piano and the bookshelves. Once-bright crayon-colored pictures were scattered on the floor and rust streaks down the walls gave evidence of a leaky roof.

I reached for Barbara's hand. The cheery little classroom we'd left behind was now a tool shed.

We had less than an hour to clean before the children arrived. As we worked frantically, I snapped from time to time, sending angry epithets into the dusty air. As I threatened to toss the junk out the door, Barbara calmed me down.

The classroom was barely presentable when cars began to arrive. Through the grime on the windows, we saw some child-sized forms approaching. We ran to the doorway to see.

It was the pastor's grandchildren. The four walked slowly toward us and passed me without a word as I greeted them. They looked hesitatingly at each other.

Barbara hugged each one, but they were uneasy. The oldest girl finished her embrace then stepped back and asked, "Why did you leave us?"

Barbara and I looked at each other. Apparently, no one had told them anything. One child thought we had moved. Another believed some government people had killed us. And nobody told them we were coming back.

"When the other children get here, I'll explain what happened," I said lamely. What could I tell them that wouldn't entangle the pastor? God only knew what they thought of us. Now I dreaded those first reactions. What would Pablo think when he saw us again? What about his cat? And his warm smile? Did they think it was *our* idea to disappear without a word?

I glanced at my watch. It was getting late. I wanted to start, but the others hadn't arrived yet. The pastor's white van drove in, and he parked close to the church. My heart skipped a beat as I realized he would not have enough time to get the rest of the children.

Only six youngsters emerged from the van. The pastor jumped out and disappeared into the church with two minutes to spare. I motioned for the children to come toward me. I didn't know any of them. They asked the pastor's grandchildren who we were.

I introduced Barbara and myself and explained a little of our history without touching on the reason for leaving, except to say we had to. Then I asked, "Does anyone know where the other kids are?"

The oldest girl looked from me to the nine small forms in postures of mistrust around her. "They stopped coming when you left the church. Nobody would drive the bus and pick them up."

Barbara's gray eyes filled with pity and a sad smile grew as she smoothed the black curls on one small head. I resolved to find those children and win them back again.

After church, invigorated, I volunteered to ride with the pastor to take the children home and learn where they lived. He shrugged.

The children climbed in and balanced themselves on two wooden benches in the back. The benches were not bolted down, and each time we turned a corner, they tilted in the opposite direction. The children all lived in the same area, so we only had to make one stop.

On our way back, I shared my hopes with Pastor Smith. "Next week I'll visit all the other children who used to come to Sunday school and invite them back."

The pastor drummed his finger on the steering wheel.

Then, to my surprise, he said that he didn't want me to build up the children's church as it had been. "I realize that the children mean a lot to you and your wife, but there's this new carpet in the sanctuary, you know, and some of our ladies can't quite see a bunch of children running around like before, trackin' in mud and the like."

He droned on and on, rationalizing, while I stared out the window as though I'd been sentenced to hard labor. "We need to leave room out there for children who attend with their parents. Having the children out with you will be a blessing to me as I minister to the adults. They won't have to worry about their children, and they can relax during my sermons and enjoy the message."

He ventured a glance in my direction. "If you have a bunch of *other* children, how will you be able to minister to the ones who come with their parents?"

Barbara and I had been recruited as babysitters for his grandchildren.

I still attempted to visit the missing children, but most had moved away. Those who still lived in the area never came back. We thought about quitting, figuring we never would have accepted the job with these restrictions, but decided to stay for the few kids who faithfully came each Sunday. Our class stayed small. The pastor was happy.

12
Caught on Tape

There was a knock at our door on the evening of February 21, 1992. Barbara took two steps backward. We weren't expecting anyone. I sighed when I saw Payan in the doorway and quickly showed him in. He held a videotape.

The tape, he said, contained evidence of an illegal strip search and physical abuse that had taken place at the camp three days prior on February 18. It was a practice search for officers being trained to look for contraband. Payan had been allowed to tape it on the pretext of providing evidence against any accusations of brutality, of which the officers were by now wary. Ruiz had supervised the search, and Rubio and Ramirez were participants.

Payan slipped the tape into our VCR and forwarded to scenes of officers wearing camouflage uniforms and visored helmets; they were wielding black batons and ordering detainees out of their beds. There was footage of men stripped naked in the midst of others who were clothed, some with hands shackled behind them; they watched as beds were searched. According to INS rules, "A strip search consists of having the detainee remove his/her clothing, searching the clothing and visually inspecting the detainee. The strip search should only be conducted in private." One of the officers held the leash of what looked like a German Shepherd with a choke-chain collar around his neck. The dog panted rapidly as Payan held the camera directly on him and his trainer.

The scene changed. Payan explained that after he had shot part of the search on Four-Bravo, he'd followed a line of handcuffed men downstairs to Four-Alpha, which was not occupied due to the low number of detainees at the camp.

He'd taped a group of detainees lying face down on the cold tile floor of Four-Alpha in their underwear, their hands bound behind them. Off camera, I heard Payan say to Ramirez, "See what's wrong with this guy." Ramirez walked over to a man writhing on the floor and knelt to ask him something. At that point the footage switched to a guard's baseball game on a sand lot outside.

Payan began to rewind the tape. What I didn't see, he said, was that the detainee on the floor was massively injured. Payan had turned off his camera and approached the man while Ramirez and another guard lifted him up. His face was bleeding, and the man was crying about his knee. Payan ordered him to medical but Ruiz, behind him, countermanded the order and sent the man to one of the unused segregation cells on that floor. That had taken place on February 18. The worst part, Payan said, was that they had forgotten him there until today, February 21.

He was discovered accidentally by another guard who left Four-Bravo by the back stairs and heard a weak voice calling from the recesses of segregation. No logbook contained information of a man on Four-Alpha. The responsible supervisor had been busy with others, and the guard usually posted there had rotated dorms and hadn't returned.

When they took the injured man to medical, he was found to have two dislocated shoulders, a broken knee, and a festering chin wound that had clotted open and couldn't be stitched. The man's name was Félix. He told them he'd hurt his knee when pulled from his top bunk and was pushed down the stairs with his hands tied.

On the twenty-first, when Ruiz received the memo about Félix, he'd called Payan and asked if he could have the tape. Payan said he told Ruiz that since the search was "only a practice, really just a show," that he had already taped over the raid with the guard's baseball game.

The tape clearly showed Payan's concern over the injured man on the floor. It clearly showed Ruiz supervising an illegal strip search. Payan was anxious to make a copy for me to hold, while he hid the original.

What Payan didn't know at the time was the dreadful story of what had happened to Félix the day of the practice search. He had arrived the day before with a high fever. When an INS officer tried to wake him the next morning, he was grabbed and thrown to the hard cement floor, and his leg hit the steel bunk beneath him. He was lifted to his feet and cuffed and shoved down the main aisle to the double doors leading to the concrete stairs. Felix's face was used to open the doors, and he was pushed down the stairs. From Four-Charlie to Four-Alpha, he lost consciousness and woke up laying face down on the floor. And this was only a *practice* drill.

■ ■ ■

A couple of months later, on April 26, 1992, I was staking out a warehouse in Harlingen in an unmarked car. With me was an officer from the Harlingen police department named Cardoza, who was working part-time for the same security company where I was employed. We had became friends, having worked together on several occasions, and were chatting about an encounter he had had the night before on his 1:00 a.m. rounds. While driving by Pemelton Park in his patrol car, he had heard breaking glass. Turning into the parking lot, he confronted an older, balding man and a young woman sitting in the back of a pickup drinking beer, pitching bottles onto the asphalt, and obviously intoxicated. In Harlingen it is illegal to drink alcohol in a public place outside of a licensed restaurant or bar.

Cardoza had arrested the protesting man and put him in the back of his cruiser to take him to the city jail. The man said his name was Ernesto Rubio and insisted that he couldn't be arrested because he was an immigration official at Bayview. Skeptical, Cardoza called in the name to the police dispatcher. Then it started to get strange. The dispatcher said she couldn't give out any information about Rubio's record over the radio, and told Cardoza to sit tight because his superior, Sergeant Eleazar Cortéz, was on his way. Cardoza couldn't believe it. His sergeant interfering in an arrest? When Cortéz arrived he spoke privately to Rubio, then Cardoza was told to give Rubio a parking ticket instead of an arrest. "Since when do we give out parking tickets to lawbreakers?" he asked Cortéz.

Cardoza vented to me as we sat in the car. "You know the law—we arrest people for doing what he did and we book them for it. Why are we giving this guy special treatment? Just because he said he was an INS official?"

Two nights later I sat in the same car in front of the same warehouse with another officer. Cardoza drove up beside us in his Harlingen Police Department cruiser and parked. He walked over to the driver's side and told me to go look in the back of his patrol car at the report lying on the seat. He said, "Now, I can't give you this information, and I'm sure, as I stand here, that I didn't see you reading it."

Ernesto Barrera Rubio's record of arrest. It said he had been arrested three times for driving while intoxicated (DWI) and that his driver's license had been suspended, except for driving to and from work. I asked Cardoza if I could have the report, but he emphatically declined. Whenever a police officer obtained a report from the computer system, his code number appeared on it. He could lose his job. I thanked him for the information—and thanked God I hadn't let Rubio use our motor home.

■　■　■

After selling one of our spring foals, Barbara suggested I buy a typewriter since I continued to bellyache about my inept letter writing. I insisted that she teach me how to use it, or I'd continue to bug her, to which she recommended the community college nearby. This was the second time she'd suggested going back to school, and I was completely, irrationally against it. "You want me to make a fool of myself in front of a whole class?" I snapped. I was dumb and unable to learn. That's what I had been taught.

Two weeks elapsed before I visited Texas State Technical College in Harlingen and enrolled in their summer typing course. The buildings were overwhelming, the other students I imagined were all brilliant, and the professors would make me feel stupid. I had to overcome all of this thanks to Jim's early tutelage. But I persisted and took the class, mostly because I felt that if I didn't, this story would not get told the way it deserved. The course lasted ten weeks and . . . was okay. It was okay.

■ ■ ■

In August 1992, while working security at the H-E-B grocery store in Brownsville, I ran into Francis Carmona. I nearly didn't recognize her; she was so slovenly and thin. Her eyes were sunken, and she looked years older than when I'd last seen her. Even her voice sounded old as she described the past seven months since she'd been fired from Bayview. I hadn't known.

She said Rubio had become increasingly obsessed with her, openly fantasizing about moving in with her and saying they would "make good bed partners." He would make comments about her breasts in front of Ramirez. In Rubio's office she noticed a box of surgical gloves on his desk and asked if she should take them back to the medical clinic. Rubio had stopped her, saying, "I use them to examine my favorite female guards."

Last October Rubio imagined Francis had an undocumented immigrant living with her. Without revealing what he suspected, he fired her, then sent a deportation officer, Daniel Pérez, to her home to confirm.

Francis reached her home and found Pérez waiting. He explained why he was there and asked permission to search her home. Livid, she allowed the search, where he discovered her ailing mother in bed and her teenage son's belongings. Shortly after he left, her neighbor told her she had seen the man try to open the locked door, then look through every window.

Rubio had called back and apologized, then rehired her. But Francis felt that she had no control over her fate. She wrote a letter to the Center for Human Rights to see if they could help her.

Then, just after Christmas 1991, Francis was working outside at the camp when Rubio approached. As she unlocked the gate for him, she mentioned that she had put on a few pounds over the holidays and needed a larger uniform.

Rubio replied that he was just waiting for her buttons to pop. Francis asked him for permission for a bigger uniform because the male detainees were making comments.

"But that is how we want you to look," Rubio told her.

Francis confided her problem to another guard in the laundry room, who gave her a larger uniform. She washed the small one and was going to hang it in the uniform closet, but the door was locked. She folded the uniform and left it on the floor beside the locked door, then heard someone inside the closet as she stepped out the door and returned to her post.

Ramirez found the uniform on the floor and discovered Francis had put it there. Ramirez wrote up an incident report against her for dereliction of company property, and Francis was sent home from work for taking a uniform without permission.

After several days off she called Rubio to apologize and plead with him to reinstate her. Her mother was dying of cancer and under expensive medical care in Francis's home. Rubio was too "busy" to listen and dismissed her calls with noncommittal replies. He always promised to talk at a later date.

A week passed, and Francis had no word from Rubio. In early

January she found a United International Investigative Security envelope in her mailbox and knew she'd been fired. The reason: poor performance.

Francis agonized. She had been told her mother had six months to live. She was not eligible for unemployment because she'd been fired for poor work habits, as I had been the first time. The two misfortunes together were almost more than she could bear.

Now her mother was dead. She described to me the ordeal of caring for her—sleeping beside her on the floor to give her medicine during the night, the horrid odor of terminal cancer, the impotence of not being able to relieve her mother's constant pain.

She had been living off her mother's small bit of social security, but now that was ending and she had no idea what she would do. She was depressed, apathetic, and overwhelmed.

"I couldn't sleep with Rubio. But then . . . why didn't I do it a long time ago?" she wondered out loud. "I would have a job again at least . . ."

I searched for good news to tell her, such as having found an attorney for the other women, but I had none. Only one lawyer hadn't given me the brush off. Our statute-of-limitations date was September 21, 1992, only a month away.

I offered some weak platitudes, but I don't know if she heard me. She was distracted and reached behind her as if clutching for something that wasn't there. She became frantic.

"Hefner, did you see my purse?" Her hands flew from her mouth to her forehead in an agitated ballet of worry. I hadn't noticed she had a purse.

"I have to find my purse," she declared, circling like a dog after its tail. "I have to go home. Maybe I left it on the table."

She quickly shuffled down the aisle in her baggy clothes. I called out asking for her phone number in case I found an attorney we could all use.

"I've got to go. I don't have a phone anymore," she replied.

I watched the shell of Francis walk out. How many others had those men destroyed?

My encounter with Francis shook me. While talking to her about her mother, I experienced a feeling that went beyond mere sympathy. Looking into Francis's troubled eyes, I saw myself as a child, desperately trying to help a parent and failing. I shook it off, but the sense that something deeply disturbing was rising within me like a black omen remained. Why did her pain seem to be my own? Why did I want to slay dragons to help her?

Francis wasn't the only guard I ran into at H-E-B while working security. Shortly after seeing Francis, I ran into Creclius. She was an entirely different picture. One of the female guards hired by United, Creclius was carefree and determined to get what she wanted. In her earlier days she must have been a very attractive woman. I figure she was in her early fifties, with long, dyed jet-black hair. She always wore wide black belts with her uniform to show off her small waistline. Creclius had dated some of the younger guards in their twenties and wasn't bashful about brushing up against me.

When Creclius saw me, she stretched out her arms to give me a hug. As I backed off, she murmured, "You're always on your best behavior, Hefner. When are you going to loosen up some?"

"Creclius, you see I'm in uniform and carrying a .38 pistol."

This seemed to satisfy her, and she kept her distance. I asked how'd she been, then quickly took the conversation in a more serious direction. She had once worked in Building 1, filling in for Ruiz's secretary while she was off on sick leave. If anyone knew anything about Ruiz, she did, and she would not be afraid to talk about it.

She said Ruiz had never bothered her or even hit on her. Then she asked if I was still trying to sue the INS. I told her the whole story, and she said she wanted to be honest with me. "You know, Hefner, I was able to keep my job, and everyone knew how I did it."

I confessed that I didn't know. I asked if Ruiz wrote a recommendation letter for her as he had for other female guards.

"Heck no," she said. "I wasn't sleeping with Ruiz like some of the other guards were." I told her I was glad about that. "Hefner, remember when I was working foot patrol on swings and graveyard?"

"Yes, I remember," I said.

"Well, it wasn't just the rattlesnakes and those smelly old polecats I had to contend with."

"What do you mean?" I asked.

She took a quick look up and down the aisle. "Many of the nights I was visited by an INS officer."

"You were?"

"Yes, and even Payan knows because I told him." With a smirk on her face, she said, "Aren't you going to ask me who?"

"Why, is it someone I know?" I asked.

"Oh, yes, you know him, Hefner. It's Jesse Rosales, you know, the assistant chief detention enforcement officer."

This was not a real surprise. When I was working swing shift as a runner, I would often be in Processing taking male detainees back to their dorms. One evening, a young woman was escorted to Processing by the female runner. Rosales opened an office door and motioned the woman inside. Closing the door behind her, he started to mingle with the rest of us. I watched Immigration Detention Officer Jiménez as he processed a few male detainees. Rosales came over and started to joke with me, making fun of me, as he always did, because I was white-skinned.

We always seemed to hit it off well, as I would join in the fun, joking about how dumb us white people were. Still, I was afraid that my joking might go too far, and I'd be faced with a situation where I would have to take sides. I knew he wouldn't like that.

Rosales roamed around some more, then slipped back into the office, where the woman was, and closed the door.

Jiménez looked over as the door was closing, a smile opening his thin lips.

"Hefner," Creclius said, "are you and the other guards who were not hired by United still beating a dead horse? If those girls did what the rest of us did, they would have kept their jobs. I believe in mixing pleasure with work."

I asked, "What other girls are you talking about?"

Without giving it a second thought she mentioned Juanita Treviño. "Treviño, she'd dated some of the security supervisors and even Ruiz."

I watched her as she walked away, and that was the last time I saw Creclius.

■ ■ ■

In mid-August 1992, Cynthia Rodriguez called and said she'd talked with Denis Downey, the attorney, and that he had found someone to take our case. I'd grown skeptical over the months. Attorneys sounded interested at first, but then their interest would wane. Every time I talked with him, Downey told me how hard it was to prove harassment. Because we had been snuffed out on every front, I was beginning to think the powerful men we fought controlled and pressured all lawyers. Cynthia, however, was undeterred.

"Hefner, his secretary just told me over the phone that they are going to file our case in court this week. Please call all the women who have a complaint. Tell them to call the attorney's office right away to make an appointment."

We decided that I would call Beatriz and other witnesses; Cynthia would contact Jovita. After trying old phone numbers, I discovered many had moved away. It was also chilling to find that our witnesses no longer working at the camp had become unavailable because they thought we had been beaten and didn't want to jeopardize themselves.

The four of us—Beatriz Huerta, Cynthia Rodriguez, Jovita Urrutia, and myself—met in Downey's office with our new attorney, Jim Sitgreaves. Sitgreaves owed Downey a favor, so he was obligated to take us on. I didn't care how we got to court—I just wanted to get there. The women needed to tell a jury what had happened.

We tried unsuccessfully to reach Francis Carmona. Sitgreaves assured us he could file a separate suit for her when she turned up because we had to push on. Hopefully, she'd read about the suit in the papers and contact us.

"There was a two-year statute of limitations," I lamented to Sitgreaves. "Are we still within the law?"

Sitgreaves assured me that our deadline was September 1992. We were hoping to settle before we went to court.

On August 28, 1992, Sitgreaves filed our lawsuit at the Cameron County Courthouse. We four were named as plaintiffs and the defendants were Vicente Ramirez; Burns International, Inc.; and United International Investigative Services. We sued for the following:

> That a citation be issued and served to the defendants;
>
> That the plaintiffs recover past and future loss of wages, seniority, and benefits, and that they collect damages for mental anguish, including pre- and post-judgment interest;
>
> That the plaintiffs recover all court costs and attorney fees; and
>
> That the plaintiffs obtain and recover any further relief to which they may be entitled.

■ ■ ■

The next morning, the *Brownsville Herald* ran a story ("Former INS-Bayview Guards Sue Employer") detailing the specific incidents of alleged misconduct by Ramirez, Burns, and United as claimed by Beatriz, Cynthia, and Jovita.

Payan called to congratulate me. "Make sure you give your attorney my name as a witness."

"Are you sure?" I asked him. I'd hate to see him stick his neck out.

"They can't fire me for telling the truth. I'll be under oath; you can go to jail for perjury, not for telling the truth. Make sure your attorney calls me as a witness."

Payan was a good man. He always treated me with respect and had great concern for others. I appreciated his wanting to stand with us in our fight for justice. We couldn't possibly lose with such a highly placed witness in the INS itself.

The new security company I worked for employed some policemen from the Harlingen Police Department part-time, who moonlighted for extra money. We were often assigned to stakeouts together, and over time, I became good friends with several of them. Taking a clear position against the status quo at Bayview drew these men to me just as it had separated me from the camp perpetrators. One of them, Claro Rocha, offered to help. He told me that he had worked for United as a security guard at Bayview for three months under Supervisor Howard Bergendahl before becoming a policeman and knew what it was like.

"I saw a lot of things going on at the camp," Claro said. "Once, while I was in the mess hall with Bergendahl, he pointed out a beautiful young woman. He told me and the other men with him that he was going to have sex with that detainee. What made him think he could do that? Bergendahl said he could get away with it because he knew Rubio and Ramirez were having sex with other detainees and so were the INS officers. So, he said, 'I'm going to get me one, too.'"

As a police officer in good standing, Claro was a perfect witness. After writing down his phone number, he told me to have Sitgreaves call him.

· · ·

On September 2, 1992, I pecked out a fourth letter to Senator Gramm. Two years had passed since I'd heard anything from him, though the television had been plastered with his "family values" announcements. What hypocrisy it was to talk, talk, talk, with Bayview in such a state, and nobody *doing* anything.

> Dear Senator Gramm:
>
> It has been twenty-one months since we've heard anything from you. I am writing this letter on behalf of the pastors here in the Rio Grande Valley. I have always voted Republican but seeing the importance of this matter, I am turning my attention to the Democrats. We cannot waste another twenty-one months. We are now taking some of these men to court because the INS cannot police themselves in this matter. Here in the Valley it is called the "Good Old Buddy System." We are for immigration laws and want them to be enforced, but the INS has no right to lock women and children up and force them to have sex with government-paid employees. These women are asked to have sex in order to keep their jobs. Let's practice more respect for these women and their families. We too believe in family values. In October of 1990, Cecilio Ruiz was placed under arrest in Matamoros for possession of cocaine. Was he guilty? Just ask some of the agents who worked for the Drug Enforcement Administration (DEA). Our government did a big cover-up for him and got him off the hook, and had all charges dropped. He wasn't punished, but promoted; a slap in the face to every taxpayer.

I sent a copy of the letter to Governor Ann Richards, and on September 8, I sent a copy to then–presidential candidate and governor of Arkansas, Bill Clinton.

Ann Richards replied on September 23, saying, "As I am sure you are aware, the Immigration and Naturalization Service is a division of the US Department of Justice; therefore, I as governor have no authority over its internal affairs. I do, however, have a concern for justice to our citizens and will continue to monitor this issue until it is settled." By the end of the next month, on October 29, 1992, Senator Gramm acknowledged my letter, but not my frustration. Bill Clinton never responded.

■　■　■

In late October, Payan's good friends, Sergeant Ramiro Sánchez and Constable Jimmy Vásquez of the Los Fresnos Police Department, notified Payan that the INS service bus that was driven to Houston with detainees to be placed on airplanes and flown back to their countries was smuggling cocaine and marijuana. Payan notified Administrator Roel Delgado and the two informed Cecilio Ruiz. Payan and Delgado planned to follow the next Houston-bound bus in their personal vehicles.

Payan gave me an account of what happened next:

> We had agreed to use both of our personal vehicles, INS portable radios, cameras, and binoculars. Our plan was to follow in one vehicle until the drugs were picked up and then continue in the other vehicle. The day before the next bus was scheduled, Delgado called me and advised me that Cecilio Ruiz had cancelled our plans because it was not our duty and none of our business. Sergeant Ramiro Sánchez called me at my office and asked if I could stop by the constable's office

on my way home. Constable Jimmy Vásquez was very upset; Ruiz had called him and ordered him to stay out of INS business.

Less than a month later, on November 3, 1992, the Democrats and Bill Clinton won. Maybe now we'd get something done.

Jim Sitgreaves filed for a court hearing in the 197th Judicial District for us, and on December 3, Judge Darrell Hester signed the agreement, placing us on the court's jury docket for trial on March 22, 1993, at 9:00 a.m.

13

The Depositions

In early January 1993, Sitgreaves, our attorney, sent each of us a copy of our lawsuit and instructed us to read it carefully as depositions were scheduled for January 12 at his office on South Padre Island.

I was scheduled to have a hernia rupture repaired on the eleventh. According to my doctor, the injury was severe, and I shouldn't delay it. I was continually in pain.

Before Sitgreaves had a chance to move the date, the Burns attorney changed the location of the deposition to the Fort Brown Hotel in Brownsville, a Ruiz hangout near the International Bridge. Sitgreaves explained that I would be hospitalized on that date but made arrangements for the women to be there. The attorneys agreed that I would be scheduled later.

I'd heard a lot about the Fort Brown Hotel. Ruiz had friends there and had dated some of the women employees. Payan told me that attorney Roberto Arias routinely paid Ruiz's bar bill there. I wondered, only half-kidding, if Ruiz would have the deposition room bugged. One of the women who worked there was with him the night he got arrested in the hotel room in Matamoros. Payan told me she had to spend four months in jail.

The hotel was also the scene of a grotesque crime just a few weeks earlier. A guest saw blood dripping from a car trunk. Police forced it open and found two male bodies with their hands lashed behind them and tied to their feet, duct tape over their mouths, and gaping gunshot wounds in each of their heads. The trusted

217

policeman friend of Payan's, Sergeant Ramiro Sánchez, came by our ranch to warn Barbara and me about it because, he said, "your neighbor across the street did the killing. Drug deal gone bad."

Every evening I watched him from the living room window, as he walked one of maybe twenty-five Pit Bulls he owned up and down the road.

"Why so many dogs?" I asked.

Sánchez said they were for protection from other drug dealers and from law enforcement. The hotel was infamous.

I imagined Jovita, Cynthia, and Beatriz being intimidated out of their stories by the opposing attorneys. I had to trust Sitgreaves to look out for them. When the four of us went to his office on January 9 to review our complaints, I doubted his commitment to us, but felt reassured afterward and thought he might even care a little.

The four of us decided that we wouldn't rest until *all* abuse had ended at Bayview. We were doing this not only for ourselves, but for everyone who had been subjected to the administration's corruption. I thought of the thin seventeen-year-old dancer with world-weary eyes. What most motivated me to press forward, though—past the pain, anxiety, and disappointment—was the possibility that it might continue, if something wasn't done now.

Optimistic about our chances, I went into surgery two days later. The doctor warned me that recovery would be painful, but I laughed and said that compared to what I was going through psychologically, it'd be a relief. Never in my life have I experienced such physical misery. The day after surgery I was amazed. Every little movement caused a sensation that felt like white-hot tongs being thrust into my side then opened up. I thought I could do without pain medication, but an hour after the anesthesia wore off, I told the nurse I changed my mind. She laughed.

At home I was good for nothing but letter writing and had to be waited on like a big baby. Barbara took a sly kind of pleasure in ordering me to be still. But she and I were both proud of my new-found independence with the typewriter.

With Governor Ann Richards back in the news that January for President Clinton's inauguration, I decided to write her again in the hopes of keeping her involved. She seemed to care about people and might have more sympathy for the women. I reminded her of what our three ex-guards and many other women and children suffered at the hands of their government supervisors, and asked if she could help me get my long list of complaints to the right person in the new administration in Washington. I closed with these sentences:

> I will gladly go to Washington as long as I can speak to the right department. After all, it was President Clinton who made the commitment that he did not want the American people to think government employees were above the law.

While I was still laid up, Sitgreaves called to say my deposition was set for February 2 at the Fort Brown Hotel, three days away. I told him I still felt miserable and weak, but he said I had to be there. He was going to send me a list of the documents the opposing attorneys wanted me to bring.

After the call, I experienced a wave of fear. I was still receiving threatening phone calls. "Watch your back, Hefner." It was so much like the agonizing uncertainty I experienced standing before Jim, my stepfather, when I didn't know when or if the blow would come. The fear was paralyzing. It made me want to put a knife to my own throat just to be free of it. I didn't feel strong enough to stand in my own defense, let alone point the finger and attack anyone else. What would they do to me? Who else knew I would be at the hotel? A fifty-dollar assassin?

I was on my second prescription for pain medication. I hated it, but it gave me relief and helped me sleep. Now I started to cut back in order to clear my mind. Rising early the morning of my deposition on February 2, I worried about the camp employees who would lose their jobs as a result of the information I was giving to the Burns and United attorneys. I was required to supply W-2 forms, medical records, the names of those who complained to me, and the complete set of letters I'd written and received back. The previous night I'd rummaged through notebooks and files and got so bleary-eyed I could hardly tell what I was looking at.

That morning I took the pain medication, brushed my teeth, and stepped into the shower, shielding the bandages on my left side. I turned awkwardly to adjust the water temperature. The movement made me light-headed and weak, and my feet slipped out from under me. Landing on my back in the bathtub, the bandages got soaked and new pain radiated from the incision. I got up trembling and finished my shower. So much adrenaline was rushing through my system, it felt as if I'd drunk four pots of coffee.

After drying off, I changed the bandages and saw that I'd ripped the incision and that it was bleeding quite a bit. Grumbling about my carelessness, I taped some more gauze over it. It hurt like before. I waffled between going to the deposition and going to the doctor's. Wishing Barbara was there, I decided to call the doctor afterward.

The drive down to Brownsville was an ordeal. Every time I had to clutch the transmission with my left foot a new wave of pain and light-headedness swept over me. Arriving at the hotel parking lot, I was breathless from the strain.

I parked close to the entrance and shuffled inside, each step burning and my breath in gasps.

Sitgreaves greeted me at the lobby desk. We were the first to arrive so I took the opportunity to find the bathroom. I opened the bandage and found new blood. I cleaned it up and put myself back together. My hand was shaking. I had no idea what to expect at the deposition. What kind of questions would they ask? Would they think I was stupid? Sitgreaves told me to concentrate on the questions before answering. But I couldn't concentrate; I was consumed by the pain in my side. I reached for my bottle of medications, forgetting I'd taken a pill an hour earlier, and washed down another one. I didn't realize I'd just taken an overdose.

I remember inching up several flights of stairs into a room with a square table. A lady with a tape recorder sat beside it. Someone introduced me and asked me to sit down.

Sitgreaves was staring at me a bit peculiarly. "Tony, are you all right?"

"Me? Sure!" I chirped. Of course I was all right. No pain!

I don't remember anything else.

When I read the transcript of my deposition several weeks later, I honestly didn't know why it was so full of mistakes. This was *my* testimony? Had it been typed wrong to discredit me? By the time I got to page eight, the horrible realization dawned.

The Burns attorney asked if I had taken any medication and I told him no. Why? I should have shown him the small bottle in my shirt pocket. What was I thinking?

I called the doctor and asked if the second pill could have caused my garbled testimony. He said I'd definitely overdosed, and two pills could also explain any hallucinations and confused speech.

I read my deposition feeling sicker at heart with each mistake. I had to fix this—here I was, blowing it for everyone.

I called Sitgreaves and told him the whole story. He wasn't surprised but said since Burns had already paid their attorneys to do this deposition, they would not be inclined to pay for another due to my mistake. By law they didn't have to.

"But there must be some way," I pleaded.

"Your deposition is not as important as the women's," he consoled. "Don't worry about it."

But I did. Each woman's questioning had lasted less than one hour. Mine had taken over four hours. It seemed to me as if the lawyers wanted to punish me more and put me through the mill. After all, if it weren't for me, there would be no case.

I wanted to go bury myself. Instead, I buried the awful memory.

■　■　■

I read the following announcement, headed "Harassment Topic At Caucus," in the January 20, 1993, *Valley Morning Star*:

> Dr. Betty Lanier, a certified psychologist, will be the guest speaker at the monthly meeting of the Higalgo County Women's Political Caucus today. Lanier will address the topic of sexual harassment in the workplace; what it is, its psychological effects, its demographics, how to recognize it, how to prevent it, and what to do if it occurs. For more information, please call Margaret Burkhart.

I called her a few days later. I told her I appreciated this caucus on helping women in the workplace, but surely she must have read about the many detained women at the camp who had been sexually abused. "Will they be on your agenda?"

She said that they would if she knew who they were. She asked me to send her all their names. Ms. Burkhart had a soft voice and sounded very concerned. A nice lady, she gave me her address.

Payan called to check up on me. We both kept each other informed. Two heads are better than one, and this time it paid off.

"You're going to do *what*?" Payan said with a chuckle. I had told him about Ms. Burkhart and that she had asked me to send her the female detainees' names. "Hefner, Margaret Burkhart is Ruiz's fiancée." He said that she was a nice lady, but what she saw in Ruiz, God only knew.

"Ruiz thinks I shred all those complaints. If he was to see those names again, he would definitely know I gave them to you, and believe me, she would give them to Ruiz."

A few days later I wrote Ms. Burkhart a nice letter. "If we can convince our government that these allegations are true, maybe our government can conduct seminars at the camp for the female detainees on sexual harassment from INS officers, security guards, and immigration lawyers." Ms. Burkhart called me on two different occasions asking for the names.

■ ■ ■

To add to my frustration, I got another reply from Phil Gramm with a copy of a letter he received from Richard J. Hankinson of the Office of the Inspector General. The allegations, according to Hankinson, "could not be substantiated." Again.

■ ■ ■

In early spring, Payan came by the ranch in an agitated mood. He'd had a horrendous day at work and wanted to tell me about it.

Payan feared that forces at work were becoming aligned against him. He had uncovered the fraudulent activities of a bond agent named Humberto Manazares who worked for Aaron Federal Bonding Agency in Houston. Payan first met Manazares in March 1988, when Payan started working at the camp. At the time, Manazares worked as a paralegal for the attorney Roberto Arias. Right off the bat, Payan was offered women and the use of Arias's condominium on South Padre Island if he would do certain favors for the two men (such as reducing bonds and releasing females under orders of recognizance).

Manazares told his female detainee clients that they had to spend the night with him and pose nude for photographs before they could leave the area on bond. The detainees thought they had to comply or risk deportation.

Manazares was also bilking them out of money by purposely misleading his clients in order to get them deported for noncompliance, then pocketing his prepaid fee. Though Payan had evidence from several witnesses, including a paralegal from a law firm hired to prosecute Manazares, he could get no action from Ruiz or authorization to release a memo he had written to warn women detainees. Besides his initial report to Ruiz, he had sent a formal complaint through usual channels to the INS center administrator, Roel Delgado, who never responded. (Delgado had sexually harassed guard Laura Zuniga in April 1991.) Payan felt he was no longer taken seriously at staff meetings. He'd been asked to shred more files and complaints.

But this wasn't what had upset Payan today. He said that Arias, Ruiz's friend, had resurfaced with his new-arrivals list. Payan had begun investigating Arias last month when a new detainee named Dilcia from Honduras confided to him the strange offers she had received from Arias.

The attorney had appeared out of nowhere, calling her by name, her first morning in detention. Dilcia thought it strange because she didn't know anyone in the country. Arias offered her a chance to work for a friend, who would pay her bond—a clearly illegal arrangement, as undocumented aliens are not allowed to work for wages. He pressured her and continued to request appointments during the week, which she kept, not knowing she could refuse.

To further pressure her, he threatened her family in Honduras, having obtained extensive knowledge of them from accomplices there. Afraid for the safety of her family, Dilcia agreed to meet the "friend." The friend offered her $250 a month to wait tables in his restaurant, of which $50 would be sent to her family in Honduras and the other $200 taken off what she owed him for bond. Dilcia refused.

When Arias summoned her again he scolded her for displeasing his friend and said he'd try to find someone else to pay her bond.

She next found herself before Manazares, who couldn't keep his hands off her and actually kissed her in the conference booth.

When Arias called her yet again that day, he warned her not to "mess this one up" as he had arranged for her to meet a woman from Houston with two small children who needed a live-in babysitter. The woman would pay her bond, and Dilcia would work for her until she paid her back. At this point Dilcia approached a guard for help and was advised to talk to Payan.

From their conversation, Payan was certain that Arias was getting the new-arrivals list from Ruiz and using it to provide his friends with undocumented workers at rock-bottom wages. The unfortunate workers could find themselves involved in prostitution, slavery, or any number of unscrupulous businesses.

Payan accused Arias in a letter to Delgado, saying it was "his strong belief that Arias is deeply involved in unethical practices" and that if someone would take the complaints and Dilcia's sworn affidavit seriously, a proper investigation could reveal other abuses as well.

In spite of hard evidence, Delgado again made no reply to Payan's charge, except to alert Arias that Payan was on his case.

Arias then wrote a four-page document of complaints against Payan for interfering in lawyer-client confidentiality and confronted him, threatening to turn those accusations over to the Office of the Inspector General if Payan continued to question Arias's potential clients.

Payan sent a letter to INS District Director Mike Trominski, asking that Arias's four pages of accusations be investigated. Payan knew that if an examination was conducted anywhere near Arias, his schemes would be exposed. Payan had nothing to hide.

Arias backtracked and turned to Ruiz for protection. Ruiz reprimanded Payan over the phone saying, "Deportation officers should not interview detainees if the detainee has an attorney representing them, unless the interview has to do with immigration matters only." But Payan knew the pressure was on both of them. He had gone above Ruiz by writing to Trominski about Arias. As in an incestuous family, stirring up outside interest was bound to bother them, and Payan knew he had their attention.

He was trumped several days later, however, when Delgado came into Payan's office and slammed his original letter on his desk. When Payan asked why he was returning it, Delgado said, "INS has no intentions of allowing this type of memo to fall into the wrong hands. We cannot afford this kind of embarrassment."

When Payan protested, Delgado became incensed and replied, "Shut up and don't bother me anymore, Payan, and don't be sending any more memos! You're not an investigator and investigations are not your job."

Later in the day, Ruiz phoned Payan to demand that he apologize to Arias for any inconvenience he had caused him. Usually mild and well-spoken, Payan snapped.

The next morning, when Payan arrived at work, he was told to report immediately to Delgado's office. Delgado received him, and Payan found a peevish, scowling Roberto Arias sitting cross-armed in a corner, waiting for his apology.

Payan became incensed. "There is no way I'm going to apologize to this man, or anyone else, for their unethical business. As of this date, no G-28 forms were ever filled out by this attorney to show client representation existed between him and the new arrivals. There was never any privileged relationship."

Now he was worried. He had no chance against them. From Trominski on down, they were like pieces in a puzzle, all linked together. He was going to lay low for a while.

■   ■   ■

In March 1993, I was gratified to see in the morning paper a picture of a smiling Janet Reno, just confirmed as the country's first female attorney general. I felt nearly euphoric about the new possibilities for reforming the government's policies. She was a woman and she had great power; surely she could stop the sexual abuse of women and children by government employees. I caught myself grinning as I visualized Reno grabbing Ruiz by the ear and forcing him to walk a straight line.

Explaining to Reno how backward southern Texas is about women's rights would be difficult. Many Hispanic men here behave as if women are second-class citizens.

People should qualify for a job based on education and experience, but from what I've seen and heard, that doesn't apply to women who seek jobs along the border. Real qualifications carry little weight in the case of female job seekers, and they know it. What's valued here are looks, charm, and sex appeal. This system teaches women to devalue modesty, intellect, and self-control.

Sexual harassment in the workplace is the rule, not the exception. Some of the more aggressive men at the camp manipulate women workers and dominate detainees without conscience and laugh about it. These men don't give their victims a second thought, because they know more will come. The pain and suffering they cause does not concern them. Is it too much to try to change a cultural bias that's so ingrained? As some of the more sympathetic male guards reasoned, you can't do anything about it—that's just the way it is.

The day that I read about Reno's confirmation, I received a second letter from Governor Ann Richards. She regretted that since the INS was a federal agency, her office had no jurisdiction over their activities.

She suggested that I contact Democratic Senator Bob Krueger, who Ann Richards appointed to fill the vacancy created by the resignation of Lloyd Bentsen, who became secretary of the treasury in President Clinton's cabinet. Her suggestion disappointed me. What could another man do? After corresponding with Phil

Gramm for so long, I was convinced it was a gender issue. Still, I continued to hold a secret hope that Governor Richards would somehow relay my information to the right people in Washington, or maybe even to Janet Reno herself.

■　■　■

A few days later I got a call from a Baptist preacher in a Harlingen Christian school, inviting me to speak and answer questions at a Valley citizen meeting about the camp situation. What I had said on the news about sexual abuse at Bayview was bothering a lot of people, and they wanted to find out if anything was being done about it. It was to be a closed conference. No newspapers and no promotions. The point was to keep the INS away for fear they would break up the meeting.

On March 16, 1993, fifty businessmen and women, several pastors from different denominations, and representatives from the police came together in a private schoolroom. The president of another security company passed out a letter stating, in part, "The US government is the number one advocate of human rights. If we denounce other governments about their human rights, why are we letting it happen in our backyard? Why should we let a handful of men bring down what the US government stands for?"

I stood there in front of them and did my best to answer their questions. Then a pastor's wife faced the group and said, "Now that we have a woman as attorney general, surely, if we send Reverend Hefner to Washington with our signatures, Janet Reno will run these men out of town."

The idea of leaving Barbara alone when we regularly received threatening phone calls made going away out of the question for me. I knew our lives were in danger all the time. I had run into a member of Pastor Smith's church a few days ago and was told that the pastor found a church window broken by gunfire. Drive-by shootings were becoming more and more common in our area. It was usually drug- or gang-related. Someone from the camp could drive by our place late at night and shoot the place up while we lay in bed. The local police department could easily say it was drug-related and steer the public away from our complaints with the INS.

Not wanting to discourage anyone, I just thanked people for their support and told them I'd keep them posted. Afterward, many came up to shake my hand—important-looking men in suits and well-dressed ladies. I'd always felt insignificant in such company. Now it seemed we were united in our idealism, and I felt accepted.

■   ■   ■

It was a balmy evening in early spring. The day had been hazy with humidity, but it had dissipated by nightfall in a fresh, salty Gulf breeze. The sunlight through the palms said spring and rebirth, though it was only mid-March. Red and yellow flowers bloomed amid the circular, prickly entanglements of cactus as Barbara and I rode Faith bareback around the perimeter of the ranch, surveying the property for the first time since my surgery. I could feel her arms clasped around my waist, and the arrhythmic touches of her bare feet against my calves. It was an idyllic evening. She leaned her chin onto my back and told me I had really changed.

"Changed?" I said. "I'm still the same old screwup."

"No," she said.

She told me how she used to suffer over my timidity way back in Bible school when the preachers there would walk all over me. "They made fun of you, and you never stood up for yourself." Now, finally, I was putting up a real fight and not backing down.

"Well, back then, I felt inferior, as I had been rejected all of my life," I said. "If I ever came off as rebellious or doubtful in their eyes, I felt that I would be rejected again as a bad Christian. And because they were godly and white, if I didn't have their approval, it was as if God himself were rejecting me. I had to be that way. I felt completely helpless."

"Do you remember I tried to tell you back then that that was wrongheaded?"

"It took awhile to sink in," I said.

Barbara told me that after having watched me these past several years, she had changed her mind. She was now proud of what I was doing. "I won't ever stand in your way again. I'm glad you're fighting them. Good people should take a stand against the bad."

We plodded along in silence as wave after wave of warmth and well-being flowed over me. I reached back and patted her leg. "And how about you?" I said. "Delivering that colt yourself? That's pretty different, too." One night, after returning home from work, I had seen a light in the barn. I found Barbara, elbow deep in amniotic fluid, delivering a foal.

"Oh, that was nothin'," Barbara said airily, with typical understatement. Her growing knowledge of horses and my being away evenings had given birth to Barbara's new willingness to pitch in. "There was nobody else here to do it."

She was no longer the squeamish, delicate girl I arrived with.

■ ■ ■

By March 17, 1993, our trial was five days away. Burns's attorney told Sitgreaves that they were going to depose Howard Bergendahl to bolster their side of the case. This puzzled me because Anna María García and Cynthia Rodriguez had both confided their harassment to him, and Bergendahl's testimony would seem to work in our favor, not Burns's. Sitgreaves was not able to be at the deposition and had Denis Downey go in his place.

I called Downey afterward, and he was discouraged. The deposition had taken forty-four minutes. Bergendahl was now at the

INS, having been promoted from United International. He had shown up in his snappy green uniform. He was professional and clear in his answers, and perjured himself over and over. He was on their side. Bergendahl denied in his deposition that Cynthia or Anna María or any other female guard had come to him with complaints about Rubio or Ramirez.

"No, sir, they did not. If they would have discussed something like that with me, I would have immediately followed up on it."

Downey asked if he knew anything about the blacklist. Bergendahl said, "No." But he was the one who had first told me about it. He also said that he *bought* a horse from me. (He hadn't been very friendly since I made him return the unbought horse.)

"Do you know who Claro Rocha is?" Downey asked him.

"No, I do not," answered Bergendahl.

"You don't recall that he was working for Burns and United and waiting to get a job with the Harlingen Police Department?"

"Oh, Claro Rocha? Yes, sir, I do know him."

"Okay," said Downey. "Do you ever recall telling him that you could get some female detainees to have sex with him?"

Bergendahl replied, "No, sir, I did not. I take my job very seriously, and I don't clown around like that."

Downey objected to the responsiveness of the question, then asked, "Do you recall that X-rated movies were shown to male detainees at the camp?"

"No, sir," said Bergendahl.

"You don't recall that at all?" asked Downey again.

"No, sir. A recreation specialist there brings in the movies that are brought in at the camp. It's a government employee."

Despite the personal trouble I'd had with Bergendahl, I was disappointed that he sold out so completely. He more than once bitterly criticized Rubio behind his back. But Bergendahl had always been afraid of confrontation. I don't know why I thought his being under oath would somehow make him tell the truth.

I shared the information with Payan and showed him Bergendahl's deposition. I told him I could not believe that Burns didn't know what was going on with its employees. A security guard, Ninfa Martínez, had once told me about a meeting Rubio had invited her and several other female guards to—with pay. It was organized by one of the big shots from the Burns San Antonio office. Before she left the meeting, she had to make up her mind which of several Burns employees she wanted to have sex with. The Burns district manager himself spoke sexually to the female guards and wouldn't keep his hands off of them. Ninfa said the women were expected to make a good impression.

According to Payan, however, because Ruiz insisted on an outstanding work review every year and felt that any problems with the security companies would reflect poorly on him, he made sure that complaints rarely saw the light of day. They were routinely filed and forgotten. "When I was co-keeper of the security contract," Payan said, "I had Rubio make a copy of every incident report and turn them in to me daily. I read every one and informed Ruiz about them. He would tell me to report only the minor ones and file the major complaints. He threatened to fire Rubio and his staff should any offensive information get out, and this kept everyone in line."

Payan urged me to get copies of the complaint files for several of the offenders. "Hefner," he told me, "if you can get Downey off his duff and have him file a Freedom of Information Act request for the files for Molinar, Delgado, and Ruiz, he'll find that each has several sexual complaints against them, especially Delgado. Creclius can tell you how many times Jesse Rosales had her perform sex on him. She told me herself, after you spoke to her last year. Jesse used his position to get what he wanted. Most of the females that did cooperate became INS detention enforcement officers, those that were thirty-five or younger."

Payan himself was not asked for a deposition because he was a key witness, and he prepared for the trial in the meantime.

■ ■ ■

The next day Sitgreaves called with news that blew me out of the water. Our trial, only four days away, was to be cancelled. According to the women's depositions, the sexual assaults in question had occurred more than two years before we filed the suit, putting us past the statute of limitations. We had been told that most judges, because harassment defendants routinely stalled proceedings, extended the statute of limitations to the court date or until an out-of-court settlement occurred. But the attorneys for Burns, United, and Ramirez had filed for summary judgments against us to drop the charges, and our judge was going to grant them.

We had been using the date of the United takeover in September 1990 as our deadline, but Jovita admitted in her deposition that her assault had taken place closer to July 1990. Burns, United, and Ramirez didn't even deny that the events took place—they merely claimed that they weren't liable anymore. Judge Darrell Hester, known locally as "hang 'em high Hester," ruled with the companies and on March 19 denied our day in court.

We were stunned, of course. But Sitgreaves told us that we could still sue for health insurance that was paid for but never provided, civil conspiracy in that we lost our jobs for reporting abuse, and sexual harassment, which created "special circumstances" to our employment. Those charges were still valid. But we would have to start all over again. We would have to file a motion for a new trial.

To me it was an enormous letdown, and I felt despair and frustration on all sides. Why was I doing this to myself and Barbara? Life was supposed to be less complicated.

Francis Carmona called from a pay phone to tell me she had talked to Sitgreaves, who would be filing a separate suit for her and Emily Davis, another guard who'd been fired illegally. She sounded more upbeat, and I was glad another guard was with her. I asked if she could think of anyone else at the camp who had been sexually harassed and could be persuaded to join us.

"A lot of guards were having sex with Rubio and Ramirez," she said and laughed bitterly. "They were promised INS jobs."

Francis also thought it would be hard to track down detainees because most would not have valid complaints. She mentioned a girl who was having sex with Ramirez and used his influence to avoid being assigned unwanted duties and gain privileges. We decided we needed to encourage those guards who were in a vise to come forward, including those who had been ordered by their supervisors to look the other way, but who could also be fired for allowing misdeeds to take place.

The next day Denis Downey called me about Emily Davis, the guard who was filing with Francis. Downey was going to listen to her story and asked if I'd be there. I came right after work and met her—a lanky, stylish Hispanic woman with an Anglo name—at the office. Emily had been a guard at Bayview for all of eighteen days before she went looking for legal representation.

Through a friend, she had contacted a female INS officer at Bayview who thought Emily would have no trouble getting employment there because she was good-looking and tall. At her first interview with the United personnel director, Vicente Ramirez, she was propositioned for a date.

Emily described her training session as "weird." She was conscious of Lieutenant Ramirez staring at her from his perch facing the class. He'd wink and smile at her. An older woman who sat close by, staring at her desktop and playing nervously with her pencil, also intrigued her.

Cecilio Ruiz came in to lecture them but talked about dating his secretary, and described her figure. "You know, my secretary was once just a security guard," he said to the women. "And it did not take her long to rise to the position she now holds. If you cooperate, promotion is a piece of cake."

During Ruiz's presentation, Emily noticed that the older woman who played with her pencil had broken it. After Ruiz exited the room, he stuck his head back in and called a name. The older woman rose and left with Ruiz.

At the front of the room, Ramirez addressed the men in the same way Ruiz had talked to the women.

"When you see some of these female detainees, you'll know what kind of goodies we have around here. And guys, let me tell you, there are *lots* of goodies out there."

During a break, the older woman's friend told Emily that Ruiz made a deal to consider the older woman for employment only if she did whatever he wanted. She was told ahead of time that Ruiz would be calling her out of the class periodically, which he did twice during each session over the course of the class. Only Emily and another young woman was hired.

When Emily reported to the security office at Ramirez's request, she found herself surrounded by four male supervisors in the room. A pile of uniforms lay on Ramirez's desk. He picked up a pair of pants and gave them to Emily. "Put them on," he said.

Emily didn't understand if he meant for her to put them on in front of them or to leave and put them on privately. Her indecision produced smiles from the men.

Ramirez took the pants from her and placed them against her body, wrapping his fingers tightly around her waist. "Say, does this look like a good fit?" he asked the others.

She had to pry Ramirez's fingers off her waist. They laughed at her distress until Ramirez threw the uniform into her arms and told her to report to work the next Sunday. The men's cackling followed her out of the office.

Ramirez began to call Emily at home to ask her out, sometimes late at night. Although she felt that she had to listen to him, again and again she refused to date him.

Eighteen days after starting work for the security company,

Rubio fired her because he said he'd only just discovered that she'd been arrested once. Emily protested that she had been arrested but not convicted, but her argument was pointless. She was out.

After listening, I told Downey that her story brought back memories of my own weird orientation and asked if he thought it might strengthen our case.

He looked up at me over his low-riding glasses as he finished jotting down his notes and smiled. "Yes," he said. "I do believe we can convince a jury."

■　■　■

Senator Gramm acknowledged another one of my letters with his usual polite but empty words on March 23, 1993:

> Thank you for providing me with the additional information. I have made a further inquiry on your behalf and will contact you again as soon as I receive a response. I appreciate having the opportunity to represent you and be of service in this matter.

I gave up hope of his being anything but ineffectual.

I received another disappointment around this time: due to some cancelled contracts and a general slowdown in business, I was laid off work again.

Then, on a black night around March 25, I received one of the menacing phone calls I could never grow accustomed to. I had finished soaping a saddle to use the next day for a retreat. It had red punch on it from our last retreat in early January, and I'd neglected to clean it until then. The ground was muddy from an earlier rain, and the wind was blowing my hair and the palm trees every which way as I trudged toward the mobile home. Barbara had gone to bed. It was dark inside except for a reading light that was on in the living room.

When I opened the door and the light spilled out, I heard the scurrying of lizard feet over the aluminum siding and knew that a hundred or so two-inch lizards were now safe in the eaves of our home. They liked to hide in the heat of the day, then cling tenaciously to the warm siding in the evening. I came in and gently latched the door. As always, I left my muddy boots on a newspaper beside it. I was going to the refrigerator for a glass of milk when the phone rang. It was after midnight.

"Hefner?" a sluggish voice asked. Faint voices and music came from the background. "This is a friend. Are you there?"

"Yes." I couldn't place the voice.

Then, almost inaudibly, he said, "Hefner, you're about to lose your key witness."

The line went dead. My heart pounded. Was someone in danger? Payan maybe? Or one of the girls? I froze, still holding the phone to my ear. My mind worked the voice over, but I couldn't identify it. I put my finger on the receiver and hoped he'd call back.

Was he a friend? Was this a new kind of threat? I hung up the phone and got a blanket from the closet. What did he mean by "lose"? I lay down on the sofa near the phone in case he called again. I felt responsible for all the people who'd given me information, endangering themselves. I couldn't stand the idea that they could be risking their life. What did it mean? Plenty of "accidental" deaths occurred in the Valley. What should I do with this information?

I decided after an hour of turmoil on the sofa that I couldn't do anything. Just too many people to warn. But, God, what if something should happen? I wished the man would call and tell me more. I tried to balance my responsibility against the constraints of my time, energy, and resources. There had to be a boundary somewhere for me, a limit to what I required myself to do. I was so tired of fighting. But what if my duty, my Christian obligation, lay beyond that boundary? Who could tell me what to do?

■ ■ ■

On April 3, I read another interesting headline: "Attorney Suggests Excessive Force Used On Haitian."

Ten Haitians claimed that on March 25, after an argument that was quelled by the INS riot squad, they had been kicked and beaten with batons by INS officers at the facility. Before the ten were shipped to a jail two hundred miles away to "cool down," a witness reported that they were forced to stand all night, handcuffed.

One Haitian in particular, a twenty-three-year-old former university student, charged that he was "kicked three times, hit with a baton, slapped twice, handcuffed and had his legs chained and left all night long on the floor." The man's attorney in Miami claimed his client was watching the others fight when he objected to being shoved by an officer, who then pushed him to the ground, handcuffed him, and left him there.

Ruiz was quoted as saying, "Nobody was beaten." He denied that having detainees stand all night was mistreatment, claiming the detainees were allowed to sit down, while handcuffed, for thirty to forty-five minutes, and that the incident was "handled in accordance with INS policy." I threw the paper across the room.

Then Payan called. He'd read the article, too. He reminded me about the video tape he had under his bed, which proved that the INS had used illegal methods of discipline before.

I popped my copy of the tape into the VCR, watching it again as I talked with Payan. Doubtless, Ruiz himself, with Rubio and Ramirez taking part, supervised the illegal exercise.

"Let me give this to the police or the newspaper," I said. "It proves what the Haitians are saying."

Payan hesitated. "Not quite yet."

"Why not? You've got them."

"You forget, I am seven months from retirement and pension."

"Yes, but—"

"I told Ruiz I had taped over the raid. I cannot admit I have this evidence until I am forced to protect myself. It is my only insurance."

Sadly, I saw his point.

■ ■ ■

On April 19, 1993, a month after Howard Bergendahl's deposition named Carlo Rocha as a witness to potential sex crimes inside Bayview, Rocha was suspended from the Harlingen Police Department.

The incident that caused his indefinite suspension occurred as Rocha and another policeman were escorting a belligerent drunk into a city jail cell. The man made a move toward his partner's gun, so Rocha quickly stepped between them and pushed the prisoner into a cell.

It was the push that the new chief of police, Jim Scheopner, claimed violated police department regulations, according to the letter of suspension he issued ten days later.

Disgusted, Rocha told the *Valley Morning Star* that "the incident . . . did not justify my termination and past incidents were trivial, trumped-up, or lacked evidence."

Rocha filed a wrongful discharge lawsuit against the city of Harlingen and the police department. It stated that he had been illegally fired and that charges of excess force with a prisoner were not true. Rocha said his suspension was "selective enforcement of rules and regulations, and resulted in a denial of equal protection under the law." He also said it was improper for the Civil Service Commission to consider evidence of previous misconduct that occurred more than 108 days prior to the April 19 incident.

Rocha rejected offers to resign with a clean record.

Our trustworthy witness was now deeply embroiled in public

controversy and legal trouble. He'd been fired from a law enforcement position. How could a jury believe him now?

Was this what the caller referred to less than a month ago, when he said I was going to lose my key witness?

■ ■ ■

That night, Waco, Texas, burst into the news. On April 19, 1993, the small northern town was thrust into the international spotlight when a zealous cult preacher named David Koresh and his Branch Davidian followers went up in flames during a standoff with the FBI. The commune had been surrounded after four Alcohol, Tobacco, and Firearms agents and six Koresh followers died in a shoot-out over the stockpile of weapons kept inside. Then, as the FBI lobbed canisters of tear gas into the compound, eighty-six people, including two dozen minors, were burned to death in the inferno that followed.

My church and I knew nothing about Koresh and his strange interpretation of the Bible, but we were now concerned about his fate. The death threats I now received came with a new twist.

"Think of Waco, preacher. You will be next."

A panicked meeting of our church congregation followed. Pastor Smith told us that the church office was receiving threats, too. "Remember Waco," a man would mutter and hang up. Bullets had broken a window in the sanctuary. The women feared we, too, were fighting the government. We could be next!

The pastor, his family, and church members were nervous and fearful. I couldn't reason with them, I couldn't calm them. Other pastors from around the Valley had called to warn us to be careful. The word was out.

The few retreats still scheduled by churches were cancelled.

"The government has our names. You know we can't take any chances." I repeatedly heard these comments and many more from church members. No pastor wanted to put his congregation's children in jeopardy.

I couldn't afford to hire bodyguards. I couldn't even allow myself to think that way. What was I going to do, shoot some suspicious trespasser? How could I shoot anybody, anyway? Was I going to become a criminal myself? The men we were fighting knew they were above the law. We were in an impossible position. The threats were eroding the foundation of our lives.

Once again, Barbara and I were discharged from teaching our Sunday school class. Children no longer came to the ranch. I sensed that Barbara blamed me for her hurt, but wouldn't admit it or express it. We withdrew into ourselves.

14

The Judge's Ruling

The *Valley Morning Star* on April 22, 1993, ran an Associated Press story entitled "White House Confirms Child Abuse Within Waco Cult." It gave explanations for Janet Reno's approval of the FBI plan to teargas the Branch Davidian compound in Waco. In essence, the White House and Reno said she was worried about the children, so she approved the plan. Who could blame her? the White House seemed to ask. According to the FBI, however, little evidence of abuse existed. She was catching a mountain of flak.

The government's alleged concern for the children was hypocritical in my mind, since they allowed their own employees at the INS to sexually abuse children at Bayview. Were Koresh's children worth more than detained Hispanic children? No one has the right to rob youngsters—brown, white, black, or yellow—of their childhood.

Maybe Mexicans are worthless. I couldn't shake the thought. Maybe Hispanics are doomed to prey on their own, one half demeaning and degrading the other half. It was like they stood on the backs of their own people to appear taller before the white world. One man couldn't stop it. Could I hide that part of me forever?

The sensation of nausea was ever-present those last days of April; it was the same feeling I'd experienced the former August when I had run into Francis Carmona. It was like a growth about to be expelled from inside me. Something was nagging, pushing at my consciousness. I did a lot of reading then because whenever I worked with my hands, I would think, and I couldn't stand my thoughts.

Around this time, the *Valley Morning Star* reported that a Proyecto Libertad attorney was filing a lawsuit on behalf of the Haitians who had been beaten, handcuffed, and left on the floor. Pat Page, the attorney, said, "This is similar to the liability of the officers in the Rodney King beating . . . INS detainees may not have many rights, but the US Supreme Court has held that many protections of the US Constitution extend to all persons in our country. A wonderful thing about the US is our concern for the rights of all people."

An asylum attorney from Laredo had interviewed the Haitians while they were in jail there and had documented and published their injuries. However, the *Valley Morning Star* article concluded with Trominski's comment that the detainees were medically examined when they were returned from Laredo's Webb County Jail and "nothing" was found that fit the description of those published injuries.

INS District Director Trominski was quoted in the article as saying that the Proyecto Libertad charges would be investigated if complaints were filed with the Office of the Inspector General. But Page, who had originally intended to file with the OIG, had by then decided that those complaints "don't go anywhere. By all accounts, it is an ineffective procedure. I understand Proyecto has filed several complaints to the office (OIG) over the years to no avail." Amen.

On May 3, 1993, the first official summary judgment was granted to Burns, and Sitgreaves sent us each a copy.

I received another set of letters from Phil Gramm in response to his "inquiry on my behalf" with the Department of Justice. Once again he wrote that "allegations of misconduct could not be substantiated." The Department of Justice would not budge: "Since it appears Reverend Hefner has not raised any new information in his current letter, we continue to consider this matter closed."

I was exhausted of trying to think of new schemes. I would often tell myself that I had tried my best. The implication was that even though I did everything I could, I couldn't succeed. But I had to, so I kept going. I felt as if someone were sitting on my chest, and I couldn't breathe. So I would write another letter, make another phone call. Was I driving myself crazy? Long ago, when I was a child, the children at school would laugh at me and say I was crazy, just like my stepfather, who was institutionalized at the time. "Tony's old man is crazy, crazy. Tony's old man is crazy, crazy." That's why I never got involved in sports. I didn't want to be out there with those kids. I hadn't thought of that in a long time.

The nagging truth was that I was doing it for me. I had to work through something desperate in me, but I didn't know what. I was absolutely determined that honest men would look into these victims' eyes, understand their sorrow, and listen to what was done to them even if it took my last dime to make it happen. Yes, that was crazy. Barbara tried but couldn't understand how obsessed I was. I could never do enough, never sacrifice enough and kept looking for someone who could tell me to rest, who'd say, "I understand. You're done. You did all you could," so I could believe it.

It was right there, the answer. Right on the tip of my tongue . . .

> Reach out and feel the victim's pain . . . Let it touch
> your heart. Wipe a tear or two away and you will learn,
> as I have seen. Beyond those soft and dark brown
> eyes . . . belief in justice, and a will to survive.

■   ■   ■

May 21 was warm and hazy. I was outside by the road replacing a rotted fence post. It was a tangled business of barbed wire and splintered wood, and I carried the Texas dirt in my sweat back to the house when I finished. I'd been thinking about the ranch and how it was so darn quiet, how we didn't need it anymore. The reason we came in the first place was gone. Twelve years of work, wasted. Nobody would trust us with their children, fearing that the threats that had been made would come to pass. People had stood up for me, patted me on the back, and told me I showed courage, but it seemed so worthless now because our life's work was ruined.

I took off my boots and set them on the newspaper spread out on the blue and white linoleum, yellowing and smudged with the powdery brown dirt from outside that seemed to find its way into the very food we ate. Through the living room window, I looked out at our little cactus and mesquite ranch. I thought about getting Barbara out of the Valley. She was determined to stand tall, but I knew she was scared to death.

The idea of leaving made me numb. So much would have to be done. I wanted to get into the truck and just drive away.

I went into the kitchen to wash up, wishing I could once and for all get rid of the cursed blood that had made me such a failure. Was that the real reason I was doing all of this, to prove that Hispanics were as good as whites, so that I would feel entitled to a sense of well-being? Did the rest of the world have that, or was it just my imagination? I only wanted to feel neutral, free from guilt and smallness for once.

When the phone rang I didn't want to answer it, but it might be Barbara.

"Hefner?" The voice was Hispanic and wheezed through a tight throat.

"Yeah?" My gut rolled up in a knot.

"Remember Waco," he said smugly.

"Who is this?" I demanded. I wanted to face this guy—I just didn't care anymore.

"You're a dead man," he growled, then hung up.

I was so angry my vision blurred. I ranted and cursed for a few minutes until I could grab hold of the notion that I was really just disgusted that these cowards still thought I was worth bothering about. The courts had dismissed my accusations. Why did they keep calling?

I began to consider that maybe I was wrong in all this, not them. Bad is good and good is bad. Anarchy reigns. I took refuge on the floor in the hallway. I was so far out of my league. I had put Barbara and myself and who knows how many others in real life-threatening danger. I had been foolish.

All I had wanted was to lift the hopes of the children, to show them what a good and honorable life meant, that it wasn't about money or prestige or color, but the satisfaction of living with integrity. I wanted to show them the inner peace that came by living your ideals. Oh, God. I was wrong there, too.

Sitting there on the hallway linoleum, watching the sun break off a candy dish into dancing rainbows while Chachalaca birds sang in the background, I felt that Jim had been right. We Hispanics didn't deserve justice. We were being forced to embrace corruption as the rule of society in south Texas. We had no recourse: the US government cared more about the children in the Koresh compound than the children in US detention camps. The difference was white and brown, ours and theirs.

Outside I could see the sign at the entrance to our ranch—"Bearing Precious Seed Ranch"—with its childish letters and foolish promise. I imagined macabre circus music playing on an out-of-tune calliope as I looked at the sign. It was a symbol of my naïveté. I jumped up, propelled by anger. I started for my axe to chop the sign down, but the phone rang again and startled me, silencing the music.

"Tony?" Barbara asked when I didn't say hello. "I'm here, is that you?" Her voice was soft and fragile and sobering.

"Yes. I'm here." We were both silent.

"There're three ledgers on my desk, so I can't really talk," she said, though we hadn't spoken.

Who was I to endanger her over this stupid mess? Who cared about what those jerks at Bayview did? It was a tough world, and we had to take care of ourselves.

"Barbara," I began, but she interrupted me.

"Tony, don't talk to me about leaving Texas. Not on the phone. You know how I feel," she said, reading my mind.

How could she love this place? It was hot and dusty and poor and had given us nothing but headaches. But she did.

"No," I said, stammering, my mind filled with questions I already knew the answers to. All I could think of was how much Barbara had endured. "I'm sorry," I said. Was she going to find me strung up in the barn, the victim of Bayview henchmen?

"Let's give it time. Everything will turn out all right."

I wanted to yell at her, oh no, it won't, not for me. But I accepted her undying optimism as blessed ignorance and let her go back to work. Barbara didn't want the bad guys to know we were licked. I couldn't bear to hurt her, but we had to leave. I had given her no children, another failure. Everything was wrong. I was a loser.

"Good-bye, Barbara."

At that point, I cried to God. Feeling small and responsible, I didn't understand why I was on the outside. I had to find out where I went so wrong.

I sat there on the floor beside the recliner for a long time. I wiped my eyes with my sleeve and thought of the courtroom yesterday when summary judgment was granted for Ramirez. His attorney had hugged him, while the women and I sat there dazed. Why, God, are these men allowed to win, and why are you allowing injustice to prevail? It is injustice, isn't it?

I saw the image of Francis Carmona in the grocery store, hollow and gaunt after spending months nursing her mother. Her haunted eyes looked like my own in the mirror.

The Chachalaca's piercing song finally shattered the lid on an old cellar jar in my memory. I saw myself as a nine-year-old, nursing my own mother. Though I didn't know it, I was killing her. The confusion I felt, the understanding of what she had asked me to do in her depression, and the paralyzing guilt that resulted all came back in a blinding, horrid picture. Although I can't say I'd forgotten the incident, I had refused to think about it. It was buried under pleasant, peaceful falsities.

Francis reminded me of my mother. Maybe it had to do with how much weight she had lost or her hopelessness. But I remember my mother looked that way, lying in bed, too weak to raise her head because of the overdose of pills I was giving her. Every hour I would try to wake her and give her one, according to her instructions. I would put my arm behind her neck to raise her head so I could put it in her mouth. Seeing her take a few sips of water as her damp hair fell stiffly around her face, I wished that my arm was longer and I was stronger to hold her head up.

A neighbor came to the house because she knew my father was in the hospital and my mother not up to caring for us. When she saw my mother she called the police. They arrived with the doctor and the woman got excited and told them that I was the one giving my mother all those pills. The policeman tried to calm her, and the doctor said that I was only doing what I was told, that it wasn't my fault.

As the ambulance took her away, I asked the doctor if she was going to be all right. He looked down at me and said he hoped so.

My mother recovered.

Here I was sitting on the floor of the hallway in San Benito thirty-five years later, crying. I'd been grieving over this my whole life. I never stopped. I never recovered. This was the thing that had fueled every battle that I fought to put things right.

I never talked to my mother about that day, and she never brought it up. Maybe she didn't remember. Maybe other things mattered more. But I was confused and devastated at nearly losing the only person on earth who ever claimed to be my own flesh and blood.

About a week after my mother had been taken to the hospital, the circus came to town, and I'd saved up for it. Anxious to go, I was on my way there after school when another emergency intervened. My mother was sitting in her easy chair on the front lawn.

Men were carrying out our kitchen table, chests, and beds. They said we didn't live there anymore. I saw our neighbors carrying what little possessions we owned away. I stayed to comfort my mother, who was crying. My place was there, beside her.

Having sat cross-legged on the floor for so long, I was getting stiff. I stretched out one leg through the doorway. I felt a numbed sense of relief. My lifelong feeling of inferiority didn't seem dependent on my Mexican blood now. Why did I need to blame anything? I wanted to believe that it wasn't *who* I was after all, but everything that had happened to me. I just didn't know anymore. So I asked God for the faith to go on.

The phone rang and rang again. I chuckled to myself because I would have laughed at Ruiz himself saying he was coming over to plug me in the chest. I hoisted myself up and crawled over to the phone, sitting down beside the end table. I cradled the handle around my face.

"Yeah?"

A much-too-cheerful voice came back at me through the phone. "Reverend Hefner?"

"Yeah?"

"This is Father Paul from the Catholic diocese in McAllen."

"Yeah?"

"Do you remember me?" he asked. "I'm a priest. We met at the town meeting at the Harlingen Christian school awhile back."

I remembered a priest. He was in a wheelchair. I had heard him shout "amen" after I said the government should show some remorse for the damage done to those poor people.

"You do remember me, don't you?"

"Okay, yes. I remember you," I said, completely puzzled. "What's on your mind?"

"Did you see yesterday's paper?"

"Believe me, Father, the newspaper doesn't cheer me up."

"Please read it, Reverend Hefner," he insisted. "There's a story about a Catholic nun. I don't know her personally, but I've heard a lot of good things about her. Her name is Sister Barbara Karal. Maybe she is the answer to your prayers."

"I don't follow."

"She's with an organization called Refugee Voices," Father Paul said. "She's the associate director, and her office is in Washington, DC. She might be able to see Janet Reno for you."

In my numbed state I had trouble understanding Father Paul as he told me about Refugee Voices, a human rights group that publicized the plight of refugees who were unable to speak for themselves. Sister Karal sent out a quarterly newspaper to churches around the country and broadcast radio programs to motivate the public to help.

"Sister Karal was here to investigate the Haitians' claim of mistreatment at Bayview, and I think she's just left the Valley. But she'd most likely know who you would need to talk to in Washington," Father Paul said. He gave me her number and reminded me again to read the paper.

"Yeah. Thanks for your concern," I managed.

"Remember, our church is praying for you and your wife," he replied. "God will keep you safe."

I returned the phone's handle to its cradle. The sound of plastic on plastic echoed in the room. A chill ran down the back of my head to my ankles. Maybe God had actually seen what happened to me. Maybe he had sent help. I plopped down in the recliner and just stared into space.

According to the picture above the article in yesterday's newspaper, Sister Karal was a modern nun of the skirt-and-blouse variety, whose weapon appeared to be the telephone.

She said, regarding her visit to Bayview, "If there is mistreatment, I am concerned about that. It is something I will definitely follow up on. I would like to come up with a way for [US Attorney General] Janet Reno to get involved." Sister Karal talked to the

Haitians still at Bayview, and she talked to the Hispanic detainees. Her group was investigating their complaints. My heart ached.

It took me two minutes to decide to call her. I waited for the sound of her voice. It was gentle, like water running over shady stones. I laid everything out like a confession, and she listened carefully, letting soft expletives escape during the bad parts, expressing her compassion for the women. Then she promised to do whatever she could to help them, even if it meant meeting with Janet Reno herself.

I needed a breath of fresh air. Was hope still possible? I was afraid to think it was.

■   ■   ■

It took a lot of nerve and stammering to explain to Barbara, as we were drying dishes, that I needed to tell her something about my childhood. I couldn't stop my tears so I knew she was probably prepared for the worst.

She put the dish towel down on the kitchen counter and looked at me as she had so many other times, her round gray eyes all liquid and understanding, her small lips pursed with practicality. She slowly came to me and slipped her arm around my waist.

■   ■   ■

The next weeks exploded with action. After speaking with Sister Karal, Cynthia Rodriguez called me with the name of another woman who wanted to help.

"Her name is María Jiménez," Cynthia said. "Her office is in Houston, and she heads up two different organizations."

I wrote down their names: American Friends Service Committee (AFSC) and Immigration Law Enforcement Monitoring Project (ILEMP).

"Does she work for the government?" I asked, confused.

"No! Just listen while I read the fax she sent me," Cynthia said. She read: "The (AFSC) is an independent Quaker organization, and was founded in 1917 to provide conscientious objectors with an opportunity to aid civilian victims during World War I. Today it carries on programs of service, development, social justice, and peace education in twenty-two foreign countries and forty-three places in the United States."

She paused, then said, "Listen to this, Hefner, this is really good." Again she read: "In 1947 the AFSC and Friends Service of Britain received the Nobel Peace Prize for their silent help from the nameless to the nameless . . ." She paused. "Hefner, they won the Nobel Peace Prize! Not everyone wins that award."

"What about the immigration agency, or whatever you said."

"It's called the Immigration Law Enforcement Monitoring Project," Cynthia said, rustling papers in the background. "It says it's 'a national accountability project working toward more humane law enforcement of immigration laws . . . This organization is intertwined with the US-Mexico Border Program to reduce the level of abuse of authority in the enforcement of immigration laws.' They might help us. You know, Hefner, we're victims," she said, trying gamely to involve me.

"Let me know what happens," I said, unable to register anything but neutrality. Maybe . . . I didn't know. I didn't know.

■   ■   ■

On May 28, Jim Sitgreaves filed a motion requesting a new trial. He argued that "there were material fact issues which could only be resolved in a trial." The public needed to judge. I still had faith in them.

I received a follow-up letter from Sister Karal on June 8. She told me she was sending letters about us to human rights groups and Janet Reno. She mentioned that, because of a tip I gave her in our conversation, she intended to ask if United International Investigative Services had a license to operate in Texas.

While I still worked at Bayview during the switch from Burns to United, INS employees and I had been required to transport detainees out of the facility to the federal court in McAllen, because United brass said that their employees were not legally able to perform duties outside of the camp. I learned from a rival guard company later (the one I had recently worked for) that this was because United's application for a license to operate in Texas had been denied.

Although, according to the INS regional office in Dallas, United shouldn't have been operating without a license in Texas at all, United had told us that they *could* provide security at the camp as long as their employees did not leave the government facility. I was pleased that Sister Karal was going to expose them and their lies.

I met María Jiménez of the two organizations Cynthia had told me about several nights later on June 11 at a seminar for regional immigration officials. Cynthia had called and told me to show up because María was going to be there. The main speaker was an internationally renowned immigration attorney from Los Angeles named Peter Schey. He was on our side.

With Barbara guiding me by the elbow, I met María in the crowd before the program began. Strands of silver wove through her shoulder-length hair and sparkled in the overhead streetlights. Short, dark, and fortyish, she wore no-nonsense clothes, no makeup, and an expression of skepticism. But her stoic face melted as she told me, "I've heard so much about you, it's like I know you already."

I was chagrined to think what she might have heard. We talked a little bit. She commended me for my activism. I told her I was just about exhausted and relieved that she and her organization had taken over.

"This is the first time anyone has come forward with so much information on what goes on inside," she told me. "Thank you for your years of work." She promised to take the complaints as high as she could. ILEMP had been logging records of abuse since 1988.

■ ■ ■

June 25 was the day we would hear whether our request for a new trial would be granted. Everything seemed to have taken an upswing since the involvement of Sister Karal and María Jiménez. I was feeling wonderfully neutral about the whole thing, although the fallout from my resurfaced memories kept me vulnerable and shaky. Taking care of the horses was good therapy.

I prepared for the hearing and the possible outcomes. Somehow I believed it was going to turn out all right. Things had changed.

The courtroom was loud that day, packed with reporters from several cities and from Mexico, all there to hear Judge Hester's announcement. As I helped Barbara sit down behind me and took my place with Jovita, Cynthia, Beatriz, and Sitgreaves, I felt gratified to look out on all those people who were interested, even excited, to see what would happen. I felt they supported us.

Sitgreaves was relaxed amid the bustle of the audience. He sat with his brief before him on the table, one foot crossed over his knee, revealing polished, ornately carved leather cowboy boots, and his arms outspread behind him on the chair backs, splaying open his suit jacket. He looked over at me, giving his head a quick tilt, and smirked, as if to say, relax, it'll be okay.

The bailiff stood and asked us to rise. Judge Hester came into the courtroom, his grim, lined face giving no clue as to his decision. He always looked the same. Or maybe that was how he looked when he denied us. He had yet to rule in our favor. My tension came back. I glanced at Jovita. She was the only one not fidgeting. She looked wide-eyed at Hester, and in her round face I saw reverence for him and the trust of someone who didn't understand but believed, like a child who'd put her life in his hands.

Hester sat down quickly and without much preamble made his ruling in favor of the companies, denying our request for a new trial without explanation. Then he called Sitgreaves into his chambers.

It was like someone hit me with a baseball bat. My heart stopped and then started again as I heard the disappointing sounds of the girls and newspaper reporters rushing out of the courtroom to nearby phones. All these years the judge had been known as "hang 'em high Hester." But today he hung us out to dry.

15

The Appeal

We were discouraged and all sat numbly in Sitgreaves's office while he explained to us that Judge Hester had in effect done us a favor by denying our trial. Hester told him afterward that he had done so to avoid the possibility of a second trial; it would waste time to try some of the issues now, then appeal the dismissed issues and try them later, doubling the legal costs and complications. So far, we hadn't spent any money.

"I've taken your suit as far as I can, ladies and gentleman," Sitgreaves told us. "Hester advised us to appeal his decision and have all the viable issues sent back to him. My advice, if you decide to appeal, is to contact Downey again. He's the appeals expert, if you choose to go on."

"Of *course* we want to appeal!" Cynthia said, looking at the others. "If we quit now, those bastards will never be stopped."

I remembered the perpetrators gloating yesterday after Hester's decision. Beatriz and Jovita added their agreement to Cynthia's. I set up a meeting with Denis Downey.

"Okay," Downey told us in his office. "Filing an appeal costs a thousand dollars."

"A thousand dollars?" I asked. Everyone's mouth fell open. Jovita looked at Cynthia and Cynthia looked at Beatriz, then all three looked at me. Nobody had a thousand dollars or even part of it. We were all out of work.

"How much time do we have before you need the money?" I stammered.

"I can't file without it." He pushed his glasses back up the bridge of his nose.

"If we can raise the money, will you take the case?" I asked.

"Yes, I will," he said.

"Then we *will* get the money," I said. The women were all smiling and relieved. Tony would pull a rabbit out of his hat. But regardless of how I scraped the money together, it was the right way to go. The way it had to go.

"I have to warn you, the appeals court could take months, even years to make a decision," Downey said. "Do you have the patience to stick it out? Because if you don't, you'll waste that money."

The women and I looked at each other with grim resolve.

"We'll consider it an investment in our future," I said.

■　■　■

A week later I was making quiet plans to leave Texas. I was scouting ranches looking to buy horses. We would sell ours to finance the move. Good homes for the horses were the priority. The phone rang.

It was a reporter for an international Spanish-language television network in Miami called Telemundo. They had a news program called *Ocurrió Así* (It Happened Like This) on which they wanted to run our story and asked if we would allow them to come to San Benito and film us. They had heard about us from María Jiménez.

On June 30, I hosted an event at our ranch for the newsmen from Miami, as well as our local newspaper and television reporters. Cynthia, Beatriz, Jovita, Emily Davis, and Francis Carmona came to testify. I was happily barbecuing chicken and making fajitas for the crowd like in the old days. We were hoping that this international exposure would encourage some of the abused women who'd been deported to come forward and strengthen our case.

After eating, the women sat around a picnic table and in Spanish, told the camera what they'd been through. It was sobering. Jovita cried through her story again, as if it happened yesterday.

■ ■ ■

I smiled as I read the return address on Sister Karal's letter. It was nice to expect good news for a change. She had composed a letter addressed to Attorney General Janet Reno and sent me a copy.

Sister Karal had asked for a new independent investigation of the INS employees and their contracted guards at Bayview because of our accusations. She asked the following questions:

- Does United International Investigative Services have a license to provide services in Texas?
- When investigations are made, are employees questioned in the presence of alleged offenders?
- What is the degree of staff turnover? What are the reasons for dismissals?
- Do personnel in the Inspector General's Office have too close a relationship to INS employees to insure just resolution of alleged violations against the INS?
- Are supervisors at the detention center using their power to dismiss employees to win employee silence regarding what they have seen and experienced?
- Is there a cover-up of violations? Are the people in charge committing violations with impunity?
- Are women treated with respect at this center? What is being done about alleged sexual harassment of female guards and detainees?

She added in bold type: "**I request that this investigation be expanded to include all INS detention facilities and include the treatment of detainees.**"

Next she included an exhaustive chronological list of events stating the names of all the witnesses and informants, the dates of the events, and corroborating newspaper articles regarding our allegations of impropriety at the detention center. Lastly, she gave my name and address and invited Reno to contact me if she wanted further documentation.

In her cover letter to me she listed ten groups that would also receive this material, from the ACLU to the Congressional Border Caucus. I was so proud of Sister Karal. Everything in this letter was correct and going to the right people. Finally.

■   ■   ■

My personal life was a mess. The stress and depression had made me an emotional wreck, and poor Barbara could only take so much moodiness. Since *Ocurrió Así* ran our segment, the phone had not stopped ringing with calls from well-wishers and the curious, but it was unnerving all the same. The occasional crank call would be thrown into the mix. Barbara would flinch at the first ring. The only stability in her life was her job, now full time, and I suppose work was the only place she felt safe. I knew she worried about my safety, but she nevertheless harbored great bitterness over our loss of the children's ministry. She blamed this loss on me for having caved in to pressure, even though she understood the reason for it. She used to rely on the church for our social life, but since we now went to a different church every Sunday, reluctant to impose ourselves on one congregation, we had little social life. She and I had become distant. We couldn't look at each other without tears welling up in our eyes. We weren't used to being emotional or identifying with our emotions, even when they were bubbling up around us. It made life very uncomfortable.

I had suggested moving out of Texas several times, but Barbara was adamantly against it. "Tony, I love it here. This is my home."

"But it's been five years since you've seen your parents. I think it would be great to go to Michigan for awhile."

Periodically, a friend who used to work at Bayview as an INS detention enforcement officer, Joe Polanco, would visit me. His aunt, with whom he used to live, lived down the road from our ranch. Polanco was likeable, tall, slim, and good-looking—a real carefree guy who drove a red convertible and always had one or two beautiful women with him. He seemed to have everything—money, cars, women. But lately, since he no longer worked at the camp, he was not the joking guy I remembered. He was more serious and would look out for my well-being. One day he told me, "Hefner, I consider you a good friend, but you need to back off. You have no idea the danger you're in. There are things going on at the camp, and you're about to blow the whole thing open."

That was the last time I saw Joe Polanco. What thing was he talking about? I had to take him seriously. His words drummed in my ears, over and over again. One thing about Polanco, he would never lie to me. I could not forgive myself if someone harmed Barbara, nor could I look her father in the eye. I was responsible for taking care of her and right now getting out was the best way to do it, even if she didn't agree.

After I had sold one of the horses I found her by the window crying.

"How can you sell off our horses and not show sadness?" she wondered.

Just recently, she had finally gotten the nerve to mount our mare Blessing. She wore a cowgirl hat and was as smiling and vibrant as I'd ever seen her. She looked so proud of herself.

"It'd be different if we needed them, Barbara," I lamented. "We'll still have Faith and some of the other horses. It's *you* I'm concerned about. You're more important to me than anything else."

"We can start again, Tony. This will all blow over, and we can have the ranch and the children back. If you sell all our horses, where will we get the money to buy them back?"

Joe Polanco's warning was on my mind. "Barbara!" I turned to her in frustration and looked straight into her eyes. All her maternal instincts and vulnerabilities, all her dreams were bound up in this place and what we once had. I wanted to scream at her to let go, that it was all over. But I couldn't. She would never have children of her own.

She angrily cried herself out of the room, convinced I was a hardheaded chauvinist.

I hadn't yet told her I was planning to leave town.

■   ■   ■

There was still the issue of the thousand dollars needed to file the appeal. I had half-heartedly asked a couple of churches for a donation toward our appeal but was denied. I didn't know where to go, and I could feel the pressure building up once again. God, if you want this appeal to go forward, I asked, provide the money.

On July 31, I read in the newspaper that a new judge had been appointed to the appeals court in Corpus Christi where our hoped-for appeal would be filed. I nearly gagged when I read the name. The new appellate judge was none other than Linda Reyna Yañez, the lawyer I had been ordered to escort off Bayview property as she was trying to arrange depositions for her injured client, José Checo. I had tried to call her with information, but she hadn't returned my calls. Could she possibly remember me?

■   ■   ■

On August 2, Sister Karal received a reply to the letter she sent to Janet Reno. I ripped open the envelope, expecting at long last a definitive answer to our complaints. Only Reno didn't answer it, a Mr. John P. Chase, director of the Office of Internal Audit, did. Not surprising. However, Mr. Chase's reply angered Sister Karal, as she explained in her cover letter.

In his letter Mr. Chase said, in part:

> We understand that most, if not all, of the matters which were brought to your attention by Reverend Anthony Hefner and Ms. Cynthia Rodriguez concern actions by employees of a former Immigration and Naturalization Service contractor, Burns International Security Service, and a current contractor, United International Investigative Services, and not by the Immigration and Naturalization Service or its employees. We further understand that the matters previously have been presented in appropriate forums, including the Equal Employment Opportunity Commission, Office of the Inspector General of the Department of Justice, and the courts. For those reasons, the new investigation you requested is inappropriate.

He then signed off with the obligatory offer of "further assistance" and provided a phone number, with no mention of follow-up to her seven concerns regarding the conduct of the INS and their contracted agencies.

When she sent me his reply, Sister Karal wrote that she was "sorry that the injustices continue without any recourse for abatement."

I called her. "Sister Karal," I said, "can you see Janet Reno? If you could only tell her face to face, I bet she'd understand and do something."

"I don't know," she answered wearily. "I'll think about it. In the meantime, I'm going to write another letter to our Mr. Chase and see if we can't get some satisfactory answers. I'll send you a copy."

She wrote to him:

> You totally ignored all of my seven questions regarding the conduct of the Immigration and Naturalization

Service (INS) and the employees contracted by them at the Bayview Detention Center. I appreciate that you contacted the District Director in Harlingen to find answers for my concerns. However, I really wanted my request to reach the Attorney General. I believe that the reason there continues to be violations at the Center is because those at the intermediate level are either ignorant of or are covering up the gross violations at the local level. To me, this is a good example of one of the statements made by the General Accounting Office in its report, "Immigration Management, Strong Leadership, and Management Reforms Needed to Address Serious Problems," published in January 1991: "Over the past decade weak management systems and inconsistent leadership have allowed serious problems to go unresolved. As a result, the agency has degenerated into a group of segmented autonomous programs, each trying to handle its own set of problems with little attention given to their interrelatedness." If violations continue at the Center, how can an investigation be "inappropriate"? I do not believe the Attorney General would have written off my request for an "independent investigation" as "inappropriate." How can the INS be so unconcerned about the conduct of the people contracted to perform duties in its name? I am not satisfied with your response.

Go tiger!

■ ■ ■

On September 2, a story broke in the *Brownsville Herald* and the *Valley Morning Star* about an INS officer who had been caught smuggling 292 pounds of marijuana through a border check-point.

Under federal law, people convicted of the possession of more than 220 pounds of marijuana face a five-year mandatory minimum sentence.

That he had not yet been suspended meant that he was protected.

Later that day I received an anonymous call from a voice I recognized as Payan's. I could tell he was calling from the camp because I heard a radiophone conversation in the background. He asked if I'd read about the drug bust in the paper that morning, then asked me to meet him at the feed store in Los Fresnos the next day.

When I arrived in the parking lot I spotted a small white INS van. I could make out a figure in the shotgun seat and another in the seat behind. The store had only one way in so I plunged toward the front door, trying to be inconspicuous to those in the van.

Payan was tall, and I should have had no trouble finding him except that the shelves separating the aisles were high. The store had the familiar warm smell of alfalfa, grain, and leather but also the distinction of selling a variety of loud South American parrots that ruined any dignity the place might have had. I climbed a stepladder against the wall and looked out over the aisles, spotting Payan's white head among the parrot cages.

I approached him cautiously and mentioned the van's presence. He scoffed, "You're paranoid." It was the van he came in; he was traveling with two other INS employees who were now eating their lunches. "They're on our side. You shouldn't watch so much television."

The squawking of a very large, colorful parrot, whose painted eyes looked back into mine, distracted me. His price tag read a thousand dollars. I strained to catch Payan's words.

We strolled away from the parrots and into the tack area, where heavily oiled leather bridles hung in rows and the birdcalls, though still intrusive, didn't threaten to burst my eardrums.

I let Payan know that Sister Karal was involved and had requested a new investigation. I asked him to please be careful of Ruiz. I had to plead with him. He didn't see the threat. I said that Ruiz might find it easier to put a bullet in him than have him questioned by an objective investigator.

Payan brushed off my concern but answered kindly, "They won't touch me, my friend. I retire in January and have a good twenty-year record. You must believe I have played along to survive, yet they know where I stand. At certain points I had to demonstrate in unimportant ways that I was more with them than against them. I have gotten more years of strong evidence locked up in my office because of it. They didn't get to shred all the evidence. Some small things lost, some large things preserved. I don't regret it."

I wanted to tell him about Joe Polanco's warning, but he would only say I was paranoid again and that would only upset me. I asked if Ruiz or Trominski had any ammunition they could use against him if it came to that. Payan reassured me that they had nothing. "I did what I had to do," he said.

I fumbled for words. "What about the drugs? You know, the smuggling in the buses?"

Another customer wandered into the bridles. Payan and I walked together a few steps around to the next aisle where the shelves were filled with bird decoys. I found myself staring back at multiple horned owls. "Constable Ramiro Sánchez is confused as to who had jurisdiction. But after Ruiz's warning they decided to drop it, reasoning that if Ruiz was involved, they didn't want to know," Payan said.

We talked about the new appellate court judge Yañez and whether she would be objective or not, and while Payan assured me that she held no love for Ruiz, the lines deepened on his forehead and around the eyes. He had a furtive look, like he never rested, only alighted for a short time on whatever perch presented itself.

"I once escorted Yañez off camp property. I hope she doesn't hold it against me," I said.

Payan reassured me with his big smile that she had probably forgotten all about it. "The other thing I wanted to tell you, Hefner," he began to search his pockets, "is that I will be leaving for awhile."

My ears pricked up. Was he pulling a getaway, too?

"I have been ordered to the Immigration Officer Academy in Georgia to teach a class. I am actually here for only several days more until I go to Glynco. My class begins mid-month and runs until November, so I will be out of touch for a time." He withdrew a card from his wallet and gave me his number at the academy, requesting I call him should there be a new investigation.

"Do you think Ruiz might know there is an investigation coming, and that's why he's sending you to Georgia?"

Payan paused, thinking, the great owl's unblinking eyes behind him. "I don't think so. I've taught there before. But . . . I was surprised to be ordered back this time. I was told on my first tour that supervisors never come unless it is for their initial training. Supervisors are never sent on detail. However," Payan regained his bearing, "I don't think so." I pitied him if the tables ever turned on him at the camp.

The last thing he said was, "We all start out much better than we end up. It's just life, eh?"

We said good-bye and good luck and ended with a firm handshake. I was always overwhelmed by how much he trusted me. I was glad he was going to Georgia.

■ ■ ■

Using the drug bust as the latest evidence of INS misconduct, María Jiménez, on behalf of ILEMP (Immigration Law Enforcement Monitoring Project), wrote to Janet Reno on September 3 requesting a special investigation.

Shortly after I received a copy of this letter, I called María's Houston office with an update of my new information. During our conversation she told me she was arranging a meeting with Congresswoman Pat Schroeder for early February 1994 in Washington. She asked if I would come and testify about what I had seen and heard. I thought about it momentarily. Washington. Last year the idea was too much to consider.

I told her she could count on me.

■ ■ ■

"Reverend Hefner?" I was surprised to hear Jovita Urrutia's soft voice over the phone. "Have you heard anything? I mean, it's been three weeks, and I wondered . . . are we still going to fight?"

Three weeks since we decided to appeal, and I couldn't find the money. They all had a right to wonder. I told her not to worry.

"But I'm not worried that we won't," she said. "I'm worried if we do." Jovita had decided she just wanted to forget it ever happened.

I knew about forgetting, moving on, putting things behind me. The sad truth was that some things don't go away. Ever. They have to be faced.

"Jovita, you can't forget about it. Don't lose your courage."

"I'm not a very strong person."

"You'll get strong. This will make you strong."

She wasn't convinced. "Will I know when the appeal happens?"

"I'll make sure you do."

"Okay." She paused. "Thank you."

"You're welcome, Jovita."

Right then I understood what I had to do.

■ ■ ■

I had owned my horse Faith since he was a six-month-old colt dodging and weaving among the palm trees, growing too fast, eating like . . . a horse. I loved him. But since the children were no longer in our lives, the ranch and the horses had lost much of their fantasy. My philosophy was "keep it simple." If you don't use it, get rid of it. But that standard didn't apply to Faith. He was our baby.

I remember the day he was given to me. Barbara and I hadn't been married long, maybe a year. My dream was to go to Texas and start a ranch ministry. One Saturday, after searching the livestock section in the newspaper, we set out to find us a horse. Still in Bible school in Ohio, I had no money in my pocket. We started out on Route 28 and ended up in New Vienna. We had just passed a horse ranch with a sign out front: Horses for Sale. I turned around and drove into the paved driveway. Not knowing if they had a dog on the loose, I honked my car horn probably more than I should have.

An old lady came out of the house and walked over to my side of the car. "Can I help you?" she asked kindly.

"My name is Tony Hefner and this is my wife, Barbara."

She said her name was Louise Hanson. "What can I do for you?"

I told her I was looking for a horse. When she asked me what kind, I told her that I wasn't sure and that it really didn't matter.

"Well," she said, "we have only two kinds of horses, Quarter Horses and Appaloosas. How much money do you want to spend?"

I told her we didn't have any money. "I'm in Bible school, and I work at a stable learning whatever I can about horses. I only clean the stalls. So there's a lot of things I don't know about horses. You see, Ms. Hanson, we're planning on going into the mission field and starting a ranch for kids. We also want to take Bibles to remote villages in Mexico. And I thought, if this is what God wants us to do, then maybe he'll give us a horse to start out with."

She laughed and invited us out of the car. The ranch was beautiful, with a big white house and a large red barn with white fencing all around the property. She took us behind the barn, which overlooked a deep valley with a pond and stream. From there we saw eight mares with their foals grazing under the big blue sky, and they looked like God had just put them there. There were foals of all varieties: spotted, black, brown, and white. The sweet smell of apple blossoms was heavy in the air.

"Come on," she said. "Let me show you what we have." Just as she was leading us down the hill through the deep grass, she turned around. "You know what?" Barbara and I looked at each other and shook our heads. "God just told me to give you a special horse."

"He *did*?" I asked. That day I became the proud owner of a beautiful Appaloosa colt. I named him Christian Faith, knowing it took a lot of faith to get him.

He had always been a special horse. I remembered the kids clapping when Faith performed the various tricks he knew: his counting trick, pawing the dirt when I gave him a sugar cube, lying down and rolling over. I remembered one skinny kid in particular, how his legs stuck out sideways when we sat him on Faith's big back.

But now I would find a new home for Faith. Maybe selling him was symbolic. I had certainly learned a thing or two about where to put my trust. The horse symbolized my childhood, lived vicariously through other children. But now the children were gone, and I had to grow up.

I knew a family with a couple of kids who had recently visited the ranch looking to buy a horse. They had just bought a nice home on eight acres about twenty miles away. The property had a small stable area and a seven-foot fence running all around it. Of course, they liked Faith, but at that time he wasn't for sale. I promised they'd be the first to know if I ever changed my mind. I called them.

I could hear the children's excitement in the background when their father said he'd love to buy the horse. Their joy and exuberance almost made me forget my sadness. He would have a good home and the affection he deserved.

The day I loaded Faith into the trailer was predictably dark and overcast. He's just a horse, I kept saying to myself. Barbara came out with her camera, wanting to take one last picture, but I almost yelled at her not to. I didn't want any pictures to remind me of this day!

We had lots of other pictures of my good old boy. People used to bring their children over to pose on Faith's back for photos they would use as Christmas cards. He was so big and proud. Sometimes he looked as if he were grinning. He loved to have his picture taken.

I was slow getting to Faith's new home and got a lump in my throat as I turned up the gravel driveway and heard the welcoming sound of the wheels grinding on the rocks. The family was waiting and swung the entry gates open. When I pulled down the tailgate, Faith had his head in the hayrack and looked around at us with a mouthful of alfalfa. The kids were delighted. Faith nickered softly.

I backed him out, and the kids stroked his tall flank. I walked him to his new pasture and opened the gate to let him in, thinking, this is it, I have to leave without him. "This is your new playground, Faith," I said. I put my arms around his huge neck and gave him a big kiss. Then I unsnapped the lead rope and let him go in. "Come on, Faith, look pretty."

He knew what to do. He took off, leaving a cloud of dust behind him, and pranced, his knees coming up high like his legs had springs in them.

I barely looked at the check in my hands. A thousand dollars. I walked back to the truck and got in, listening to the family cheer their big, beautiful new horse. I drove through the gates and headed down the vast, lonely highway, the empty trailer bouncing behind me.

I looked up at the fence bordering the road and saw Faith running parallel with my truck. He whinnied loudly, and I accepted that as his good-bye. Would he forgive me? He looked so free and beautiful with his mane and tail waving in the wind. Memories of living in Windham as a child, wishing I had a horse, came rushing back. I was practically giving my dream away. Don't look back, I kept repeating to myself. Keep your eyes straight ahead.

A mile down the road I pulled over. The tears hurt as they began to fall. I had held them back as long as I could. I looked back to see if Faith had found some way of getting out of the pasture. If he did, he'd be coming down the road soon.

I waited five minutes or maybe longer. Why didn't he come? Didn't he love me? I sat there and cried.

16

Payan Is Framed

Our appeal was filed at the Nueces County Courthouse on September 15, 1993, and sent to the 13th Circuit Court of Appeals for review. We had no idea when it would be ruled on.

The jury listening to us would make the difference. The money didn't matter. Although we were all tapped out, none of us wanted to settle out of court, even if offered that option. We needed the public to stand with us and repudiate the behavior of these public employees. If these men get away with it, I thought, then crime pays and honesty is the policy of the naïve. Our country would move that much further away from the moral authority and discipline that made it great. I wanted to be part of its greatness, not a peasant abused by every petty official with a little power. We had to be heard.

More and more fearful for our safety, Barbara and I finally decided to move out of Texas. We no longer had the ministry, and without it, our main reason for staying in the Valley was gone. Busy packing up the things we had accumulated over the years, I was amazed to see how we valued each object differently, depending upon our state of mind and finances when we bought it. The hundreds of dollars' worth of tack out in the barn I could have given away for all I cared. But the four blue glasses we bought during our poorest years—of themselves not great glasses—we prized highly because we had sacrificed food money to buy them. I wrapped them with care and placed them at the top of the box.

I had made arrangements to store our belongings at the new

country home of some friends who had moved to Georgia. I would drive one truckload at a time, spacing my trips over three months, so that no one could tell we were going until we were already gone. These friends had invited us to stay with them as well, but I'd already decided to go up to Ohio where my old pastor friend Tim Roeser of the Barberton Baptist Temple was hoping we could start another ranch ministry. Guilt gnawed at me about going. But I had to.

I saw myself as a foreigner, a Yankee boy who had come down from the North to a foreign country, where the game was played by different rules. I spent years trying to impose my understanding of our country on them. No wonder I had been shocked. It *was* shocking for someone who didn't understand the culture.

In the meantime, María Jiménez wanted me to go to a press conference in Weslaco, Texas, given by Proyecto Libertad. The women and I wouldn't be the only ones talking. A panel of authorities, including the director of the South Texas Immigration Council, the field director of the American Civil Liberties Union, the senior immigration policy analyst for the National Council of La Raza, and María herself, in her capacity as the director of ILEMP, would all speak.

More than two hundred activists, reporters, victims, and citizens showed up in Weslaco for the press conference on September 18. Barbara and I were among them. I had never seen a more purposeful-looking group. Fortified by their righteous indignation as well as the law, simple decency, and good education, they gave the impression of being important people who got things done.

As the discussion turned to the exact nature of the problems in the INS and different testimonies were heard, including ours, it became apparent that what was needed was a complete overhaul of the accountability system. At stake was a new bill before the House Judiciary Subcommittee on International Law, Immigration, and Refugees that would create an independent agency for the investigation of abuses by immigration authorities. Many of the human rights groups' representatives argued in favor of the bill. All of us victims were urged to send our testimonies to the subcommittee. If this bill were passed, how much time would elapse before any changes were actually made and someone like Ramirez was prevented from running his hands over an unwilling guard? It was difficult to know. Our case in the courts was still important, but we needed to involve the INS somehow.

María summed up the conference during a television interview afterward when she said, "It's a system that does not work. Like most internal systems, the police policing themselves has always been questioned."

I felt a great machine of activists working behind me when I told the *Valley Morning Star*, "We've been fighting this for three years, but we're not going to stop until something gets done."

Before we left the conference in Weslaco, María handed me a long memo on ILEMP letterhead, telling me how to write my letter of testimony to the House subcommittee. The bill before them was HR 2119, "A Bill to Create an Immigration Law Enforcement Review Commission."

"But María, where do I begin?"

"Don't worry, I'll help you. It's important to get as much of this testimony as we can as part of the public record. If we can get your letter and Cynthia's and Jovita's and everybody's in before the hearing, it will be given to the committee members before they decide. If we don't make that deadline, it won't have any bearing on their decision, but it will be included in the printed record. I'll call you."

The next day, with María's help, we put together a long letter describing everything for the subcommittee in Washington. I wanted them to understand that it wasn't just adults who were singled out for immoral advances by INS officials, but children, too. I used the young girl from El Salvador who was forced to dance for officials as an example. We also pointed out the many errors in the

Justice Department's handling of our complaints, including deciding that an investigation of the INS would be "inappropriate" because INS employees were not being directly accused, only employees of the companies the INS had contracted. We told them that INS employees, including the camp director, now promoted to assistant INS district director of detention, were indeed engaged in the sexual abuse of detainees and harassment of female guards. We sent the three-page letter via certified mail, and I brushed the dust of its evil off my hands.

■ ■ ■

I was wrapping two antique lamps in the bedroom when the blasted phone rang for the umpteenth time.

"Barbara, can you get that?" I yelled out.

A minute later Barbara stood quietly in the bedroom doorway, her eyebrows raised in an expression of surprise.

"Well? Who is it?" I asked.

She sighed, then answered, "It's some man."

"Tell him I'm not home."

"I'm not telling him you're not home. He's from the *María Laria Show*," she continued, "and wants to know if we will fly to Miami to be on the show. All expenses paid." Laria's show was hugely popular and aired nationally on the television network Telemundo.

Before the day was over, Barbara, myself, Cynthia, Beatriz, and Francis Carmona were booked on an all-expense-paid trip to Miami. We were all but jumping out of our skin with excitement.

Jovita Urrutia refused to go. The producer tried to convince her, but she declined to make any more public appearances due to the embarrassment it had caused her family. Jovita was raised in a culture that discouraged women from asserting themselves and placed a high priority on compliance. The family name was a source of pride and was protected at all cost. For Jovita to be caught in the middle of a sex scandal, even as a victim, mortified her parents.

On October 6 we flew to Miami. The women were nervous and excited before the taping. They had been bowled over when the producer took us out to dinner the night we arrived and couldn't believe they were actually going to talk to María Laria, a celebrity they'd watched on television.

As they told their stories to the studio audience, the reactions were stunning. People were incredulous, gasping with disbelief and outrage, their hands over their mouths. Laria skillfully drew them out, asking, "What was going on in your head when this was happening?"

Laria praised them for their strength in overcoming their fears. A cameraman told Beatriz afterward that he would have busted heads if those things had happened to his sister. Cynthia told Laria she felt as if the show had come to their rescue. Sympathy. The healing had begun.

After our appearance on the *María Laria Show* was broadcast I was contacted by the news shows *Dateline* and *Inside Edition*, both wanting personal interviews. Geraldo Rivera also wanted us to appear on his talk show. With all this national exposure, I began to feel better about leaving. Others were taking over. They really cared.

Craig Rivera, Geraldo's younger brother and a correspondent for *Inside Edition*, came to Texas in November to interview us for the show. If we gave our story to him instead of *Dateline*, he promised us that his brother would have us on his show. It surprised all of us when Jovita consented to be interviewed. Rivera didn't expect Jovita's depth of emotions to surface so dramatically. When he asked, after several minutes of conversation, what had happened to her in the closet, the tears started to flow. At times, as she told her story, she sobbed openly.

Gently, Rivera asked, "This happened over three years ago, and it still hurts you, doesn't it?"

"Yes," she wept.

"And this man still works at the detention center?"

"Yes, sir, he does."

Her depth of sadness that day made me realize that many abused women carry disgrace and guilt with them the rest of their lives. I hoped they would one day be strong enough to help someone else through the trauma and thereby help themselves. That was what had helped me.

During the three days of interviews with *Inside Edition*, Payan was with us. Rivera didn't ask him for an interview, but Payan did talk to Rivera about the INS being involved in drug smuggling. The reason I know this is because Rivera asked me, "How well do you know this Eduardo Payan?"

"I know him real well," I responded. "A lot of my information comes from him. Why do you ask?"

"Because Payan said he knew the INS was smuggling drugs in INS buses." Rivera shrugged and looked at me, expecting an answer.

"The only thing I can tell you is that I am out of here. I'm concerned about my wife. Where this whole matter will end up is unclear and out of my control. If you're asking me if the INS is involved in drug smuggling, I don't know. But I will contact you once I have my wife in a safe place."

■ ■ ■

Due to the television appearances and increased publicity, former detainees and officers came out of the woodwork to speak about sexual abuse in the camp. An article entitled "Bayview Charges to be Corroborated" appeared in the *Valley Morning Star* on November 15 and referred to our appearance on *Inside Edition*. Finally, others were coming forward. It had been a long, brutal battle.

By Christmas, the bulk of our belongings and our few remaining horses were settled in Georgia. The mobile home was clean and bare except for two chairs and a table, which we'd take later. I had sold our little home and made arrangements to have the new owners pick it up on moving day. On Christmas Eve Barbara and I went outside with a cup of hot chocolate and looked at the stars powdering the broad black night and for the first time in a long while felt close. Barbara had forgiven me back in Miami. It's funny how God works things out in a woman's heart. It's got to be him; otherwise, how could any woman on her own forgive the things Barbara has had to bear? She didn't require that life be fair to her.

On December 29, Sister Karal heard back from INS Commissioner Doris Meissner, to whom she had sent a letter urging an investigation. It was good news.

> As you know, some of these allegations were previously investigated by the EEOC and the Office of Inspector General of the Department of Justice, and could not be substantiated. However, based on the information supplied by Ms. María Jiménez of the Immigration Law Enforcement Monitoring Project, it is now the intention of the Inspector General's Office to pursue an investigation into offenses against aliens and any alleged misconduct by INS employees at the Bayview facility.

She hoped this was "responsive" to our concerns. Yes, it is finally responsive. Thank you.

As I finished reading the letter the phone's ring echoed through the empty living room.

"I've been contacted by the FBI, Reverend Hefner," María Jiménez said. "I gave them your phone number; they'll be calling you, too."

"The FBI? But I just now heard that OIG is opening another investigation."

"They're out of it, Reverend Hefner. We've been upgraded."

"Upgraded?"

"By Ms. Reno herself. It's now a full FBI investigation."

"Hallelujah!" I was scratching my head at the turn of events.

"Amen."

"María, we're leaving."

"When?"

"Not for another week. I'm afraid for Barbara and—"

"You don't have to explain. I understand. Will you be able to make our meeting with Congresswoman Pat Schroeder in February?"

"Oh, yes, I'll be there."

"Good. You know, Reverend Hefner, you've done so much. You can rest now, it's okay."

"Thank you, María. See you in Washington."

The following day it was official. The *Valley Morning Star* ran an article entitled "FBI Probes Sex Abuse Charges."

On January 2, 1994, between good-bye visits to our few remaining friends, the FBI contacted me. I gave them the phone number of our friend's house in Macon, Georgia, as the best way of contacting me in the future. I later met with them in Macon and handed over all documents to FBI special agent Fred C. Stofer.

Two days later, on January 4, I drove our truck through the front gate for the last time. Earlier, a tractor had hauled the mobile home out into the road where it evaporated from my reality. I got out of the truck and locked the gate for the last time. I stood looking over our empty little ranch and couldn't let go of the gate. It was as if a magnet held me there against the rails. I didn't want to let go.

A hundred thoughts swirled around my head: visions of the children we loved, the new palms growing as the dead ones fell, the sad eyes of the women who were victimized, my warning to Payan, and his discouraged call of a few nights ago.

Payan told me that he had been relieved of his teaching assignments in Georgia and was ordered to report back to the Harlingen district office in Texas. Shocked, he had called Ruiz to ask why his detail was cut short. Ruiz replied that Payan had to return and take a polygraph or be indicted, and would not give any more information. Payan learned later that he was suspected of stealing twelve thousand dollars in detainee bond money from the office safe, even though he was on annual leave in San Antonio on the day it was stolen and others had the safe combination.

When he reported for the polygraph at the district office, he was told he no longer needed to take it. Payan immediately asked for annual leave and went to Bayview to retrieve the records and evidence he had been saving for this day, but was denied entry.

At his lawyer's request, Payan had his own polygraph done on November 3, which exonerated him. Despite the evidence, he was suspended from work on November 5. On November 9, he was formally indicted, then legally maneuvered by Ruiz and Trominski into an indefinite suspension without pay until the indictment was resolved. Like many others who had done the same thing, Payan had indeed borrowed money from the safe for job-related business but had paid it back. It was to cost him his good name.

Given the indictment and the coming investigation, Payan was no longer a credible witness. I had often feared that something like this would happen.

Leaning against the gate while the Chachalacas laughed in the distance, an old sensation came over me. I could feel the pulse in my neck. The pasture where our mares and foals had once grazed stretched out before me. I had once felt so lucky to be standing here watching our horses cavort on the rolling, cactus-dotted terrain.

I started to turn toward the steady hum of the truck's engine and Barbara's patient figure when something caught my eye. A dead palm leaf had blown off a tall tree and was floating in the gusty wind. It fell across the path of a small figure standing near the barn. My heart beat faster as the light-skinned Spanish boy stepped out of the shadows and into the open. I pulled myself up and stretched my neck to see. He looked to one side as if expecting someone to follow him. Just then I saw Faith's tall shoulders emerge from behind the barn. He walked to the boy and stood beside him with his ears pricked forward, looking proud. Tears started falling down my cheeks. I could hardly see. The boy looked at Faith and then at me.

"Thank you," I whispered. I have seen you in the eyes of every Hispanic boy who set foot on this ranch. I heard you laugh and saw the excitement in your face when I picked you up and put you on the hay wagon. I comforted you when your cat was sick. I saw the hope stir in you when I told you about a great God who loves you.

"Thank you." I promise I'll never forget you or be ashamed of you again.

With his left hand he grabbed Faith by his long, thick mane, and I yelled out, "I love you," but he didn't hear me.

I could feel Faith's wiry mane between my fingers and his smooth coat and the smell of his slick hair as the boy threw himself over that broad bare back. You are the reason I came. You are the reason I fought so hard for the victims. I fought so that *you* could finally be heard.

Raising his hand high, he waved good-bye. The two of them turned toward the open pasture and disappeared in the dust. I raised my hand and waved.

"Good-bye, Pancho! You're free. You're finally free."

Postscript

Many years later, in 2010, we are still waiting for justice.

Sister Karal's meeting with Janet Reno became unnecessary when Reno ordered an FBI investigation after reading all the evidence. We had hoped the investigation would lead to real change. However, while it confirmed that the INS was indeed smuggling drugs in its own buses, it played down the sexual abuse of female guards and detainees. Several INS officers were sent to prison for drug smuggling, but no one was held accountable for abuse of detainees or female guards. Another disappointment came in February 1994 when the meeting María Jiménez had organized with Congresswoman Pat Schroeder was cancelled due to a blizzard that paralyzed Washington.

Our appeal was finally heard later that year, in November 1994. I'm happy to say that we were successful.

Meanwhile, evidence of abuse continued to surface. On November 5, 1994, the *Valley Morning Star* ran a story with the headline "Police Crack Down In Gutierrez Park." It reported that "in an effort to curtail prostitution, Harlingen police are running a prostitution sting at the park." The arrests included "INS and Custom officers." One of these officers was Aaron Lee Cabrera, who was on his lunch break driving a government van when he allegedly offered two undercover policewomen money for sex. Payan had told me that Cabrera was a good friend of Ruiz's. The case was dropped, and Cabrera is now the officer in charge at the Bayview facility.

In the years that followed, Barbara and I eventually settled in Michigan to live a modest life. I remained in touch with those who had fought alongside me and managed to keep informed about those we fought against.

Cynthia Rodriguez remained firm, fighting our case all the way, tooth and nail. She had found another good job and was determined to go the extra mile.

Beautiful Beatriz Huerta was also able to find another good job, but the abuse and pressure took its toll on her marriage. She and her husband separated.

My fragile, rosy-cheeked china doll, Jovita Urrutia, became pregnant by her boyfriend who then deserted her. She moved from one family member's home to another, still without a job and trying to cope.

Ernesto Rubio and Vicente Ramirez lost their jobs when United's contract was not renewed. The new security company declined to hire them.

Cecilio Ruiz remained at Bayview until he retired in 2002.

Pastor Smith changed the name of his church, and I heard that other churches with which we had been involved were thinking of doing the same.

Mike Trominski formally terminated Eduardo Payan sixty days before his retirement and the federal court decision that dismissed all charges against him. During Payan's trial his attorney proved time and time again that no money was missing. The government spent close to $800,000 of stolen bond money; the total amount that was stolen is unknown. While trying to sue the government for back pay and pension, Payan eventually spent eighteen months in prison.

■ ■ ■

On occasion, Washington showed signs of taking steps to address the abuses I continually sought to bring to their attention. On May 13, 1993, a bill to create an independent agency to investigate INS abuses was introduced to Congress (HR 2119). However, no further action was taken. The INS acting director opposed the legislation in order to protect INS employees against frivolous accusations. The INS instead funded, but never implemented, a program to form citizen advisory groups designed to afford complaints the same recourse as the bill would have.

Several years later, on May 21, 1998, INS Commissioner Doris Meissner addressed the House Subcommittee on Immigration to introduce a plan to completely restructure the INS. She told the committee members, "When I took over the agency five years ago, it had been so badly neglected that we had to urgently triage a number of problems that had seriously undermined immigration enforcement in the country altogether. As you know, the southwest border was completely out of control."

Even though previous investigations had been fruitless, I continued to hope that an investigation conducted by the right government agency would lead to action. This appeared to be a real possibility when I received a letter from Associate Counsel to the President Benjamin A. Powell on April 25, 2003. I had sent Senior Presidential Advisor Karl Rove a copy of this manuscript, and according to Powell, Rove had read it and thanked me for the information. Powell said the manuscript would be turned over to the Office of the Inspector General of the new Department of Homeland Security (DHS).

With the help of Congressman Camp, I sent a letter to the Department of Legislative Affairs, requesting information about the findings of this investigation. A reply, with the DHS seal dated June 27, 2006, finally came from Chief of Investigative Operations R. E. Martin, stating, "The DHS will review the information you provided to determine the appropriate course of action." As of April 2010, I have yet to hear from DHS.

■ ■ ■

In August 2009, the *Wall Street Journal* reported that the Immigration and Customs Enforcement Agency (ICE) had discovered records of ten previously unreported deaths of detainees, which brought the total number of reported deaths since October 2003 to 104. This alarming discovery prompted calls for an agency-wide review. It is an opportunity to demand honest investigations into our country's immigration detention system, which detains 400,000 individuals annually.

As Attorney General Eric Holder considers a Justice Department recommendation to reopen and pursue prisoner abuse cases in Guantánamo, so too should the Justice Department reopen the investigation into abuse at the Port Isabel Service Processing Center. I believe the same inappropriate tactics that may have been used in Guantánamo were used on some of the immigrant detainees in Texas.

Trouble at Bayview continues. There are reports of hunger strikes and complaints of abuse from detainees within the center today. In March 2010 I was subpoenaed to appear in federal court in Texas as a witness on behalf of a detainee who was wrongfully accused of using force on two security guards. I testified that I had never seen a detainee raise a hand against a guard or federal employee. The abuse will not stop until we as good citizens stand up for human rights in honor of our great country, even if this means we have to go to federal court to stop it.

Acknowledgments

I'd like to thank my wife Barbara for standing by me through the good times and the bad. She is my best friend and has always encouraged me to stand up for what is right, despite all we've been through.

I'd like to thank Maria Jiménez and Sister Barbara Karl for all their hard work in reaching our representatives in Washington, DC.

I appreciate Jovita, Beatriz, and Cynthia, and all the other men and women who put their lives on the line in order to expose the abuse they endured and witnessed.

Thank you to my attorney, Denis Downey, for all his hard work.

A special thank you to Eduardo Payan, who risked everything in the struggle to help people who will never know of his sacrifice.

And finally, thanks to my publisher Seven Stories Press. Without their help and vision, this book would not exist.

About the Author

TONY HEFNER is a human rights activist and founder of the Bearing Precious Seed Ranch ministry in southern Texas for local Hispanic children. He has reported the abuses taking place at Port Isabel on *Inside Edition*, PBS, and many other radio and television news programs. Tony and his wife Barbara now live in northern Michigan, where he continues his fight with national officials for new investigations. For more information visit www.torchlake.com/hefner.